Old Tales of the Maine Woods

Steve Pinkham

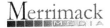

Merrimack
MEDIA

Published by Merrimack Media
ISBN: 978-1-939166-25-8
Library of Congress Control Number: 2013948188

Manufactured in the United States of America, or in Great Britain, when purchased outside of North or South America.

Merrimack
MEDIA

For further information, contact info@merrimackmedia.com

www.merrimackmedia.com

Cover design by Merrimack Media

DEDICATION

With everlasting love and wonderful memories, this book is dedicated to Lillian Ellingwood Smith, my grandmother, teacher, friend and mentor, who told me stories of growing up in Rangeley, who inspired me to read and learn all I could, to follow my dreams and who helped instill in me the passion that lead me on this wonderful journey.

ACKNOWLEDGEMENTS

The journey that created this book took me from Northern Maine to Washington, D.C. and introduced me to many wonderful people who helped me along the way. Outside of Maine I visited many research facilities and am especially grateful to the librarians and staff members who helped me find so much material – The Library of Congress, New York Public Library, New York Historical Society, Yale University, Brown University, the Providence Athenaeum, University of Massachusetts at Amherst, the American Antiquarian Society in Worcester, the University of New Hampshire at Durham and Dartmouth College.

Much of my initial research was done in institutions in Greater Boston where I found a great wealth of material in old bound volumes and microfilms. I am especially indebted to the staffs of the Boston Public Library, New England Historical Genealogical Society, the Appalachian Mountain Club, the Thomas Crane Library in Quincy and the Lamont, MIT Archives and the Lamont, Widener and Ernst Mayr Libraries at Harvard University. Special thanks go to Mary Sears and Ronnie Broadfoot at the Ernst Mayr Library at Harvard, and Henry Scannell and Joe Maciora at the Boston Public Library, who faithfully tracked down much obscure material and numerous photos for this book.

In Maine I am thankful for the use of materials and generous assistance at the public libraries of Portland, Skowhegan and Bangor, as well as the Longfellow and Hawthorne Library at Bowdoin College, Mallet Library of the University of Maine at Farmington, the Maine State Library and the Maine Archives at Augusta.

Valuable assistance came from the staffs at Bethel Historical Society, Maine Historical Society, the Old Canada Road Historical Society, Moosehead Historical Society, the Registry of Deeds at Houlton and the Maine State Archives. And I am forever grateful to State Historian Earle Shettleworth who allowed me access to the wonderful collections at the Maine Preservation Commission.

There were also individuals who helped and stood by me on this decade long project and I am thankful for their unconditional love and everlasting friendship. Thanks to my Mother, Charlie, Chai and Joe Cove, who helped and supported me in many ways to see this project through to the end.

TABLE OF CONTENTS

INTRODUCTION

Ten years ago I began collecting articles for my first book, "Mountains of Maine," and started finding wonderful stories of the Maine Woods that were not about mountains, but were none-theless, fun and exciting tales. Quickly getting the idea of collecting stories of the Maine Woods for a separate volume, I went back to the beginning and started over, methodically perusing through all the old sporting magazines, journals, newspapers and other periodicals for any and all articles about the Maine Woods. I soon found that if I looked for mountain articles, I would find stories; if I looked for stories, I would find mountain data.

This journey has taken me from northern Maine to the Library of Congress and to numerous libraries and historical societies to locate the stories and to date I have collected, copied and filed over 22,000 articles and photographs on the Maine Woods, choosing the best stories for this volume.

Running from 1851 to 1913, many of the stories came from Forest and Stream, the foremost sporting magazine of the latter 1800s. After 1910 most regions of the Maine Woods had been visited and written about and stories about the Maine Woods became sporadic and often redundent. Also, as the nation expanded, the focus of the sporting magazines also turned westward, and less and less was written about Maine.

The tales in this book are separated into specific regions of the State of Maine, running east from the New Hampshire border to the northern tip of Maine and Down East, and include exciting tales of hunting and encounters with wolves, catamounts, bears, moose and other wild animals as well as great fishing tales. The majority of tales are the adventures of known authors, while others are fictional stories, written in the ever popular juvenile books and novels and collections of stories.

If you ask anyone today, who went to the Maine Woods in the 19th century, most people would mention Henry David Thoreau, the man credited with coining the title "Maine Woods." But thousands of others including well-known and lesser known individuals ventured into the woods and also penned articles about their experiences. Some of the well known authors are Seba Smith, Henry David Thoreau, James Russell Lowell, John Burroughs, Lucius Hubbard, Thomas S. Steele, Charles A. Stephens and Fannie Hardy Eckstrom.

Where the author is known, we have included some biographical information and a photograph, and in the case of an unknown individual, or an unknown pseudonym, we have often included some appropriate information on the region, setting, or if a story has been extracted from a longer narrative, and have included appropriate old photographs.

Finally, there are plenty of more stories which we plan to put in a sequel to be published later. May you enjoy these stories as much as I did discovering them.

– Steve Pinkham

Chapter 1

THE ANDROSCOGGIN AND MAGALLOWAY RIVERS

Beginning in the Rangeley Lakes, the Androscoggin River does not actually gain its name until it flows out of Lake Umbagog in New Hampshire. While the majority of its water's come from the lakes through the Rapid River, it also receives water from the Magalloway River, which begins in the far northwest section of Maine and runs south, paralleling the New Hampshire line. The Androscoggin then enters New Hampshire, makes a wide arc and re-enters Maine at Gilead.

Settlement along the Androscoggin River began in 1774, when Bethel was known as Sudbury, Canada. The surrounding river towns were settled in the next six or seven years. Upton, located on Lake Umbagog was settled in 1823, access being by way of the "Coos Trail" through Andover. Two years later the first families arrived in the remote townships along the Magalloway River.

Sporting in this region did not begin until about the 1860's when the railroad reached Bryant's Pond and Bethel. A daily stagecoach left Bryant Pond for French's Hotel in Andover and another left Bethel, stopping at the Poplar Inn on the Bear River, on its route through Grafton Notch to the Lake House at Upton. The earliest account we have of this region was by the noted historian Francis Parkman, who came over the mountains from New Hampshire and paddled down the Magalloway in 1842 and by a tourist from Cambridge, Mass., who had his account published in the *New York Times* in 1852 under the pseudonym "Quahog," In 1860 an anonymous writer published his adventure in *Harper's Magazine* and the following year Marshall Tidd, a lithographer from Woburn, Mass., travelled through Grafton Notch on his visit to Parmachenee, keeping a journal and sketching various scenes. In 1864 another anonymous account was published in *Harper's Magazine*, further advertising the great fishing to be had in this region. Capt. Fred Barker and John Danforth trapped in the Parmachenee region in 1876 and wrote about their adventures in *Hunting and Trapping on the Upper Magalloway River and Parmachenee Lake.*

Only a few sporting camps were located in this section. Hotels in Upton served sportsmen on Umbagog Lake, Capt. Wilson took in travelers in Wilson's Mills, and sportsmen could stay at Camp Caribou, John Danforth's famous camps on an island in Parmachenee Lake. Camp Caribou's most famous guest was President Eisenhower, who stayed there in the summer of 1955. Later sporting camps were Bosebuck Camps on Aziscohos Lake, Big Buck Camps on Sturtevant Pond, and Indian Rock Camps at Howard's Pond in Hanover.

THE OLD HUNTER'S STORY

By Daniel P. Thompson, from *Gaut Gurley*; or, *The Trappers of Umbagog,* 1857

Daniel Pierce Thompson

Daniel Pierce Thompson (1795-1868), a noted lawyer, was called "The Novelist of Vermont." Graduating from Middlebury College in 1820, he set up his practice in Montpelier and was appointed clerk of the Vermont Legislature in 1830, then Clerk of the Vermont Supreme Court and later Secretary of Vermont from 1853-1855. An avid abolitionist, he owned and edited "The Green Mountain Freeman," from 1849 to 1856. Thompson loved both literature and history and was one of the original founders of the Vermont Historical Society. He authored numerous novels, and his "Green Mountain Boys" became a standard in Vermont schools for over a hundred years. A noted historian, he also wrote a "History of Montpelier, Vermont."

In his novel, "Gaut Gurley," Thompson based the flowery, romantic story loosely on the kidnapping of little Jim Wilber, who was abducted in western Maine by the notorious David Robbins and sold to the Saint Francis Indians. In the novel, a trapper and a hunter settle it in front of a campfire and each tells a story in an attempt to out-perform the other. This is the hunter's story.

"It was about a dozen year ago, and on the borders of lake Parmagena, a squarish-shaped body of water, four or five miles in extent, lying twenty-five miles or so over these mountains to the northwest of us, and making up the chief head-waters of the river Magalloway. My camp was at the mouth of the principal inlet, and my most frequented hunting route up along its bank. On my excursions up that river, I had often noticed a deeply-wooded, rough, and singularly-shaped mountain, which, the distance of four or five miles from the nearest point of the stream, westward, reared its shaggy sides over the surrounding wilderness, and which I thought must make one of the best haunts for bear and moose that

I had seen in that region. So, once having a leisurely day, and my fresh provisions being low, I concluded I would take a jaunt up this mountain, thinking that I should stand a good chance to find something there, or on the way, to replenish my larder. And accordingly I rigged up, after breakfast, and, setting my course in what I judged would prove a bee-line for the place, in order to save distance over the river route, I took up my march through the woods, without path, trail, or marked trees to guide me.

"After a rough and toilsome walk of about three hours, I reached the foot of the mountain of which I was in search, and seated myself on a fallen tree, to rest and look about me. The side of the eminence next to me was made up on a succession of rocky, heavily-timbered steeps and shelves, that rose like battlements before me, while, about midway, it was pierced or notched down by a dark, wild, thicket-tangled gorge, which extended along back up the mountain, as far as the eye could penetrate beneath, or overlook above the tops of the overhanging trees.

"To think of trying to ascend such steps was out the question; and I was debating in mind whether I would attempt to go up through that forbidding and *pokerish*-looking gorge, or, giving up the job altogether, strike off in the direction of the river, and so go home that way, when a hideous yell, which brought me instantly to my feet, rose from an upper portion of the ravine, apparently about a hundred rods distant. I at once knew it came from a painter, or "evil devil," as the Indians justly call that scourge of the woods; and, from the strength and volume of his voice, I also knew he must be a large one, while, from its savage sharpness, I further conjectured it must be a famine cry, which, if so, would show the animal to be a doubly ticklish one to encounter.

"Feeling conscious that it was but the part of wisdom to avoid such an encounter as I should be likely to be favored with if I remained where I was, I soon moved off in an opposite direction, steering at once for the nearest point of the river, which was at the termination of a long, sharp sweep of the stream to the west, and nearer by a mile than in most other parts of its course. I had not proceeded more than a quarter of a mile before the same savage screech, ---which was more frightful than I can describe, being seemingly made up of the mingling tones of a man's and a woman's voice, raised to the highest pitch in an agony of rage or pain, --the same awful screech, I say, rose and thrilled through the shuddering forest, coming this time, I perceived, from the mouth of the gorge, where the animal had so quickly arrived, found my trail, doubtless, and started on in pursuit. I now, though still not really afraid, quickened my steps into a rapid walk, hoping that, now he had got out of the thickets of the ravine, he would not follow me far in the more open woods; yet thinking it best, at all events, to put what distance I could between him and me, without too much disturbing myself. Another of those terrific yells, however, coming from a nearer point than before, as fast as I had made my way from him, told me that the creature was on my tracks, and rapidly gaining on me in the race. I then started off at a full run; but even this did not insure my escape, for I was soon startled by another yell, so near and fierce, that I involuntarily turned around, cocked my rifle, and stood on the defense. The next moment the animal met my sight, as he leaped up on to the trunk of a lodged tree, where he stood in open view, eagerly snuffing and glaring around him, about forty rods from the place where I had brought to a stand, --revealing a monster whose size, big as I had conjectured it, perfectly amazed me. He could not have been much less than six feet from snout to tail, nor much short of nine, tail included. But for his bowed-up back, gaunt form, and mottled color, he might have passed for an ordinary lioness. The instant he saw me, he began nervously fixing his paws, rapidly swaying his tail, like a cat at the first sight of her intended prey, and giving other plain indications that he was intent on having me for his dinner.

"I had my rifle to my shoulder; it was a fair shot, but still I hesitated about firing. My experience with catamounts, which, though of the same nature, are yet no more to be compared with a real panther, like this, than a common cur to a stout bulldog, had taught me the danger of wounding without killing them outright.

If *those* were too dangerous under ordinary circumstances, what would this be, already bent on destroying me? And should I stand, at that distance, an even chance to finish him, which could be done by putting a ball through his brain or spine, or directly through his heart? I thought not. The distance was too great to be sure of any thing like that; and besides, my nerves, I felt, were getting a little unsteady, and I also found I was losing my faith, which is the worst thing in the world for a hunter to lose. While I was thinking of all this, the creature leaped down, and, the next instant, I saw his head rise above the bushes, in his prodigious bounds towards me. With that glance, I turned and ran; ran as I never did before; leaping over logs, and smashing headlong through brush and bushes, but still distinctly hearing, above all the noise I made, the louder crash of the creature's footfalls, striking closer and closer behind me. All at once, however, those crashing sounds ceased to fall on my ear, and the thought that my pursuer had sprung one side into an ambush, from when he would pounce on me before I could see him, flashing over my mind, I suddenly came to a stand, and peered eagerly but vainly among the bushes around me for the crouching form of my foe. While thus engaged, a seeming shade passing over the open space above caused me to glance upward, when, to my horror, I saw the monster coming down from a tree-top, with glaring eyes, open mouth, and outspread claws, directly upon me! With a bound, which at any other time I should have been utterly incapable of making, I threw myself aside into the bushes just in time to escape his terrible embrace; and, before he had rallied from the confusion caused by striking the ground and missing his prey, I had gained the distance of a dozen rods, and thrown myself behind a large tree. But what was now to be done? I knew, from his trotting about and snuffing to regain the sight and scent of me, which could now distinctly hear, that he would soon be upon me. If I distrusted the certainty of my aim before this last fright, should I not do much more now? I felt so; and, as I was now within a mile of the river, ---where, if I could reach it, I thought it possible to find a way to baffle, at least if I did not kill, my ruthless pursuer, ---I concluded that my best chance for life was to run for the place. But, in peering out to ascertain the exact whereabouts of the painter before I started, my ear caught the sound of other and different footsteps; and the next moment I had a glimpse of a bear's head, bobbing up and down in his rapid course through the bushes, as he ran at right angles, with all his might, directly through the space between me and painter, which, I saw, was now just beginning to advance towards me, but which, to my great relief, had seen and was turning in pursuit of the flying and frightened bear.

"But still, fearing he would give up that pursuit and again take after me, I ran for the river, which I at length reached, and threw myself exhausted down on the bank. As it happened, I had struck the river at the intended point, which was where a small sand-island had been thrown up in the middle of the stream. To this island, in case I kept out of the claws and jaws of the painter till I reached the river, I had calculated to wade; believing, from what I knew of the repugnance of this class of animals to water, that he would not follow me, or, if he did, I need not fail of shooting him dead while coming through the stream. But I soon found that I was not the only one that had thought of this island, in our terrible extremity.

"I had lain but a few minutes on the bank, before I caught the sounds of near and more distant footfalls approaching space through the forest above me. Starting up, I cocked my rifle, and darted behind a bush near the edge of the water, I had scarcely gained the stand, when the same bear that I had left fleeing before the painter, made his appearance a few rods above me, coming full jump down the bank, plunging into the stream, and swimming and rushing for the island. As soon as he could clear the water, he galloped up to the highest part of his new refuge, and commenced digging, in hot haste, a hole in the sand. The instant he had made an excavation large and deep enough to hold his body and sink it below the surface, he threw himself in on his back, hurriedly scratched the sand at the sides a little over his belly and shoulders, and lay still, with his paws stiffly braced upwards.

"The next moment the eagerly-pursuing painter came rushing down the bank to the water, where the bear had entered it; when, after a hesitating pause, he gave an angry yell, and, in two prodigious bounds, landed on the edge of the island. Having raised my rifle for a helping shot, if needed, I awaited, with beating heart and eyes wide open, the coming encounter. With eyes shooting fire, the painter hastily fixed his feet, and, with a long leap, came down on his entrenched opponent. A cloud of dust instantly enveloped the combatants, but through it I could see the ineffectual passes of the painter at the bear's head, and the rapid play of the bear's hind paws under the painter's belly. This bout between them, however, was of but short continuance, and terminated by the painter, which now leaped aside, and stood for a moment eyeing his opponent askance, as if he had found in those rending hind-claws already much more than he had bargained for. But, quickly rousing himself, he prepared for the final conflict; and backing out the water's edge, he gave one short bound forward and, leaping ten feet into the air, came down again, with a wild screech, on his still unmoved antagonist.

"This time, so much more furiously flew up the dust and sand from the spot, that I could see nothing; but the mingling growls and yells of the desperately-grappling brutes were so terrific as to make the hair stand up on my head. Presently, however, I could perceive that the cries of the assailant, which had been becoming less and less fierce, were now turning into howls of pain; and, the next moment, I saw him, rent and bloody, with his entrails out and dragging on the ground behind him, making off till he reached the water on the opposite side of the island, when he staggered through the current, feebly crawled up the bank, and disappeared in the woods, where he must have died miserably within the hour.

"I went home a grateful man; leaving the bear, that had done me such good service, to depart in peace, as I saw him doing before I left, apparently little injured from the conflict."

IN THE WILDS

By George Shephard Page, from *Forest and Stream*, August 22, 1878

George Shephard Page

George Shephard Page (1838-1892) was born in Readfield, Maine and in 1845 his father moved the family to Chelsea, a suburb of Boston. In 1858 he went into the chemical business, inventing a form of creosol to preserve wood, and patenting several of his products. Moving to New York in 1862 to continue his profession, he resided in Stanley, N. J. However, it was the propagation and preservation of fish that endeared him to the brotherhood of anglers.

He first visited the Rangeley Lakes in 1860, where he caught his first trout, a seven-pound beauty, at Upper Dam. He subsequently was "hooked" by the lakes, built a camp, and continued visiting the rest of his life. Fascinated with the behavior of trout, he took some five-pound brook trout back to Boston, but was met with doubt by other anglers until Professor Agassiz verified the authenticity of the species. In 1867 he formed the Oquossuc Angling Club, an association of fellow anglers, who built a lodge on Mooselucmeguntic Lake, the first fishing clubhouse in the country. In 1874, through his expertise and extensive knowledge, the club built a successful fish hatchery on Bema Stream, one of the first in the nation. Mr. Page became president of the American Fishcultural Association in 1882 and was a champion of education.

On the 15th of last October I left Camp Kennebago, Rangeley Lake, Maine, for Megantic and St. Francis Lakes, Canada, via the Wilderness. My system was fully charged with the terrible malaria, imbibed during the six months mainly spent at the Philadelphia exposition of 1876. A month's stay at Camp Bema, on Mooselucmaguntic Lake, had not affected a cure, and friends and physicians advised a hundred-mile tramp through the wild woods of Maine and Canada. Accompanied as a companion by that sterling gentleman, E. A. Rogers, Esq., of Rangeley, Maine, whose courtesy is so well known to many anglers, sportsmen and tourists, and with the famous Capt. F. C. Barker, of Andover, as chief guide, and Stephen Taylor and Addison Long, of Byron, and Frank Hewey, Jr., of Rangeley, as packers and boatmen, we went by Cupsuptic Lake and stream and the Five Mile Carry to Parmachenee Lake. We were cordially welcomed by Uncle John Danforth at his unique camp on a raft, anchored in the middle of the lake, and in a short half-hour made a clean sweep of his well-supplied table, the prominent and most delicious dish being "beaver hash." Having reached the region famous as the ranging ground of deer, moose and caribou, of which I had heard for the seventeen years during which I had frequented the Rangeley Lakes, I interviewed Uncle John immediately after supper as to the probability of my getting my first shot at a deer. "Oh, yes," he replied, "I can give the opportunity tomorrow morning." With full faith in Uncle John, I retired to rest and slept sweetly, gently, but literally "rocked in the cradle of the deep." Awakening early and breakfasting at half-past seven, we sent two guides ashore. At 8 o'clock we heard three shots. Springing into our boats we started from the camp. As we rounded the point of an island a half-mile distant, we saw a deer swimming. As we approached I exclaimed, "Fred, that is a caribou!" He turned. A look was enough. The forest of branching antlers looming five feet in the air, together with his great length and the exquisite dark-gray color of his skin informed his practiced eye that a veritable specimen of the American reindeer was before us. He swam rapidly, but not with the speed attained by our Adirondack boat, propelled by the muscular arms of Capt. Fred. At long range I fired my first shot at a member of the deer family. Eleven buckshot rattled around him, but only served to quicken his speed and turn him directly toward the shore, but a short distance away. I urged Fred to increase his speed, and standing in the stern of the boat with the gun at my shoulder I calmly awaited the moment for the last shot. "Fire," shouted Fred, as he glanced at the noble animal now within close range. "Not yet; I don't want to ruin those antlers with the twelve buck-shot in my left barrel." Aiming steadily at the line formed by the broad neck and rippling water I pulled the trigger. Almost at the report he ceased swimming. The majestic head slowly drooped, and as the antlers touched the surface of the lake I was alongside and caught the upper one in the crook of my right arm. "All-right, Fred; I told you ten minutes ago that was my caribou. Now for the camp." The other boats came up and in tow line we returned to the camp. It was half-past eight as we touched the raft. The hunt was exactly an hour. The next morning as we set out for Lake Megantic, Uncle John's assistant, Perry started for Colebrook, N.H., sixty miles down the Magalloway. He carried the head and the antlers, the skin, the feet and the two hind quarters of the caribou, which were expressed to New York. A rustic sign over the main entrance of Uncle John's camp on the raft, placed there by our hands, reads, "Camp Caribou."

We had many delightful and exciting experiences during our three weeks through the wilderness to Lakes Megantic and St. Francis and return to Rangeley, and I may jot them down for the entertainment of your readers. Suffice it to say that the main object of my trip was accomplished. I returned home fully recovered. No lingering evidence of malaria was left in my system. I can therefore earnestly recommend a similar tour to the victim of this widely-prevalent malady…

– GEO. SHEPHARD PAGE, Stanley, N. J., Aug. 12

BEAR HUNTING IN MAINE

By Stephen Taylor, from *Forest and Stream*, November 22,1882

An Apparition (From Canoe and Camera, by Thomas S. Steele, p. 66)

Most of the accounts of trips and adventures in the Maine Woods were written by the sportsmen and travelers who ventured there. Sportsmen would often correspond with their intended guides by mail, but here we have a more infrequent letter from a guide with whom George Shephard Page had built a lasting friendship.

Stephen Taylor (1842-1923) was born in Byron, Maine, a small hamlet along the Swift River and remained there his entire life, farming, logging, guiding and obviously, bear hunting. He taught school for a few seasons and tried his talents at dentistry, probably the kind of barber/dentist who basically just pulled teeth, using whiskey as the sedative. Taylor raised a large family of boys and girls and lived to be eighty-one years old, being buried in his hometown, the last of the great guides and hunters of that region.

The following letter (writes Mr. George Shephard Page) may be of interest to your readers. The writer has frequently served as my guide at the Rangeley Lakes. As his story indicates, he is a man great courage and endurance. He is very well informed, having been employed in teaching school for several terms. In meeting him for the first time, one would hardly realize that a noted bear slayer was hidden in the courteous, intelligent person with whom he was conversing. Mr. Taylor has killed nearly thirty bears. His letter is Byron, Maine, May 3, 1882' it had been awaiting my return from Europe. He says:

I have had some exciting bear hunts since I saw you. Last winter I hunted a little. Bears are very plentiful, and quite bold. I lost quite a large number of sheep last spring and summer, killed by bears – one large sheep was killed in my pasture and dragged about twenty rods in the woods before she was eaten. It must have been a large bear, for he dragged her over a log, which was about three feet high.

Two winters ago I spent twenty-nine days hunting bears. I saw six and shot three. A. S. Young was with me part of the time, and part of the time I was alone. On Bald Pate Mountain in "Andover Surplus," we had been following a large bear several days, and were going over the smoother, hard, frozen snow and ice, cutting places for our feet with the ax, when we suddenly came to a fresh track of an old bear and two cubs. There was a little light snow on the hard crust. Add Young, Ben Mitchell and myself were together. We followed these tracks about twenty rods, when we came to their den, in a cave in the rocks. We, of course, thought that we were sure of all three of them, as Add had a Ballard rifle, Ben a 44-calibre Remington revolver, and I my two-barreled shotgun, one barrel loaded with a ball, and the other with buckshot; but I changed with Ben, and took his revolver, as I was going into the mouth of the den to start them out, while the others were to take stations around and take them when they came out. But they didn't start easily, and I got a pole and was trying to punch them out, when Ben cried out, "There comes one above them." Of course we all looked in the direction.

The old bear came out first and her two cubs followed her. We fired eight shots at them, and we thought that we had killed the old one, but she finally came on to her feet again and went off, leaving a trail of blood. We followed till dark, then went to a logging camp in the valley below and stopped all night. The next day we drove one of the cubs out of another den on a high bluff and followed him two days, when we decided to divide the crew, and Add was to follow this cub, while Ben and I went back to look after the old bear and the other cub. We found their trail and followed it to another den, which they had found among a pile of huge boulders. It was a hard place, and we were not certain that they had stopped there till we had cut the ice away sufficiently to get down and look into a cave about twenty feet under the flat side of a large rock. I got a long pole and punched in till I saw their eyes glisten, then I knew they were there; but we couldn't drive them out, so we cut the ice away and I got down flat on my belly and crept in about half my length so as to let the light shine in over my head, and with my pole I punched her till I could see her eyes shine, then I took as good aim as I could and fired. I backed out pretty soon. I fired twice before I hit her. The second time I put a large bullet in just to the left of her right eye. Then the cub curled down behind his mother so snug that I could only just see his eyes and ears, and when I stopped punching him he would be entirely out of sight. I fired three times before I killed him. It was almost dark when we got them out of the den. We left them there that night. The next day we got help and hauled them down to the road and took our team and went home. I have the pictures of the bear and cub. Perhaps you would like to see it? Addison S Young has killed two or three lately. A very large bear was shot in Weld last week.

– STEPHEN TAYLOR

CAMEL'S HUMP AND THE RANGELEY LAKE MOUNTAINS

By Rosewell B. Lawrence, from *Appalachia*, 1885

Taken While on a winter trip (Courtesy of the Appalachian Mountain Club)

Rosewell Bigelow Lawrence (1857-1921) was born and raised in Medford, Mass. graduated from Harvard in 1881 with a law degree, and was admitted to the bar the next year. Active in civil affairs, he served a number of years as chairman of the Medford School Board and in 1906 was elected as a trustee of Tufts College. In 1907 he was chosen chair of the Scholarship Committee of the Medford Club of Harvard University.

An avid outdoorsman, Lawrence was also chair of the Medford Park Commission and was instrumental in the formation of the Middlesex Fells, a vast wooded park, north of Boston. As one of the earliest members of the Appalachian Mountain Club, he served as secretary for over 25 years. He also lead several of the club's first trips to the Katahdin region and being interested in venturing into new areas, he took the following trip in September of 1885, to a little known region of western Maine.

The clouds the next morning did not interfere with our starting. A short row brought us to the head of Cupsuptic Lake, and it was two miles more to the falls in the river of that same name. We walked the half-mile carry, took a different boat above the falls, and continued up the river, about seven miles, in a general northerly direction, till we reached Camp Parmachenee at the eastern end of the Parmachenee Carry. The heavy rain during the night had raised the river so that the oars could be used nearly all the time, and the pole was needed but little. The vegetation was luxuriant, and the trip so delightful that I was loath to leave the boat and shoulder a pack. We were just two and a half hours going from Billy Soule's to Camp Parmachenee,--very good time. At the camp we ate our lunch and at two o'clock started on the seven-mile tramp to Parmachenee Lake. The height of land on this carry is half-way across, and about 600 feet above the Cupsuptic and 450 feet above Parmachenee. The path is much used and is in very good condition. The tramp took us two and three-quarters hours. It seemed more than seven miles, and I really think it is more. A short row on Parmachenee Lake brought us to Camp Caribou, the paradise of the sportsman, far away in the Maine wilderness. The proprietor, John Danforth, gave me a hearty welcome, and suggested that I knew how to make myself at home. Danforth is the best man I have found in the woods, and his camp is a delightful place to stop. At first he built a raft, until he obtained a lease on the island where he now lives. The building or rather buildings, have been erected piece by piece, so that the result is quite fantastic and corresponds with the wildness of the scenery.

Danforth has several excellent guides, especially for hunters and fishermen. My guide, John Olsen, is one of the best, and as a woodsman and chopper is famous in that section of the country. A Norwegian by birth, he retains the good characteristics of his race. Honest, faithful in his work, and quiet in his habits, he made a good companion and an excellent guide. He considered me, however, an unusual specimen of humanity; and in fact I was an object of curiosity to guides, hunters, and fishermen alike. They all thought it strange that a man who did not care for hunting and fishing should come so far into the wilderness; and I wondered that they should sit in a boat or stand in mid-stream all day, or lie in tree-tops all night, and not care to enjoy the wild and beautiful views from the mountain-tops.

September 6 proved a cool day, fair, with heavy clouds. John and I took our boat, and, rowing to the head of the lake and up the Magalloway River, arrived in fifty minutes at Little Boys Falls. Pulling our boat over the rough ways, we started again, rowing or poling according to the depth of the water, until we reached the first east branch. Beyond this point the river was filled with logs, which had been cut several miles above, and had stuck in the river because the spring freshet had not been heavy enough to float them to Parmachenee. Had it not been for these logs, we could have continued in our boat to the base of the Camel's Rump, and thus accomplished our journey much more easily. There is an old tote-road all the way from Parmachenee to Canada, and this we followed. It is in very bad condition, and after a rain the traveller at times wades in mud and water and otherwise pushes his way through wet raspberry-bushes six to eight feet high. After passing two dilapidated loggers' camps, we reached in a few minutes the small clearing opposite Rump Pond, about five miles from Camp Caribou.

The Camel's Rump was indeed before us, but we could see no more than I saw the previous year,--it's base. We selected a site for a camp, and I made up my mind to remain a week, if necessary to accomplish my object. During the afternoon the clouds were slowly breaking up and disappearing, and at sunset I was rewarded by seeing the whole mountain from base to summit. It was not so wonderful, after all. The inclination of the southern slope was not what previous writers had described it to be. It was steep, to be sure, but nearly covered with trees, the ragged ledges appearing only here and there. Nevertheless, it was a beautiful picture,--the black river in the foreground, the pond and foot-hills just beyond, and then the rough mountain with its summit about two miles distant from us.

That night I stretched myself on the fir boughs before the fire, anticipating a glorious day on the morrow. The moon shone bright, and the temperature fell until the moist air, rising from the warm river, spread a gray mantle about us, obscuring the mountain, the moon, and even the river and trees. The frost-work the next morning was beautiful, every leaf being covered with the white crystals. At 6:30 A.M. the temperature was 33°, and the aneroid 28.37, indicating an elevation above sea-level of about 1,700 feet.

At 7:30 we crossed the river upon a raft which John had built the afternoon before, and started for the top of the Rump. After crossing some wet land we began to ascend, bearing to the right in order to climb a ridge which would lead us to the top. The plan worked successfully, and in two and one-half hours we reached the southern summit, and in ten minutes more the middle one, which is the highest point on the mountain. The whole ridge was once well covered with small trees. A few have been cut, so that one gets an unobstructed view east, west and south. Going about ten rods north, I found a place where I could catch glimpses of Canada; and John, by felling a few trees, soon gave me a clear northern view.

For hours I studied the mountain peaks and enjoyed the scenery of forest and lake. The White Mountains were a little west of south; but Mt. Washington, sixty-five miles distant, was in a cloud. The Presidential Range was seen nearly over a high ridge which John called Bull Ridge. Many of the Green Mountains were visible. In the north was Megantic, about twenty miles distant, forming one of the most striking features of the view. Of the boundary mountains none are worthy of special mention, except Double Head.

There are several fine mountains in the Ox Bow, much farther east. The Cupsuptic Mountains filled the east, the sharp summit of East Kennebago, east-southeast, being very marked. South-southeast were Rangeley Lakes and Bald Mountain. Then came the symmetrical Deer, and finally the double-topped Aziscohos. This sketch can give only a faint idea of the numerous peaks, the billowing sea of gray and green. I do not remember a sign of civilization, but possibly farming-land on the First Connecticut Lake was visible. The First and Second Connecticut Lakes were very beautiful, being only a few miles distant southwest, while northeast and southeast stretched the valley of the Magalloway, with the water of the river, and its bogs and ponds showing here and there.[1]

The view from the Camel's Rump is interesting especially on account of the isolated position of the mountain and the wildness of its surroundings. It divides the waters of the Connecticut from those of the Androscoggin (Magalloway), and overlooks the sources of the St. Francis, Chaudiere, and Kennebec (Dead River). It is distant from the Crown Monument--the common bound of Maine,

1 The map which accompanies this paper was taken mainly from the State map of New Hampshire, with more or less help form Captain Farrar's map, a map of the Magalloway by Charles I. Adams, also a map of the Rangeley Lake and Dead River Regions by A. W. Robinson, and from guides and personal observation.

New Hampshire, and Quebec--only about seven miles; and the boundary-line between Maine and New Hampshire passes over it just as it begins to slope to the west. Its position was determined by chaining south from the Crown Monument that point having been determined astronomically by Colonel Graham under the treaty of Washington.

You will not find the "Camel's Rump" on the New Hampshire State map, but in its place "Mt. Carmel." I was much pleased, however, to notice that the popular name was used by the United States Coast and Geodetic Survey. Dr. C. T. Jackson, in his final report on the geology of New Hampshire, 1844, gives the elevation of this mountain as 3,615 feet. Colonel Henry O. Kent, who perambulated the boundary in 1858, gives it as 3,711 feet. The latter, at least, is barometrical, and probably correct. It was adopted in the "New Hampshire Geological Survey," by Professor C. H. Hitchcock, 1878. The summit is just about 2,000 feet above Rump Pond and Parmachenee Lake, which are, therefore, about 1,700 feet above sea-level.

After spending six hours on the summit, we began the descent at 4.20. "Now for the southern slope," I said, and called to mind the description by Professor J. H. Huntington in the "Geology of New Hampshire." He says that the descent is almost perpendicular to the debris formed from the fallen rocks. My recollection was of a very steep slope, and such it proved to be,--steep, without being precipitous; nearly covered with tress; but very ragged. Some of the cliffs overhung so that it was necessary to zigzag in descending, following down one shelf till a break allowed a descent to the next. The raggedness was increased by the great masses of rock which had broken from their strata and fallen to the lower shelves. On these shelves and among the rocks there is considerable vegetation and many trees, so that at a distance of two miles the slope appears to be covered with trees except in a few spots where the ledges and cliffs crop out. After the leaves fall the slope must look very bare and rough.

Probably the same geological structure continues to the mountain's base; but as we made slow progress, and were going too far to the right, we concluded to take a more easterly course.

After some travelling we came to logging operations which we had crossed on our ascent. Knowing that the logging-road would lead to the river, and wishing to escape the swamp we had crossed in the morning, we followed the road, and struck the river at a place about a mile above our camp. Crossing upon the logs, we continued our tramp on the left or east bank. Again we had a clear evening, cold night, and foggy morning, the temperature at six A.M. being 35°. We returned to Camp Caribou the way we came. The next day was stormy, and I could but congratulate myself as I joined the circle of senators, plenipotentiaries, authors, and guides around the large fire. Conversation was not confined to fishing and hunting, but included politics and economics; the whole was seasoned with some of Danforth's matchless stories.

The morning after the storm, the sky was perfectly clear, the rain having cleansed the air of all impurities. John and I started in our boat at nine for Bosebuck Mountain, situated about two miles southwest of the lake. We landed at the head of Bosebuck Cove, and then pushed on to the mountain, the summit of which we reached at quarter past twelve. The mountain is said to have derived its name from a hunting adventure; a buck having been run down on the mountain's side by a dog named Bose. I estimate the summit to be about 1,500 feet above Parmachenee, and 3,200 feet above the sea. It is covered with a good-sized growth of timber, which necessitates some climbing to secure views. First, however, I found a lookout south where, by shifting my position several times, I was enabled to sketch a quarter of the horizon. The view of the Presidential Mountains was like that from the Camel's Rump, except that Mt. Washington was clear. Aziscohos was more interesting than when seen from the Rump, because it was several miles nearer. After enjoying this view, I strapped on my climbing-irons and walked up a tree, thus obtaining a fine view of Magalloway Mountain and the intervening ridges, and especially of the Camel's Rump. To enjoy this latter view was my object in climbing Bosebuck, and I felt well repaid. There was nothing between us and the mountain, except a low ridge called Prospect Hill, which gave the forest an undulating appearance. The steep southern slope of the Rump directly faced us, and the steep eastern slope was outlined against the sky. The Camel's Rump is quite long, and runs northwest and southeast; the middle summit is the highest. The sag between the southern and middle is slight, and the distance about one third of a mile; while the other sag is deeper, and the distance greater. Megantic was behind the Rump, and therefore invisible. As Lake Parmachenee affords a good view of Bosebuck, so the mountain commands a beautiful one of the lake, embosomed in the forest two miles to the northeast; it is, in truth, the gem of the Magalloway wilderness. The return to Camp Caribou took two and a quarter hours. The day had been perfect for mountaineering.

Having enjoyed the view from the Camel's Rump and a view of it from Bosebuck, I was ready to set out on my return, home. Deer Mountain, however, was on the way. My view from Aziscohos the previous summer had created a desire to climb Deer, and this wish had been strengthened by the views from Bald, the Rump and Bosebuck. I could find no one who had been on the summit of Deer; and of those had been near the mountain, no two gave the same advice as the best way to ascend. So I adopted Danforth's plan, and found his advice good, although, if I were going again, I should follow a course entirely different from what any one advised me. We left Caribou Camp about nine, rowed down the lake, crossed the carry, and floated down the Cupsuptic River as far as the falls. There at three o'clock we took and old tote-road to the foot of a spur which Deer Mountain sends out to the north. By this ridge we began to ascend about four o'clock; and the ascent through the heavy growth was so gradual that we were obliged to depend upon the compass, and several times John climbed trees to assure himself that we had not deviated from our course. At quarter-past six we camped well up on the side of the mountain, about 900 feet above the river.

A tramp of two and one-half hours the next morning brought us to the summit. It was thickly wooded, but by going a few rods north of the exact top I found a tree high enough to overlook all others. In the top of this I sat for two hours. At first the black flies bothered me, although it was the middle of September; but my guide kindly built a smudge at the foot of the tree and relieved me of the nuisance. I was rewarded of my toil, for there was spread before me the finest view northwestern Maine affords. Again I had a fine view of Washington; also Bosebuck, Camel's Rump, and Megantic near together, with a beautiful foreground embracing Lincoln Pond and Parmachenee Lake. Even Camp Caribou twelve miles distant, was clearly visible. But the charm was the view of the Rangeley Lakes to the south and east: Cupsuptic at the mountain's base; beyond, Oquossuc and Mooselucmaguntic, with Bald Mountain between them; while to the right was Molechunkamunk, and to the left Kennebago. The background of this beautiful picture was formed by the Kennebago Mountains, Bigelow, Saddleback, Blue and Grafton Mountains. I estimate the elevation of Deer to be over 3,500 feet, and 2,000 feet above Cupsuptic Lake, 1,000 feet higher than Bald Mountain, a few hundred feet higher than Aziscohos, and a trifle lower than the Camel's Rump. The best way to climb it, I think, would be to land at the northwest corner of Cupsuptic Lake, ascend the southern spur, and follow it to the summit. We descended the way we went up, reaching the tote-road in two hours, and the carry in one and one-quarter hours more. At half-past six we arrived at Billy Soule's camp, six and one-half hours from the summit.

Sunday morning I arose at half-past eight, after twelve hours of rest. It was another beautiful day, and a part of it was delightfully spent with friends who have a camp on the lake. At five o'clock I took the steamer "Metallic," and went with Captain Barker to the Upper Dam and then to Camp Bemis. I was much pleased with the little village of log camps, and can recommend Captain Barker as an excellent host. Monday I went to Phillips. Tuesday I ascended Mt. Blue by taking a carriage ride of an hour and a half, and climbing the mountain very leisurely in an hour and twenty minutes. Mt. Washington was again visible, but hazy. The farming country with its numerous ponds and villages was very pretty, but the chief attraction to me was the stately view of the Saddleback and Abraham Mountains. This is worth a journey in itself. I descended in fifty minutes, and then drove back to Phillips in one and one-half hours, --a very easy one-day excursion.

One may be inclined to ask whether this attractive region is available for a Club excursion. A camping-trip enabling a party to see what is here described would be practicable, but the magnitude of the task for a committee of arrangements is somewhat appalling. A few days could be spent by a party at that pleasant hotel in Phillips, the Elmwood, and day excursions made to Blue Mountain, Abraham and Saddleback. The delightful trip from Phillips to Rangeley, or Oquossuc, Lake could be taken, together with the steamboat ride down to the outlet, where the Mountain View House is located. From this point Bald might be easily ascended. Then Mooselucmaguntic Lake could be done on Captain Barker's steamboat, with his village of log camps as headquarters. Good climbers could also go up Deer Mountain. But to carry a party to Parmachenee Lake, the Camel's Rump, or Aziscohos would require serious labor in planning and in execution. An August trip would be practicable only by camping from the outset, and the flies would be somewhat troublesome. Camp Caribou is filled with sportsmen until late in September. I have hope, however, that some year a party may be arranged for the last of September and the first of October, which is, after all, the best season of the year for the woods and mountains.

BLACK FLIES ON THE MAGALLOWAY

By Edward A. Samuels, from *With Fly-Rod and Camera,* 1890

Dr Edward A. Samuels

Edward A. Samuels of Boston (1836-1908) was employed by the Massachusetts State Department of Agriculture and became a curator at the State College of Natural History. An expert on ornithology, he became an associate editor of "The Living World, and authored a number or works on birds and other animals, particularly those of the eastern part of the country. Among his works are: "A Descriptive Catalog of the Birds of Massachusetts," "The Ornithology and Zoology of New England and Adjacent States and Provinces," and "Our Northern and Eastern Birds." He later became President of the Massachusetts Fish and Game Protective Association.

An avid fisherman, in 1890 he published, "With Fly-Rod and Camera," a narrative of his recent fishing trip to the Maritime Provinces, which included numerous photographs he had taken. When he and his fellow fishermen were being attacked by hordes of black flies, he related the following story.

"Never shall I forget an experience that I had in the summer of 1860 on the upper waters of the Magalloway. It was a wild country then, and one would not meet a hunter or fisherman for weeks at a stretch. Now it is quite different, and fishermen are numerous, and on an island in Lake Parmachene there is a comfortable house for their accommodation kept by the popular guide John Danforth. On the occasion I refer to, I had with me as canoe man, a son of dear old Captain Wilson, one of the whitest men that God ever created. We were coming down the river on our return from a trip to its headwaters, and had just reached "the Meadows," so-called, when young Wilson was taken ill. He seemed in great pain, almost as if dying, and was of course quite helpless. What his sickness was I could not understand, but I did the best I could for him. I laid him in the bottom of the boat on the blankets, and gave him a dose of Jamaica ginger, which I happened to have among my stores. I felt sure it could not hurt him anyway, and it did in a short time give him relief, for he soon fell asleep. But the black flies! Like a dense cloud they settled upon us, and I was literally streaming with blood. Wilson I had covered with the blanket and his face was protected by his hat, with a handkerchief thrown over it. But I, while I was tending him, was completely at the mercy of the little pests, and no mercy did they show.

Not a breath was stirring, and the weather was very warm; the perspiration streamed at every pore, and consequently tar ointment would not adhere to my skin. It would have been useless, anyway, against such hordes as pounced on me.

It took but a short time to convince me that unless I had a smudge in the canoe the situation would be critical, for I had heard of cases of terrible poisoning from black flies, which were followed by insanity and helplessness. Seizing the frying pan and iron pot, I started a fire in each, and when it was fairly burning, I covered it with damp moss, leaves and turf. I placed one in the bow close to Wilson, and the other at my feet, and began my long paddle of, I think, over thirty miles down to Aziscohos Falls.

The river was low, and once or twice I was obliged to get out of the boat and haul it over bars and windfalls, at which times I was at the mercy of my tormentors.

The load was also heavy for a single paddle, and tired enough I was at nightfall when I landed at an old logging camp on the river side, and got my patient out of the boat and into the camp. However, I started up a big smudge, for although the flies had finished their work for the day, the mosquitoes began to show up in clouds.

I then built a fire and got supper. I contented myself with hard tack, fried bacon and tea. For Wilson I made a dish of flour porridge; and through the evening I laid cloths steeped in hot water across his abdomen, changing them as fast as they cooled off to the temperature of the body.

This treatment seemed to do him good, and glad and thankful enough I was to see the poor chap coming around, for it was a pretty serious matter for me have a sick man on my hands alone in the wilderness, particularly as I did not know what ailed him, and what the best treatment would be.

At length I smudged out the camp and turned in, leaving a big smoke going outside.

On the following morning Wilson was so far recovered that he could move about without my assistance, and we got an early start on the river, he, however, still too weak to paddle. The flies, however, soon put in an appearance, and I was obliged to kindle my smudges again. I sped the boat as rapidly as I could, but it was noon when I heard the oh, how welcome roar of the falls, and knew that the end of my journey on the river was at hand.

Wilson, though still feeble, was now able to walk the carry (portage) around the falls with me, although we had to travel slowly; and it was late in the night when we reached his home at Wilson's Mills, and I was relieved of my responsibility and anxiety.

We were both so badly poisoned by the virus from the insects that we were in high fever for a day or two, but good nursing brought us out all right.

My hands were in a terrible state, for, in addition to the soreness from the bites of the flies, they were badly blistered by the hard bout I had had with the paddle.

Yes, that was an experience with black flies never to be forgotten. The region about the Magalloway is one of the favorite haunts of this pestiferous insect, and I do not remember ever seeing it in any other section in anything like the abundance in which it exists there. In old times we used to think that the Schoodic Lake country, particularly around Grand Lake Stream, was bad on account of these diabolical insects, and I have seen them so thick on the Miramichi that the air was black with them--but I have never anywhere seen anything like the prodigal plenty in which they are found on the Magalloway."

THE BIG TROUT OF THE STONE DAM

By Ompompanoosuc, from *Forest and Stream*, November 6, 1891

From Frank Leslie's Magazine

Here we encounter not only the grand-daddy of trout, but also the grand-daddy tale of "the one that got away.".

In the summer of 1890 it was my good fortunate to spend a couple of weeks with two companions in camp at the forks of the Magalloway, about four miles below Parmachenee Lake. In the last few years I had met a number of anglers who had been in that region, and each and every one had sung the praises of the pool at the old stone dam on the Little Magalloway, and told, as only anglers can, of the number of two or three-pound trout taken at this pool, but they added that there always remained the giant of the waters, whom many had seen, a few had hooked and had with him a few moments of anxious and expectant pleasure; but none had been able to become intimately acquainted and to place their hands upon his gleaming sides. I had heard so much of this talk, that the one spot on earth, or rather water, where I longed to cast my fly was that stretch at the old stone dam on the Little Magalloway.

It is needless to say that as soon as we got camp well fixed we made a call at the old stone dam, which is about a mile up the Little Magalloway from the forks. A glorious morning's walk over the trail past Sunday Pond brought us to the stone dam. The sun was just giving the pool its early morning greeting as we reached it. It was indeed an ideal spot, and if beneath its rippling surface the patriarchs of the trout tribe were taking their morning swim and were ready for breakfast, I also would sing its praises. Jointing our rods, we commenced casting the fly from the head of the pool; and at the first cast they were ready for business. We caught a goodly number before they stopped rising to the fly. They were nice, fat, handsome fellows from a quarter to three-quarter pound in weight, and made glorious sport on a light rod, as we frequently took two or three at a cast. We did not get any of the old "he busters," but I, too, saw the father, nay the grandfather, of the trout of the Magalloway.

I had hooked a good half-pound trout, and it had made a gallant struggle for life and freedom, but the constant spring of the rod was too much for him, and he lay upon his side at the top of the water, and I was slowly reeling him in, when a giant trout rose directly beneath him, opened up a pair of monstrous jaws, slowly brought them together again, and my half-pound trout disappeared from view as would a two-inch shiner in the mouth of a 5lb. bass. What happened next I do not know, for I lost my head, had "buck fever," or something else, and the boys said I jumped about two feet in the air and gave an awful "yank." The first thing I realized was that my trout was in the air, and I had a glimpse of a fan-like tail as it disappeared from view. Perhaps it will be best to drop the curtain on the next few moments. Suffice to say that every angler has had some such experience and can picture the scene for himself and I sincerely hope he can do it justice. I cannot.

For the next few days by common consent that pool was my property, and I spent at least an hour there every day. I was there in the early morning before the sun was up, and at night when it was so dark I could not keep the trail by Sunday Pond---and climbing windfalls after is not pleasant traveling. I cast upon its waters flies of every size, shape and color, from tiny midge to large and gaudy bass fly, and when these failed I descended to bait, the abused angle worm, wood grub, a strip of fish, the fin of a trout, and live bait from a two-inch shiner to a half-pound chub. Many a handsome trout did I get, but not one glimpse of the old patriarch of the pool until the last day of our stay.

I was making my farewell visit to the stone dam alone, and was idly casting a fly upon its waters, and was just ready to reel up and leave, when, throwing my fly in the rapids near the dam, it was taken by a small quarter-pound trout and I commenced to reel him in. But he was a gamy little fellow and was darting here and there as quick as a flash; and the thought struck me, why not try him for bait! But, no, I will never be guilty of piercing the sides or lip of a lordly trout and using him for bait; but as this is my last cast, and I can see that you are likely hooked in the lip, for the gaudy wings of the Parmachenee-belle can be plainly seen, you may take one run down through the pool, and if you do not get away I will gently release you and you shall go free. I drew the line from the reel to give him all the play he wanted; and down to the center of the pool he went, and there he stopped for a few playful darts this way then that. Then he started again down the pool, until I had all the line from the spool and thought it about time to reel him in. But I could not start the reel, and still he went. I involuntarily struck and raised the tip, and for an instant a big fin shoed above the water and I knew I was fast again to the old patriarch of the waters. What a predicament. There I stood on a rock at the head of the pool with one of Chubb's little 4oz. "Raymond" rods in my hand, not a single turn of the line upon the spool of my reel, and 140ft. away, hooked with a No. 8 Sproat, was the giant trout of the Magalloway. There was one thing to do, and I gave him the butt. Whether the little rod was too much for him or he concluded he had that way far enough I do not know, but he turned and started for the head of the pool diagonally from me, and I had time to get a goodly lot of line on the reel; and then I took a good long breath. It was useless for me to attempt to describe the battle that followed. How long it lasted I do now know; but it was down the center, forward and back, cross over and all hands round and repeat, until at last he lay upon his side and was drawn across the landing net, and I had barely strength to lift him from the water. What a big one he was. Four, five pounds; yes, we will call him a six-pounder; as handsome in form and as brilliant in coloring as a half-pound trout. And why should he not be, this cannibal of the waters, who would refuse every kind of bait or fly and would have naught but his own spotted tribe, his relatives, or perhaps his own children. But you have had your last one, you old rascal, and the other trout can now swim in peace.

To understand the "subsequent proceedings" it will be necessary for me to describe the stone dam. This was not made by man, but was a natural ledge, running clear across and extending up the river for perhaps a couple of rods; but the fall was mostly in the last rod before the water fell in the pool below, somewhat more than halfway across when the water was at its usual summer height the ledge protruded from the water. This was worn smooth by the action of the water, and formed a flat table-like surface with rounded sides. The water upon each side of this ran with the swiftness and force of a raceway; but with care and a cool head it was possible for one to wade and jump on this rock without having the water come above a pair of high boots. Directly below this ledge, and jutting into the pool, were two large rocks, which could be reached from the ledge by a little careful wading; and from these rocks a good caster could reach all the best parts of the pool below. It was from this rock that I had been casting and upon which I now stood with my prize; and I wanted to get to shore with the fish soon as possible. Grasping the net above the trout, I crept to the ledge above and attempted to cross to the shore; but I was so weak I could hardly stand and hold the fish. With my first step the water nearly took my feet from under me; and I realized that I must rest before I could cross in safety. I therefore lay the landing net down pointing upstream, and stepped upon the frame in such a way that the fish could not get out. I had hardly straightened up when I heard a grating on the ledge, and just caught a glimpse of a long handle as it swung and rolled into the water. The moment the full force of the current caught it my feet flew out from under me and I sat down with a "dull thud," and the only reason why the ground did not shake was that I only weigh 130 lbs. and there was no ground to shake; it was all rock.

The current was fast drawing me in; I was wet all over before I could manage to grasp a protruding rock and drag myself out to look for my landing net and fish. The frame had caught in the rocks and the handle was playing shuttlecock on top of the racing water. Quickly grasping it, I began to raise the net; and as I did so the big trout came to the top of the water, some little way below, and with a dash was carried to the pool beneath. As he reached the more quiet waters of the pool and lay upon his side, he gave one "spat" with that giant tail, which was plainly heard above the roar of the waters, and disappeared from my view forever. No, not forever. Many a time during the past winter, as I have sat by the open fire, my feet upon the fender, watching the fantastic shapes the blaze would assume, have I seen the handsome form of that monstrous trout, and the scene at the old stone dam was all before me. And many a time in my dreams have I fought that battle over and over again and have been awakened by the "spat" of that fanlike tail as the trout disappeared from view--only to find that the noise was made by the alarm clock.

I told my companions that day that I had not got the big; that I had slipped into the water and was now ready to go home. From that day to this I have never told the story of the big trout. It was a very sore spot in my memory (and I had another one somewhere else) for many a day, but time works wonders. The sportsman only remembers the pleasure of a trip, the trials and discomfiture are forgotten or are made light of; and now I am enabled to look back with some degree of pleasure and think of that royal battle with the monstrous trout of the big pool at the old stone dam on the Little Magalloway.

– OMPOMPANOOSUC

BUCKSKIN SAM'S LAST BEAR FIGHT

By Samuel H. Noble, from *Life and Adventures of Buckskin Sam*, 1900

Buckskin Sam

Samuel H. Noble (1837-1908) was born and raised in Kennebunk, but left early in life, traveling around the globe seeking adventure and fortune. According to his biography, which is evidently highly exaggerated, he took the name Buckskin Sam, fought with the British Army in India, was at the Battle of Big Horn aside Custer and worked in Wild Bill Hickock's Wild West Show.

He returned to Maine, where he lived in a log cabin near Lake Mooselucmeguntic and worked as a guide, and later in life married and lived the remainder of his life in Mechanic Falls. This incredible tale is the last story in his autobiography, evidently occurring upon his return from the west, though some historians deem it to be fictitious.

One pleasant morning, the seventeenth of October 1898, in the town of Byron, Oxford County, Maine, myself and Mr. J. Louis Houle started out on a deer hunt. Louis carried a 45-70 and I carried my famous old 44 Winchester rifle. We started off in the direction of Houston Mountain. When we arrived there Mr. Houle said,

"Sam, let's separate. You may drive a deer to me, and I may drive one to you."

"All right, but remember, if we separate you have what you shoot and I have what I shoot."

"All right, Sam, go ahead."

Louis went around the west side of the mountain and I on the east side. I kept on until I came to West Mountain about one mile beyond. Not seeing any game of the kind, I still kept on and around the east side of West Mountain, and on up to the top, where I had a good view of the surrounding country.

After standing there a while and admiring the grand scenery I turned and west and commenced the descent. For a little ways the bushes were so thick I had to crawl on my hands and knees for some distance. All at once I came to the edge of a high ledge, and I looked over and far down into a canyon for two hundred feet.

I went to my left a little and on down to a little level spot of ledge about ten by twelve feet, in the edge of a "blow-down." There were some small trees, and one tree standing between two large logs. This one had some gum on it, so I stood my rifle up against a tree. Not thinking of wild animals being in such a place as that I had only three cartridges in my rifle at the time.

I drew my hunting knife out and was picking the little lumps of gum. All of a sudden I heard shuffling noise behind me and the breaking of a small stick as though you would break a pipe stem between your fingers. At that instant I caught hold of my rifle and turned around quickly, only to be confronted face to face, by five hungry bears within ten feet of where I stood between the logs.

One of them got around behind me, another stood at the end of the two logs, while the other three were circling around me. I aimed my old Winchester at number one bear, "bang" and down she fell, dead at the first shot. Then the other two turned to go to my left and bang went another shot. Number two bear fell dead, and the ball going through and striking number three bear in the fore shoulder, he, with a snarl, went down over the ledge a hundred feet or more. Then I turned around to see what the bear behind me was doing. She was standing behind a tree so I could not get a shot at her head, so I got up with the rifle and sent a ball whizzing through her ribs. With a howl of pain and rage over the ledge went the same as number three. When I turned back again number five bear stood erect on his hind feet within three feet of me, his little eyes twinkling like two stars.

Just at that moment he struck at my head with his right paw and I dodge the heft of his blow. He only tore my hat and struck me on my right hand. I worked the lever of my rifle and found it empty of cartridges. I shifted my knife to my right hand, and with my left put my rifle over my head as a guard. He struck me a blow with his right paw on the breast, tearing the whole of the sweater and vest from me, and knocking me back against the tree. I recovered myself, as quickly as I could, and with lightning like spring forward I plunged my hunting knife to the hilt in his shaggy breast.

Over he went on his back and rolled under one of the logs at my left. I took two steps forward to finish him with my knife, then I thought as I had wounded him I had better reload my rifle. I stepped back and began to reload, and by the time I got the cartridges in he had crawled out on the opposite side of the log and got behind a large rock. There he stood with blood dripping from the knife wound in his breast, and peeking around a tree at me. I yelled at him to make him show his head, but he would not. So I put up the old Winchester and fired at his eye. The ball just missed, and cut the skin from his ear so that it hung down below his jaw. He backed back a little and gave me a chance at his neck. Then I gave it to him in the neck—one, two. He thought I was making it too warm for him, so he fetched an angry snarl, and with a couple of jumps forward he went down over the ledge, taking sticks, stones everything with him into the cave below.

I went after him with knife in one hand and rifle in the other and hunted all around one cave and out into another, but I could not hear or see him. I circled around for half an hour, but all in vain, he had crawled in somewhere out of sight to breathe his last.

Then I climbed back up over the ledge to where my two dead bears lay and got down between them for half an hour to see if some other bears would not come on the scene, but all was still. Then I arose and examined my spoil. Two fat bears, how is that for Buckskin!

Then by means of my compass I took my course down the mountain, and with my knife blazed the trees from my bears out to the main road. The next day I got a number of men and got them out. This finishes my last bear hunt.

Chapter 2

THE RANGELEY LAKES

The Rangeley Lakes in western Maine consists of five lakes – Rangeley, which was originally called Oquossuc Lake, Mooselookmeguntic, Upper and Lower Richardson, and Umbagog Lake. They are the headwaters of the Androscoggin River and are basically fed by the Kennebago and Cupsuptic Rivers.

Originally called the Androscoggin Lakes, for many years they competed with the Adirondacks as the best fishing resort in the East, and in Maine these lakes and Moosehead Lake were the most frequently visited regions. The region was not settled until 1815 and soon Squire James Rangeley purchased the town, which he operated like a feudal estate for a few years before moving on, leaving his name on the lake and town. Several dams were built at the foot of Rangeley Lake, Mooselookmeguntic and Lower Richardson, controlling the flow of water and the lake levels. Early on Upper Dam had a lumber camp where sportsmen could stay and at Middle Dam at the "Angler's Retreat," which was opened by Joshua G. Rich about 1860. In 1878 Middle Dam Camps were rebuilt on the site of the older camps, and are the oldest continually operating sporting camps in Maine.

George Soule, an old guide, had a small cottage near the outlet of Rangeley Lakes which was later enlarged as the Mountain View House. The Oquossuc Angling Club was founded in 1867, was the first private sporting club in Maine and their camp, the Kennebago House, was open for many years. Here they operated one of the first salmon hatcheries in the nation at a brook that empties into Bemis Cove.

Access to the Rangeley Lakes was first made from two points. Travelers could take the train to Bryant Pond, a stagecoach to Andover, a buckboard to South Arm and steamers to their hotels or camps. The other approach was by way of Farmington where a daily stage ran up the Sandy River to Phillips, and where visitors could stay at the Barden Hotel. The next day they would take a stage over the mountains to Greenvale on Rangeley Lake. Here they could stay at the Greenvale House or take a steam boat to Rangeley City, or the Mountain View House, where you could obtain a guide. A third approach was opened in the 1890s, when a train track was built up the Swift River to Bemis on Mooselookmeguntic Lake. This train station claimed to be the only log cabin railway station in the country. Also the Sandy River Railroad was built through Redington, affording a new approach to Rangeley City.

In its heyday the Rangeley Lakes had many large hotels available for hundreds of guests, several run by Capt. Fred Barker, who also ran steamboats. Here they were apt to meet Fly Rod Crosby, who wrote about the establishments and the many people who visited them. When the Maine Guide System was inaugurated, she received badge number one for her tireless promotion of the region.

Trips could also be taken to Kennebago Lake on a buckboard, where they could stay at the Forest Retreat and later at Grant's Kennebago Camps, where they could be entertained with Ed Grant's wonderful stories. Later sporting camps were erected on nearby Saddleback Lake, Loon Lake and Dodge Pond, and today there are fewer hotels at Rangeley, but there are available sporting camps, cabins and other hostelries.

SIX-POUND TROUT

By Thomas S. Steele, from *Forest and Stream*, October 9, 1873

Thomas Sedgewick Steele

Thomas Sedgewick Steele (1845-1903) was born in Hartford, Conn., where he attended Hartford High School. Showing a talent for art and drawing, he went into the jewelry business with his father and ran a successful firm, Thomas Steele and Son, from 1866 to 1875, that allowed him to vacation summers. In the early 1870's, when about twenty-five years old, he began taking his annual vacation trips to the Rangeley Lakes, where he enjoying fly-fishing, one of his favorite hobbies. In 1873 he published one of his first articles, relating the catching of a trout in Mooselucmeguntic Lake.

EDITOR OF FOREST AND STREAM; -- My six-pounder was a genuine *Salmo Fontinalis,* or speckled brook Trout, and was caught in the Mooselucmaguntic Lake, Maine, twenty miles from the Canada border. It was in the early part of June, and the snow had hardly left the ground, when our merry party started for camp to throw care aside for two brief weeks, and enjoy in the depths of the woods that stimulant which nature seems so ready to impart. As we journeyed over the road on one fine morning, Mounts Saddleback and Abraham stood out in their brightest livery, while up and down their rugged side were patches of snow, and from a bank by the roadside we had the audacity to form balls and return to our younger days of snow-balling.

To be suddenly transported from a State where trout weighing a quarter of an ounce are looked upon as gold dust, to a region where they *average* from one to two pounds each, was a little too much for my senses, and I really had to shake myself occasionally to whether I was in the body or out of the body. It really seemed like the realization of my boyish dreams of the "Indian's happy hunting grounds." As I started out with my guide the last day of my vacation, a fellow angler suggested that if I was going out to the lake to troll (I had fished mostly in the brooks which emptied into the lake) I had better take a heavier rod, my eight ounce split bamboo fly rod being too light for that purpose. We were soon at the mouth of the river and upon the placid waters of the lake. It was a lovely morning, and as the mist drifted off the surface of the lake, away to the north loomed up that finest shaped mountain in these parts --Mt. Kennebago--while on our right in other's good company, lay Mts. Iscohos, Deer, and Observatory. Away to the western horizon was the pride of New England, the "White Hills," the distance producing that elegant purple so peculiar to mountain scenery, which was shaded by the different ranges form purple to blue, and then to the green of the nearer mountains, making a scene to be enjoyed without trout being thrown in to heighten its color. We fished with live minnows at that time of the season, it being too early for flies, although strange to relate, no one dared even to whisper *bait* from New York to camp; but after a few days unsuccessful trial, how quickly and how naturally they all took to it. I believe with Mr. Prime, that if trout will not take a fly, put on something they will take; and it was intensely interesting to see our noted *fly fishermen* changing gaudy flies for sombre-colored minnows, when there repeated casts failed to produce even a rise, while someone in the next boat was meeting with the best of luck by using bait. Mooselucmaguntic Lake (a person wants a hard cold to pronounce it to perfection) is twelve miles long and about three miles wide, one of the Androscoggin chain, one of the largest, I believe, and certainly one of the most beautiful. It was under the shadows of old Bald Mountain, which lies to the northeast of the lake, that I first felt that magic pull that went like an electric thrill to the ends of my fingers. I had been trolling with about one hundred and twenty-five feet of line, and had caught a few small trout from a half to one pound each, but had decided that my last would be the poorest of all the days. You are apt to get a little careless when trolling for some time without success. In fact, I was so interested in the landscape that I had just returned my fly-hook to my pocket, having made a rough hasty sketch of the White Mountains, which were in full view. Just then a trout struck and aroused me from my reveries. Before I had recovered from the first shock another followed, until I had no doubt of the quality of my game. Then all was quiet again, and wondering what had happened I gently reeled up a few feet of the line, my guide remarking that he thought I had lost him. But I very soon discovered that it was not so, but that his lordship had taken the matter in to his own hands and was heading directly for the boat, thinking, I suppose, that our shadow in the water was a lone rock under whose protection he might find rest. For a while it was about an even chance whether the line could be gathered on to my repeating reel as fast as the fish dropped the slack of it in the water, for it was with the greatest difficulty I could retain a consciousness of the fish. But finally, after a hundred feet of the line had been stowed away on the reel and twenty-five feet only remained, the trout became motionless as a rock. Now came the time to see which should be the master. Nervously I held him, expecting some new freak would start him the next moment and I had not long to wait, for the next instant he shot like an arrow for under the boat.

"Quick! guide, quick!" I shouted, and with a sudden dip of the paddle we shot out into the lake, the trout coming up on the other side of us, but not in a way he most desired. Before I had recovered sufficiently from this movement he plunged for the bottom. I endeavored to check him by "giving him the but," but it was no use, for in less time than it has taken to tell it, I had lost fifty feet of line and he was not contented even with that. Slowly again I reeled him in, foot by foot, inch by inch, and drew him so near that I could see his entire length. Guide said "he would weigh hard on to four and a half pounds, but never having caught a trout weighing over two and a quarter pounds, I did not offer my opinion. Backwards and forwards I swayed the giant until four feet of my single gut leader showed itself above the water, and I could see the mottled sides of the trout, and in my anticipation he was as good as mine. With head down and his caudal appendage moving backwards and forwards, he lay, stubborn and obstinate. My guide dropped a stone into the landing net to keep it in the right position, and slipped it overboard, but his majesty was so fagged out as we had anticipated, for with another tug at the line he sought the bottom, doubling in this way again and again, one moment seeming to be mine and the next knocking over all my air castles by running fifty feet away. Finally, finding all efforts to get free were useless, he came again to the surface and with a dexterous movement of the net he was safely landed in the boat. Quickly seizing my scales I held him up to my guide's admiring gaze. Immediately the indicator marked *six pounds*, and passing around his body a cord he measured fourteen inches at the dorsal fin and twenty-five inches in length. Looking at my watch, just twenty-six minutes had been spent in his capture. As he lay there in the net still heaving with excitement, his sides spotted with gold and rubies, his gills distended, and his dark fins edged with snowy white, to say that I was happy would tells half the story, for such an experience is but one in a life time.

– T. S. S.

IN THE WOODS OF MAINE

By D. H. E., from *The American Sportsman*, December, 1873

A View from Snowman's Point (From Farrar's Illustrated Guide Book of The Androscoggin Lakes, 1883)

When earlier sportsmen made a visit to Kennebago Lake, they had to build shelters to camp in, but by 1873 a rustic log cabin was available, but still no boats. It would be another five years before "Forest Retreat," a log lodge with twenty beds, would be built at the southern end of Kennebago Lake by Grant and Richardson, offering much better accommodations to those willing to make the nine mile trek from Rangeley.

Last fall, myself and two friends, Fred and Dick, started for Lake Kennebago, in the northwestern part of Maine, quite near the mountains, which form the boundary between Maine and Canada. We first went to Portland, from there to Farmington, then to Phillips, by stage. We stayed at Phillips all night, and early the next morning we started in a wagon for the woods, and struck the "tote-path" or trail, that led to John's Pond, nine miles distant, and upon the shores of which we intended to camp that night.

After a very hard tramp, we at last reached our destination, and our canine friend, "Cato," (a fine setter) came in for his share of duty, and succeeded in flushing a fine covey of partridges, five of which were quickly brought to grief, and made ready for supper.

After building a rousing fire, which is the main comfort of a camp, winter or summer, we next proceeded to build our camp. This was done by planting some forked sticks firmly in the ground, and placing a pole across them, and then some sticks, reaching from the cross pole to the ground, forming the rafters. These were covered with hemlock branches, and our house was finished. Our beds were made of small branches of fir, which form a very fragrant and soft couch.

While all this was going on, our guide was preparing supper, and when was all ready, we gathered round the festive board (said board was an old log) and partook of a supper of broiled partridge, fried pork, brown bread and coffee; and our appetites being well sharpened by our unusual exertions, we did ample justice to the repast. A short smoke, and then, after replenishing the fire, we all turned in, being too tired for story-telling that night.

When I awoke it was day. Rousing my comrades, we washed ourselves at the lake and then prepared breakfast. This eaten, we discharged our guide and pack-horse, determined to cut loose from all that was *civil* or civilized, for a time at least.

The pond must next be crossed, and a raft made for the purpose. This was done from logs, which were lying on the shore, and making our traps fast, we embarked and after an hour's time, and some trouble in finding a good landing place, we disembarked, made our raft fast, for future use, shouldered our packs and started off boldly in the direction of Kennebago, about three miles off. Each man's pack weighed about one hundred pounds, besides gun, rod, etc. We pushed on and at last found ourselves at the top of a hill, and there beneath us, lay the longed for haven of rest. There was a log-hut, which was to be our home, and there was the lake and stream just visible through the trees, while huge mountains in the background showed the dividing line between us and the Canadas.

We hastened forward, deposited our packs on the ground. Rods were soon brought out, flies overhauled and selected, and while I stayed to fix up a little the other two went down to the stream to try their luck with the trout. About dusk they returned, having had some excellent sport, and bringing five trout, from 1 lb. to 3 ½ lbs. with them. We cooked them for supper and after having eaten them, took a long smoke and retired.

The next morning I was awake before light, and after getting things ready for breakfast, I took my gun, called the boys and Cato, and just as the son rose above the mountains, started out to see if I couldn't get a partridge for breakfast. It was rather early for shooting, but in a few minutes Cato struck a scent, and pointed as staunch as a rock.

I walked on and flushed a small covey of partridges, from which I killed one as they rose, and another when they were about fifteen yards off. Cato retrieved them handsomely, and I started back to camp. After breakfast, I started again with my gun and dog, leaving the others to try their luck at fishing. We went some distance before Cato stopped, and I knew by the way his body quivered, and by the gentle waving of his tail, that there was something right under his nose. Sure enough, as I went forward, I flushed a large covey of twenty odd partridges. I killed one, but missed fire with my second barrel, and the rest got away. Soon another covey was flushed, and two killed; then another rose as I was walking away, so close to me and so unexpectedly, that they got clear away before I knew what was the matter. Suddenly I heard the chattering of a squirrel, and looking, saw a large squirrel overhead. My gun was at my face in a minute, but as I moved the squirrel darted off. I followed, and after a long chase, had the satisfaction of bringing him down, and found that it was a large black squirrel, the first and last I saw while in the woods.

So the sport went on--first partridges, then squirrel, besides one rabbit which I almost stepped on before it started, and when I got back to camp almost 4 p.m., I had six partridges, three squirrels, one rabbit and the black squirrel. The others had been back some time, having made with only fair luck, getting seven small fish.

Almost dusk, I took my rod, and selecting a large white miller, went to try my luck with the fish. A few rods from the camp was a log bridge, and thither I went, as the most favorable place for fishing. The pool was still and deep and scarcely had my fly struck the water when with a rush a large trout rose to it. A sharp turn of the wrist, and I struck him. For one second of time he waited, and then started down stream. I let him go until my line ran short, and then I gently slackened, and succeeded in turning him. Back he came, leaping out of the water, and it took all my skill to prevent his getting a bite of line over his body, and breaking it. At last, when within thirty feet of me, he stopped, and I could not induce him to move. All at once, with a rush, he started directly for the bridge, on which I stood, intending to pass under it. I knew if he did this I should lose him, and checked him again. Now came the tug of war. My pole bent nearly double. My line was of the best braided silk, my leader of the whitest gut, and my fly strong and new. Would they bear the strain? Slowly the rod began to spring back, and then I knew that the fish was giving way, and would soon turn down stream. I was ready for him, as with a plunge he started in his career. Again I slackened and turned him, and as he came slowly towards me, I saw that he was beginning to feel my efforts, but I well knew that I was to have one more struggle before I conquered him. He turned on one side till I could dimly see his glistening form, then with a desperate plunge, he went straight to the bottom, and gave a few jerks at the line, then, as quick as lightning, reappeared and commenced again the same evolutions that had tried my skill when I first hooked him. Such efforts could not last long, however, and indeed this proved to be the last struggle, and as I found myself victor I breathed freer. Slowly I led him to the bank, where he was landed by one of my friends. A noble fish he was, and as game a one as it had been my fortune to kill. His length was 21 ½ inches, and he weighed 4 ¼ lbs. Darkness had now fairly come, and well satisfied, we returned to camp for supper and rest.

This was the beginning of the some splendid sport, and many a noble trout and fat partridge graced our table, cooked in all the different ways we could invent. For two short weeks we wandered in the woods with our guns, or up and down the stream with our rods. Well do I remember a dark deep pool at the foot of the rapids, some half mile from camp, when in one short hour we landed six fish weighing twenty-five lbs. total.

But all such things have an end, and early one rainy morning we started for home, fully resolved that we would either return next fall, or at least seek some other part of Northern Maine.

TROUT-FISHING IN THE RANGELEY LAKES

By Edward Spencer Mott, from *Scribner's Monthly*, 1877

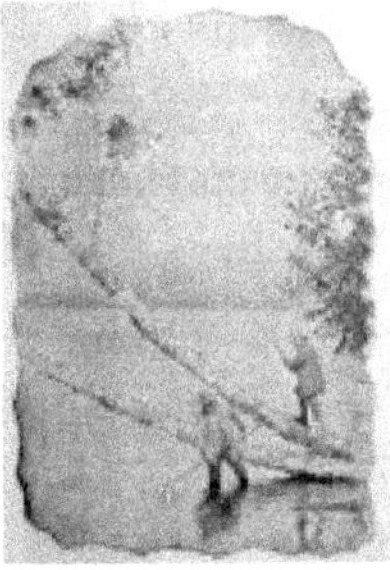
A Rangeley Beauty

Edward Spencer Mott (1844-1910), a respected short story writer from New York, who went under sever pseudonyms, published many articles, often on sociological themes, for Harper's Monthly, Putnam's Monthly, Scribner's Monthly, The Atlantic and Galaxy Magazine. Later he tried his hand at literature, producing a three-part story, Tristan and Isolde, that was published in Galaxy Magazine.

After vacationing in the Rangeley Lakes Region, he wrote a long article about the wonderful fishing found there, including this story of Mr. Page's trout. George S. Page, who was originally from Readfield, Maine, and later resided in Stanley, New Jersey, was the founder and first president of the Oquossuc Angling Club, whose clubhouse was Camp Kennebago, on Mooselookmeguntic Lake.

I very well remember an incident which happened upon the occasion of my first visit to Camp Kennebago, when I was a tyro in trout fishing, and had not been fully initiated in the use of the fly. My boat was at anchor some distance below "Stony Batter," and with humiliation I confess that I was angling with a minnow. For a half hour or more there had been no sign of a trout in my vicinity, and I had carelessly laid my pole across the boat, with the butt under the thwart. Suddenly there was a "strike." Before I could seize my pole, the trout had carried the line directly under the boat with such a rush as to snap the rod--which I ought to say, in justice to the professional makers, was a cheap store rod--into two or three pieces. The trout escaped, as he deserved to do, and for once I could not help confessing myself outgeneraled. This mishap, of course, put an end to my fishing for the day, but fortunately it occurred quite late in the afternoon, and this left me at leisure to enjoy a scene which was in itself singularly beautiful, and which was an appropriate setting for a striking incident.

As the sun was sinking behind the hills, close under which we are fishing, it threw their long shadows far out on the lake, while the waters on the eastern shore were still bright with the golden light of the gentle June evening. In the distance, we descried three specks upon the water, which gradually grew in size as they steadily approached us, until we made out three batteaux laden with the "river-drivers," who were returning from their perilous and tedious journey down the Androscoggin with the great log-rafts,--the results of the previous winter's lumbering. The first sound which disturbed the Sabbath-like stillness of the lake, as the batteaux came nearer, was the steady thump, thump, thump of the sweeps in the rowlocks. Then we heard the sound of voices, but at first too indistinctly to determine whether it was the echo of boisterous talk, or some river-driver's song, with which the oarsmen were keeping time. But soon the sounds, as they became linked together, grew into that grand old tune, "Coronation," and the words,

"All hail the power of Jesus' name!"

came to us over the peaceful waters, snug with all strength, steadiness, and fervor which might be expected in a congregation of religious worshipers. Nothing could have been in more perfect harmony with the scene, and yet nothing could have been a greater surprise than to hear this tune and words, with which it is so inseparably connected, coming with such zest from the throats of men who have gained an undeserved reputation for roughness, not say profanity, of speech.

Mr. Page, although the most expert and enthusiastic fisherman of our number, had devoted himself so assiduously to caring for the comfort of his quests that his own chances of catching the big trout had been seriously lessened. In was our last afternoon together, and as the hours waned toward sunset, the surface of the lake became as smooth and as brilliant as burnished steel. Our three boats were anchored within a short distance of each other, and we were condoling with our friend upon his lack of luck, when suddenly, a few rods away, there was a quick swirl and splash which told of the presence of a big fish. "That's my trout!" exclaimed Mr. Page, as he ordered his guide to haul anchor and scull him quietly over the spot where the fish had appeared. Two or three casts of the fly, and in an instant, with a ferocious rush, the trout had hooked himself so firmly that his final capture became only a question of time,--but of what a time! After two or three desperate struggles, during which he was met at every turn with the skill of a practiced fisherman, he settled sulkily at the bottom of the lake. Meanwhile, a gentle east wind had sprung up with the setting sun, and Mr. Page's boat began to drift with it gently to the westward. Fifteen minutes, half an hour, three-quarters of an hour passed, and from our anchorage we could see that the trout had shown no signs of yielding,--nor did Mr. Page. As it gradually grew dark to "cast" with satisfaction, my companion in the other boat and myself decided to haul up anchor and "got to see the fun," which at our distance from the scene of conflict, seemed to be growing decidedly monotonous. By this time Mr. Page had drifted fully half a mile to the westward, and not once had the trout given any sign of yielding. When we came up with Mr. Page it was quite dark, and the contest, which did not seem so very unequal after all,-- for it was yet doubtful which would get the best of it,--had stretched out to a full hour and a quarter. Then at last, the trout showed signs of exhaustion, and, yielding to the inevitable pressure of the elastic rod, was once brought to the surface, but not close enough to net. Settling again to the bottom, he had apparently made up his mind to stay there; but the gentle, steady persuasion of the faithful seven-ounce Murphy split bamboo fly-rod again proved too much for him, and straining his tackle to the utmost, Mr. Page brought his victim gradually toward the surface. The three boats had now come so close together that the fish was shut in on all the sides. But it had become so dark that it was difficult to discern objects with any distinctness, and to shed all the light we could upon the puzzling problem which was at last approaching solution, we got together all the matches we had with us, and made in each boat, a miniature bonfire. Soon a commotion upon the surface of the water showed that the critical moment had arrived.

There, with his back fin as erect as ever, was a magnificent trout, which was soon in the landing-net and in a moment after in the boat, after precisely an hour and a half of as steady and persistent a fight as a fish ever made for his life. But his capture was a full reward for all time and trouble it had cost, since he weighed by the scale full seven pounds.

This trout and one weighing eight pounds which had been taken by Mr. Crounse were among the magnificent trophies which were carried away from Bema when we broke camp a day or two afterward…

A TRIP TO HATHAN BOG

By D. S. Thomas, from *Forest and Stream*, October 27, 1881

A Study in Trout (From Canoe and Camera, by Thomas S. Steele, 1882)

In this account, D. S. Thomas for Sherbrooke mentions the changes at Megantic since his first trip there twenty years previous. His story also gives us a good sense of the fishing and hunting on the Quebec side of the Boundary Mountains as well as the early routes across the border that were used prior to the formation of the Megantic Fish and Game Club, which later owned this entire region. After several days at Spider Lake, the group decided to cross over Boundary Mountains into Maine and fish at Hathan Bog.

After several days fishing and shooting with fair success, we concluded to go through to Hathan Bog, in Maine, and Ball spent a couple of days in blazing line and hauling through a small boat capable of carrying two, but so tottlish that a quid of tobacco couldn't be shifted from one jaw to the other without the danger of a capsize.

On the 19th, we started from the upper river, and after six hours tramp over the mountains reached the bog, distant four or five miles, about 3 P.M. Our party consisted of four and owing to the difficult nature of the route, were unable to carry anything but provisions - a light cotton tent, one blanket and firearms. Large game were plentiful, and it was necessary to keep very quiet. The tracks of deer and moose were abundant. Every rod of ground in the vicinity of the bog and its inlet was tracked like a cattle pasture, and numbers of freshly cut paths through the moss led to the water on all sides. We concluded to camp on the "burnt land," some two miles lower down, where we could pick up camp wood with out being obliged to use an axe. While two of us took the range the other two, with the traps, took the boat through the bog and down the outlet. In doing so we were obliged to haul boat over two strongly-constructed beaver dams, the upper one of which floods the bog to a depth of five feet, making a sheet of water about a quarter of a mile across, which was covered with lily-pads. These pads had been eaten by the moose through the whole extent of the bog. The lower dam, constructed some distance below the other, is very substantially built at a point where it has the support of two large granite boulders, and is evidently to prevent the total escape of water in the event of the upper dam being unable to withstand the pressure. Both these dams are covered with a dense growth of grass and bushes. Ball said the upper one was an old one when he first saw it, some fifteen miles ago. Under each of these we caught some fine trout. Our tent was pitched a little back from the river and about two and a half miles above the uppermost of the chain of ponds in Maine. Here five considerable ponds, and several minor ones, may be struck within a circumference of a mile, namely: Arnold, Crosby, Moosehorn, Horseshoe and Hathan Bog. All abound with trout, while Arnold and Crosby contain lunge. The waters of all unite and form the principal tributary of the chain of ponds. In rear of our camp stands the finest granite ledge we have ever seen. Near the edge fissures extend to a depth of twenty to thirty feet, with smooth perpendicular sides. God help the fisher--or any other man--who should fall into one of these fissures. Unaided, his chances of escape would be small, and he would be provided with a sarcophagus not made with hands.

At night two of us rigged a jack-light and went back to the bog. The night was warm and perfectly still. The hoot of the owl and the alarm signal of the beaver were the only sounds. We had never heard the beaver before, and when the alarm was given so close that the water almost splashed over us, it caused a shiver in the back and our hand took a tighter grasp of the rifle. It is given by slapping the tail paddle-like on the water, and the sound is similar to that of a twenty-pound stone thrown into deep water. On our return we heard a large moose walking through the marsh close by, occasionally stopping to feed or reconnoiter. It kept just within the edge of the timber, and although we remained perfectly still for ten minutes within one hundred feet, we failed to get a sight of it. We tried for two nights more to get a shot at it, but without success. On nearly every stream moose tracks were seen in which the water was still muddy. Several deer were also seen one a very large buck, with antlers seven or eight pronged. One of our party was within shooting distance, and raised the site of his rifle to three hundred yards. Afterwards he managed to get some bushes between him and them and got within sixty yards, when he fired, forgetting to lower the sight. He then fired a second shot, the buck in each case merely looking rough at the crack of the rifle. A third shot must have touched his ear, for, giving his head a savage shake, he started for the timber. The same day this party had a bead drawn on another buck, standing in a tamarack grove, and lost his shot by waiting for him to come out into the open, which he didn't.

Trout in the vicinity of our camp was abundant. On the last evening Ball took out over thirty in a few minutes with the fly, without moving the position of he boat. Our supply of bread and pork being exhausted, we took our back track on the 22d, making the distance from the head of the Hathan Bog to the Spider in four hours and reaching the Chaudiere at ten o'clock the same night, feeling that we had exercise enough for one day

– D. S. THOMAS

TROUT FISHING ON RAPID RIVER IN '74

By E. L. C. from *Forest and Stream*, October 14, 1899

Another fisherman visits Angler's Retreat in the early days, finding good fishing and good room and board. Arriving at Upton, they took a ride on the steamer "Diamond" to Sunday Cove then walked the seven mile carry to Middle Dam. On this carry, which the author called Cedar Stump Carry, can be found Forest Lodge, the home of Louise Dickenson Rich, whose books about her family's life there in the early 1940's, became national bestsellers.

We arrived at Middle Dam Camp a little before 8 o'clock, tired and hunger, but not too far gone to feel interested in a smudge at the end of the piazza, over which stood the horse and cow, to rid themselves of the mosquitoes, which pest reigned supreme at that season.

After regaling ourselves with one of Asa Frost's delicious suppers (he was a fine cook), we sat be a large open fire, while the men had their evening smoke, and planned the morning work. We agreed to get up at 4 o'clock and go down to the Dam. I had been in bed about five minutes, it seemed to me, when there was a rap at the door, and our guide said it was 4 o'clock. I insisted his watch was wrong and I would not get up for all the trout in B. Pond (and there were many in those days), but Gethro knew it was the early bird that caught the trout, as well as worm, and he went down to the Dam to get the big string of trout we had walked so far to catch. He was repaid. When I appeared at 7 o'clock there lay twenty-seven trout--such beauties! None under a pound and the largest 3lbs.! Gethro stood up to his knees in water; a few yards below him the guide with his net. As Gethro cast into the middle of the stream, often hooking two fish at one strike, an old guide who sat on the rocks watching the performance said: "They seems to be a reg'lar flight er the critters." Gethro wanted me to try my luck. I had never thrown a fly, and like everything else, it needed practice; but I managed to get one into the water, and the second the fly touched the surface a trout had it and was off. I was told to play the fish till the guide brought the net. I could not wait for all that ceremony, so I snatched my trout out, doubling my rod terribly. The two men nearly had a convulsion; they thought the rod would snap, but I thought I should lose my trout and I did not wait for the proper way. I ran off, dragging him into the bushes, where I was sure he could not get away from me. I dropped the rod, seized him with both hands, took him off the hook myself, and ended his life.

We had caught all the fish we needed for ourselves and friends, and after a breakfast of trout baked in cream we packed our finny prizes for the walk back to Cedar Stump. I was so lame I could not walk, and Bony was called to carry me down. (He was so named because he ate fish bones and all). I was strapped on to his back. My whole day was to look out that the branches didn't sweep me off his back, or the black flies devour me. Reins were not needed to guide this remarkable horse; he picked his way among those boulders as man could not--never stumbled. But the pitching down and back was very peculiar--quite sea sickening in effect. Occasionally I would exclaim "Oh Bony! Do wait a minute till I regain my equilibrium," which language he always understood and cheerfully waited. He often made the journey over the carry with people strapped on his back; no less a personage than Gen. Ben Butler had been carried in the same manner a few days before.

At last we reached Cedar Stump. I was taken off dear Bony's back, and I bade him an affectionate farewell and told him I would drink his health from Cold Spring nearby. I was dying of thirst, and proceeded at once to the spring, a little in advance of the men, who were collecting materials for a fire to cook our lunch before the twelve-mile row down the lake. As I neared the spring a man was lying down, drinking. I had often seen Gethro do it, so thought nothing of it. As he finished and moved, behold! a bear before my very eyes! I stood gazing at the shaggy creature, when the guide, a few feet away, called out "I smell a bear," I thought it was rather circus-like in odor in that lovely dell, but did not connect it with bruin. I could not move--whether fear or interest beheld me, I was unable to say. After a satisfactory gaze at me, the bear with great dignity marched into the bushes. The guide was much excited and wanted to chase him with his gun, but I told the guide it was my bear, for I saw him first, and as bruin was polite enough to leave me unharmed and enough water in the spring to quench my thirst, I should protest against molesting him. The guide, too, belonged to us, for in those days we actually bought guides.

We had what I call a wild lunch--no dishes to cook in, but trout and thin slices of salt pork stuck on a green stick (which would not burn easily), and frizzled, and delicious water from Cold Spring, the quality of which cannot be excelled.

We found our little rowboat just as we had left it the night before. I was so tired I was made to lie in the bottom of the boat and an umbrella spread over me, to keep me from being sun-burned, for I was already a wreck from lameness and the miserable black flies. We arrived at the mouth of the Cambridge River as the sun was going down behind Squaw Mountain, and I forgot all my ills in my admiration of the surroundings. I cannot describe the grandeur. Please, readers, all go there and see for yourselves the beauties of nature in that region.

When we reached Upton we found an audience ready for us--guides who had been to B. Pond and Parmachenee Lake with Gethro in the old days, and who thought him a wonder because he could throw a fly so far, and several woodsmen who had many a time enjoyed his good stories round the open fire. In we stalked, carrying the big string of trout. "There! I tole ye so! The biggest ketch yit!" said one of his old friends.

The next morning we were up before the lark even, because we must reach Bethel early--before the heat should wither our trout--and as the driver said it was a "dreffu han'some drive down to Bethel." I suspect by "han'some" he meant the downhill drive as well as early morning scenery, and with our own horse we were able to make the trip more rapidly than the stage. The news of our good luck had preceded us, and never were mortals more warmly welcomed than we that morning by our friends at the Bethel House.

To-day Cedar Stump carry is much like any other piece of wooded road, and a span of horses attached to a three-seated buckboard makes the journey from Middle Dam to Sunday Cove, morning and afternoon. Middle Dam of '90 is quite different from Middle Dam of '74. The lake, mosquitoes and flies can be found the same. The old log cabin, Asa Frost, the man of the place, the dear horse and cow, as well as most of the trout, have disappeared.

– E. L. C.

KENNEBAGO MOUNTAIN CAVE

By J. R. Rich, from *Forest and Stream*, August 15, 1889

Joshua G. Rich

In about 1847 Joshua Gross Rich (1820-1897) moved his family to an abandoned farm at Metallak Point in Upper Richardson Lake. Here, twenty-three miles from Andover, they made a living farming, hunting and trapping. In about 1860 he moved his family to Upton, but they were soon back at Lower Richardson Lake where Joshua ran a store for loggers and outdoorsmen for seventeen years and opened the original Middle Dam Camps, then known as Angler's Retreat.

Rich travelled all over the Rangeley region in search of moose, deer, caribou and bear and wrote about many of his exciting adventures in the Bethel Courier and in Forest and Stream magazine.

The following story is a fictional account of a trip. A thorough search on caves and geology of Western Maine does not locate any such cave in the Kennebago Mountain region. The type of bed rock and granite that makes up the region would not have created the kind of limestone cave that Rich used as the basis for his tale.

In 1850 the State of Maine placed on the market certain townships and parts of townships of public land in the Bingham West Kennebec Purchase, so-called. Most of these lands were remote from civilization, in which were high, rugged and precipitous mountains, deep ravines and rushing cascades, although in the valleys between the mountains there were beautiful lakes and smooth running rivers, also open meadows of tall grasses and reeds, where the moose, caribou and deer roamed in freedom and peace; also timber lands where the woodsman's axe had never struck a blow. These lands were advertised for sale by the land agent of the State, and were situated in the northern part of Oxford, Franklin and Somerset counties, inland many days journey from settlements or roads, or in the deep recesses of the mountain wilderness. In the year

1835---fifteen years after Maine had become an independent State--there sprang up a great excitement in timber lands, and speculation ran so high that the authorities found it necessary to township off the untrodden wilderness of wild lands belonging to the State. These lines were run by competent surveyors at that time. Many of these townships had been sold by the State to individuals and corporations, leaving the most remote and least valuable portions still in the possession of the State. Many speculators were now on the qui vive, looking up township lines and making explorations. Among that class was Mr. E. S. Prentiss, ex-mayor of Bangor, a prominent lawyer, and he employed the writer of this article to guide and assist him in exploring certain tracts of land situated in the counties named, more especially some parts of townships bordering in the Canada line.

It was in the month of August 1850, that we started out in our light birch canoe well stored with camping outfit. The basis of our supplies was salt pork and hard bread, with pepper and salt, sugar and tea, a ball of butter, and a little flour. Our cooking utensils consisted simply of fry-pan, wire broiler and two-quart tin pail. Then we had each a blanket, also a light axe and a small gun. Our ammunition consisted of powder and bird shot No. 6, with bullets for bear, moose or other large game, should any come in our way. We started from Lake Mollychunkemunk and made our way up through Moosluckmeguntick and Cupsuptic, sacking our canoe and camping kit across the carries between the lakes, and landed at the head of the last-named lake, where we hid our boat and made up our packs for the journey.

We had charts of the township lines as they were run out in 1835, and a good compass, and our plan was to make up our course every morning and go entirely by compass. We allowed one mile an hour through the thick woods as an average progress, and kept a sharp lookout for old blazed or spotted trees, and when we found one we cut into it to see how many years old it was---counting each ring or grain of the tree since the blaze was made, as signifying a year's growth. Thus we distinguished between our township lines and lines made by Indians years before or after the survey of these lands. When we were sure we had struck a township line we followed it up to the corner, where the surveyor marked on a tree the number and range and whether it was the northwest, southwest, northeast or northeast corner; thus giving us our exact position in the forest, and on the chart, and making a true starting point for our next object.

As we struck into the thick woods from our canoe we soon saw marks and signs of wild beasts--deep paths--worn into the ground a foot or more; and fresh tearings on the bark of trees made by bears; also foot prints of denizens of the forest. The further we proceeded northward and away from the habitations of man, the thicker these signs became, until we not frequently got a glimpse of some heavy animal escaping out of sight. Partridges and other birds were extremely tame and abundant; indeed we did not pretend to shoot them except just before a meal; and we never lacked for game at our meals on this trip. We made our time pass pleasantly by each in turn relating some adventure either of his own or some one else's experience.

Two persons traveling together in the woods make much more noise than one, and I think if there had been but one, or in other words, if I had been alone, I should have got chances to shoot many large animals of various kinds. But we were not on a hunting excursion; still we were amid wild animals. On coming to a brook we would try for a trout and soon catch enough for a good meal. I often saw them jump out of the water and take the hook before it touched the water. And all the streams and ponds on or way seemed to be just swarming with fish life. Camping at night we cut large trees and built big fires at our feet, spread fin-pick evergreen boughs on the ground for a bed, and stretched out in the open air covered with our blankets--with the starry heavens over our heads--minding well to keep up a good blaze, for we well knew that our best protection from wild beasts was our fire.

Everything went on pleasantly for several days. We traveled about ten miles a day over swamps, mountains, streams, large or small, and this would have grown monotonous only for the spice of hearing the cries of wild animals every night, some of which seemed to come uncomfortably near, especially when we awoke to find our fires growing low and detecting in the howl not far away the well defined voice of the wolf. But after a few days our tired bodies would give away to slumber in spite of the varied noises all about us after nightfall. It stirs the blood of the fatigued woodsman to sit on a log in the early evening and listen to the calls of the denizens of the forest. They seem to take that time to try their voice and see what reply they can get. One unaccustomed to this manner of life would expect to be eaten up alive before morning.

After ten days steady traveling northerly we found mountains growing more abrupt, ravines deeper, timber short-bodied, and very little level ground, and the general face of the country rough and rocky, as if nature began to form an impenetrable barrier to our advance, the whole region looking cheerless and forsaken, imparting to us a forlorn feeling of hopeless insecurity. Often while reflecting in these woods we could not but realize the horror of our situation should either of us get injured by any accident, either with gun or axe or in any other way, so that we could not travel. Surely the sick one would have to be left to the mercy of the elements and wild beasts that even one us might be saved.

Our object of exploration having been secured, we turned our faces homeward. The morning we started back was cloudy and ominous, the rising winds soughed through the treetops, the smothered roar of the distant waterfalls, and all nature seemed pregnant of some fearful uncertainty.

We had gone so crooked about in our wanderings, exploring various townships, and estimating their timber capacity and cash value, and other objects connected with our enterprise, that to make a comparatively straight course home necessarily took us in an entirely new course. The East and West Kennebago Mountains were all the landmarks we had seen that we knew since we left our boat, and our course must be made entirely by compass home, as it had been on our journey out. In setting our compass for a start a large high mountain not very far away loomed up exactly in our course, and somewhat dampened our ardor, as we had had a taste of climbing many such eminences on the trip. We had materially lessened in weight our knapsack, and so considered ourselves in light marching order, and started off as if every step carried us nearer home. The day grew darker as the afternoon wore on, but nothing of note occurred until two or three o'clock in the afternoon, when we found ourselves gradually ascending a mountain. We set our compass and found our course correct and traveled on, the ascent growing steeper as we advanced. I heard a subdued rumbling and called the attentions of Mr. Prentis to the fact. We had before heard the shaking of the ground under the heavy tread of wild animals, but this was different, and we unwillingly had to admit that a thunder storm was approaching, and we were with no protection from the elements except our common clothing. We held a council of war, and decided to go on and run our chances.

The mountain grew steeper and the storm nearer and the timber growth shorter, until we emerged up and out of green woods into an open, ledgy, bare mountain top, and about the same time the storm broke on us in all its fury, with wind, rain and lightning. The duel of the elements was tremendous; no adequate description can be given of its fury. The play of the lightning below us on the mountain side and in the valleys, the flood of rain beating through our clothing to the very skin, the awful roar and reverberation of the thunder among the mountains, all gave us a feeling of awe, seeming more like something supernatural than a common storm.

It was growing toward night and we were on top of a barren mountain; but we had great hopes that by pressing on with our utmost speed we might cross the top and descend far enough on the opposite side to reach the timber, and so make a fire and shelter for the night. The short brush and vines spread out thickly under our feet and retarded our progress, and occasionally threw us sprawling upon hands and knees by entangling our feet. The whole top of the mountain was a ledge, having been burned over by fire, leaving an occasional stub of short wood or sharp stick stub to help trip us up. Reaching the top we found it comparatively level for half a mile or so; and as the storm cleared off we stopped, wonder-stricken with the majestic view before our eyes. To the south we could see one of the Rangeley lakes, and to the north Moosehead Lake and intervening many ponds and sheets of water and high mountains in a wilderness of woods as far as the eye could reach on every side.

But we must push on, for the sun was lowering fast, and we knew not the distance we must yet travel to get a comfortable place to camp for the night. As we descended the south side we found the mountain much more precipitous and dangerous traveling. The northwest side of our hills and mountains in Maine, as a rule, are very gradually sloped, and the southeast sides are abrupt and often perpendicular. Naturalists say this formation was occasioned by the drift from northwest to southeast in the glacial age of the world. Our drift was southeast, and we hurried on, often finding large seams or openings in the ledge well grown over by the wild vines. A stifled cry caused me to stop and look around, as I was a little in advance of Mr. Prentis, who had fallen into a crevice or fissure a little on one side from the path I had taken; and in answering his call I found he had slipped down fifteen or twenty feet in a narrow seam in the ledge, and was sitting on a shelf of the rock that protruded out over a large, dark place, which appeared to be a room. I asked if him if he was much hurt, and he said he had sprained his wrist--he guessed that was all. I worked myself down toward him with difficulty, and found it next to impossible for us to get up again that way; so worming our way carefully down by stepping on and clinging to the projecting spurs of the ledge, we soon found ourselves in a large room, and fearing to advance in the darkness, I gathered some dry sticks and leaves that had fallen or been blown into the crevice and lighted a torch.

And now my pen fails me to describe the beauties of that cave, with its stalactites of various hues hanging pendant from the roof, golden, silvery and all shades of the rainbow, as the fire cast its light against their tremulous sides. We have read of fairy tales, of mountain retreats and wonderful sights in the recesses of the earth; but I never imagined anything one-half as beautiful as I now saw.

The room itself was oblong, perhaps 20X40ft., and its irregular sides might be 20ft. high. We did not stop long to examine the beauties of this cave, feeling it possible that we were prisoners in this lonesome den, but began to search for some opening to make our way out; but what was our surprise and horror on looking about to find bones and skulls of animals scattered promiscuously about the place, some of which were very large and different from anything we had ever seen before, although we had hunted and killed all kinds of wild animals indigenous to this part of the country.

Going around the unequal sides of the room we discovered a passage way, long and narrow, leading into another apartment, through which ran a small stream or brook out of whose sands we brought away specimens having the appearance of gold; and listening we could hear the growling and snarling of some large animal, which appeared to be some distance further into the mountain. This gave us quite an impetus to escape if possible from our seeming prison.

Creeping along a well-worn pathway on the south side of the cave, we discovered a glimpse of daylight in the distance and lost no time in following the pathway out to the light. We were not, however, one moment too soon, for the animal, whatever it was, had discovered us by scent or our taking, and came toward us fiercely growling and gnashing his teeth, until we had gained the open air through what appeared to be a common pathway for wild beasts.

We made the best of our way down the south side of the mountain until we reached the timber, when we cut spruce and white birch and made a roaring fire, stripped ourselves of our outer garments, and commenced the process of drying our clothes and cooking our supper, after which we laid out our tired bodies down to rest and sleep. Although the stream in the ravine beside which we were sleeping roared like the elements in a thunder storm, and the wind howled among the craggy rocks of the steep mountainside, and the proximity of wild beasts we had heard, all would, in the beginning of our journey, have kept sleep from us, and scary night of frightful visions before us, we slept on, and awoke in early morning refreshed and ready to devour our frugal meal. After breakfast, our courage being somewhat renewed, and the morning clear, I said to Mr. Prentiss, "Let us go back to the cave and look it over a little." "Well," said Prentiss, "if you feel like it, and have got some bullets left, I am willing, but we may have some serious business with that varmint that followed us out last night." "We must run our chances," I said, "but this is once in a lifetime, and too good to be lost." So we were soon climbing up the steep side of the mountain on our back tracks again, with a good-sized roll of birch bark for a torch.

Arriving at the entrance we came out of the night before, we were amazed at the perpendicular height of the mountain over our heads, very near seventy-five feet, along the whole side as far as we could see. Had we not come down the crevice into the cave and out on the lower side, we should have had to go the length of the mountain around to get down its steep side.

We now cut a stick three feet long and split one end of it, and filled the split with the bark, touched a match, and started in. Watching the signs beside the little stream that ran along the passageway, we discovered in the golden sand a footprint of a large animal with long toenails or claws--a round foot pressed deeply in, as if the creature was a heavy fellow. We also saw lesser tracks in the sand of various animals; some we thought were of the loup cervier, others bear, wolf, badger; in fact it was a well-trodden path into the cave. The avenue we were following narrowed after leaving the brook, so that we had to stoop and sometimes crawl through narrow holes. After going 100ft. or more we came into another room, not so large as the first, but darker and covered over the top with small stalactites and on the bottom with bones and skulls much the same as the first.

Looking, with our torch in hand, we found another passageway leading further in, and on starting in a short distance we got a draft of air strongly impregnated with the odor of wild beasts, such as we had smelled in a menagerie. We hesitated; and listening intently we heard the crying of what we thought was young panthers. After listening intently for some minutes, I said to Mr. Prentiss, "Shall we go on or go back?" "Do as you like," said he, "but I think it foolhardy and dangerous." And I was as willing as he to retrace our steps.

On reaching the great chamber into which Mr. Prentiss had fallen the night before, we heard the well defined growl of the animal that so frightened us before coming through the narrow passage from the outside; we involuntarily crept back to the further side of the cave. I cocked my gun, which was loaded with two bullets, and as the animal rushed along the passage I fired. The sound stunned us both, and the effect lasted several days, feeling very disagreeable. As our torch was now almost gone out I hardly think I hit him, but he gave an unearthly yell as he leaped along toward the room we had left before. We had only got a glimpse of his receding form, but that was all we wanted of him.

We took some specimens of what was in the cave and made our way out as fast as possible and down the mountain to where we had camped the night before, and packing up, again started on our journey homeward.

Our trip back was very much like the first, only we shot a fisher, a black wildcat and a martin, which we had mounted, and of which I still have a specimen.

When we struck out on the shore of the Cupsuptic we were not ten rods from our birch canoe.

This was thirty years ago last August, and I have never seen that cave since, but I have a great desire to once more visit the wild animal den of the Kennebago mountain cave.

– J. G. RICH, BETHEL, Maine

GRANT'S TAME TROUT

By Francis I, Maule, from *The Tame Trout and other Backwoods Fairy Tales, as narrated by that Veracious Chronicler, Edward Grant, Esq. of Beaver Cove, Me.* 1904

Ed Grant

Francis I. Maule (1846-1910+) owned a printing house on 402 Samson Street in Philadelphia where, according to his advertisement, he made "Catalogs, Booklets, Price lists, Folders, Circulars, Mailing cards and slips, etc." Having come to Maine annually on fishing trips he became fascinated with the region and especially Ed Grant. Collecting a few of Grant's stories, Maule had them printed in 1904 as a small booklet, using a small press in Phillips. The same year he published "Only Letters," a description of his travels in Europe and in 1910 published another book of stories known as "El Dorado "20" Along With Other Weird Alaskan Tales. "

A few of Grant's stories were later published in the Boston Transcript in the 1920's and several more collections of his stories were published in 1939, 1941 and in 1961 by Harold Felton "World's Most Truthful Man: Tall Tales Told by Ed Grant in Maine."

Ed Grant (1839-1919) began his career as a part owner of the "Forest Retreat," a small inn at the foot of Kennebago Lake. Later he sold his share and opened a set of well-known sporting camps at the head of the lake. People would join Ed on the porch each evening, listening for hours to his wonderful tall tales and everyone's favorite, "The Tame Trout..."

The sage of Beaver Camp sat sunning himself on the bench beside the cook camp, the bench so widely known as the scene of countless weary hours of that perpetual toiler. He seemed to be smoking an old black pipe, whereas he was only dropping matches into its empty bowl at intervals of three minutes, agreeable to the terms of his contract with the American Match trust.

As he sat and pondered, the writer, at that time a recent arrival, approached and said: "Mr. Grant, I wish you would give me the true history of your wonderful success in taming a trout. I have heard of it in all parts of the world but I have always longed to hear the story direct from headquarters."

"Well, it really ain't so much of a story," replied the famous chronicler. "It was this way. Nine years ago the eleventh day of last June, I was fishin' out there in the pads, and right under that third yaller leaf to the right of the channel---yes, that one with the rip in it--I ketched a trout 'bout six inches long. I never see a more intelligent lookin little feller--high forehead, smooth face round, dimpled chin, and a most uncommon bright sparklin' knowin' eye.

"I always allowed that with patience and cunning a real young trout (when they gets to a heft of 10 to 15 pounds there ain't no teachin' them nothin') could be tamed jest like a dog or cat.

"There was a little water in the boat and he swims around in it all right till I goes ashore and then I gets a tub we had, made of the half of a pork barrel, fills it with water and bores a little small hole through the side close down to the bottom and stops the hole with a peg.

"I set this tub away back in a dark corner of the camp and every single night after the little feller goes to sleep I slip in, in my stockin' feet, and pulls out the peg softly and lets out jest a little mite of the water. I does this night after night so mighty sly that the little chap never suspected nothin' and he was a-livin' hale and hearty for three weeks on the bottom of that tub as dry as a cook stove, and then I knowed he was fit for trainin'.

"So I took him out o' doors and let him wiggle awhile on the path and soon get to feedin' him out of my hand. Pretty soon after that, when I walked somewhat slow (I'm naturally quite a slow walker, some folks think) he could follow me right good all around the clearin', but sometimes his fins did get ketched up in the brush jest a mite and I had to go back and swamp out a little trail for him; being a trout, of course he could easy follow a spotted line.

"Well, as time went on, he got to follerin' me most everywhere and hardly ever lost sight of me, and me and him was great friends, sure enough.

"Near about sundown one evening, I went out to the spring back of the camp, same one as you cross goin' to Little Island, to get some butter out of a pail, and, of course, he comes trottin' along behind. There was no wind that night, I remember, and I could hear his poor little fins a-raspin' on the chips where we'd been getting' out splits in the cedar swamp. Well, sir, he follered me close up and came out on the logs across the brook and jest as I was a-stoopin; down over the pail I heared a kee-plunk! behind me and Gorry! if he hadn't slipped through a chink between then logs and was drowned before my very eyes before I could reach him, so he was." Here a tear started from the good old man's eyes on a very dusty trip down this time-stained cheek.

"Of course I was terrible cut up at first--I couldn't do a stroke of work for three weeks--but I got to thinkin' that as it was comin' on cold (it was late in November then) and snow would soon be here and he, poor little cuss, wasn't rugged enough for snowshoein' and he couldn't foller me about all winter no how, and as he couldn't live without me, mebby it was just as well after all that he was took off that way. Do you know, Mister, some folks around here don't believe a word of this, but if you'll come down to the spring with me right now, I'll show you the very identical chink he dropped through that night, so I will. I've never allowed anyone to move it. No, sir! nor I never will."

Here the old man dropped match number thirty-seven[1]* into his pipe and sucked at it hard in silence, while I crept softly away on tiptoes. I never could bring myself to speak of it again, after seeing him so deeply moved--I never could.

1 * Ed Grant's regular allowance is one pound of tobacco to each gross of matches used.

Chapter 3

THE DEAD RIVER, UPPER KENNEBEC AND MOOSE RIVER REGIONS

The Kennebec River's headwaters are located near the Canadian border in western Maine where they are known as the Moose River, which flows east through Jackman, emptying into Moosehead Lake. The river leaves the lake at both the East Outlet and West Outlet, which later rejoin and empty into Indian Pond, pass through a long high-walled gorge, coming to The Forks, where it is joined by the Dead River.

The Dead River, which is sometimes known as the West Branch of the Kennebec, has two branches. The North Branch begins near the Canadian Border and flows south through the Chain of Ponds to Flagstaff, while the South Branch begins at Saddleback Lake and flows east. The two branches converge, forming the Dead River, which got its name from the barely discernable current on its traverse through the valley and is well-known for Benedict Arnold's trek in the fall of 1775. Today the river is dammed up at Long Falls, producing Flagstaff Lake. From here the river flows easterly, passing over Grand Falls and meeting the Kennebec at West Forks.

Bingham, which was settled in 1784, is the gateway to the Upper Kennebec Region and formerly had hotels and daily stagecoaches that ran to Moose River via Parlin Pond, where a large hotel also stood. Later the Somerset Railway followed the Kennebec, ending at Rockwood, where it brought visitors to camps on Pleasant Pond, Bald Mountain Pond, Moxie Pond and Knight Pond. Outer lying camps could be reached via buckboard at Rowe, East Carry, Pierce, Otter, Enchanted, Grace and Chase Ponds.

The Dead River Region was also known for its great trout fishing and moose hunting. Originally it was approached through the Carrabassett Valley, which had a stagecoach that started in Kingfield. Another daily stage was available from North Anson, approaching

Dead River though New Portland. Finally a narrow gauge railway was built up the Carrabasset to Bigelow, bringing more sportsmen to the region. The first camps in the Dead River valley were opened by Kennedy Smith at Tim Pond in the spring of 1878 and by O. A. Hutchins at King and Bartlett Lake that fall; both were famous for their excellent trout fishing. Other camps could be found at Tea Pond, Jim Pond, Deer Pond, Blakesley Lake, Spencer Lake, Spring Lake, Black Brook and West Carry Pond. The Ledge House offered rooms and cabins on the road to New Portland.

In 1888 Gus Douglas, a Dead River guide, killed a large moose near Kibby Mountain, which was mounted and displayed in the Smithsonian Institute. And in 1913 Joe Knowles, a former guide went into the woods naked at King and Bartlett Camps, to survive on his own, and adventures he told about in *Alone in the Wilderness,* but it is still argued whether it was truly survival or just a publicity stunt for the Boston Post, where he was employed as an artist.

Access to the Moose River Region was eased by the building of the Canada Road in the early nineteenth century and settlement was begun there in 1820 by Samuel Holden. Later the Canadian American Railroad passed along the Moose River, affording access by rail. Camps were located at Skinner, Holeb Pond, Attean Lake, Crocker Pond, Heald Pond, Long Pond, Mackamp and Misery stations.

NARROW ESCAPE

By John S. Springer, from *Forest Life and Forest Trees,* 1851

The Common Wolf
(from Springer, 1851)

John S. Springer (1811-1883) was born in Robbinston in Washington County, and at the age of fourteen, went to work as a lumberman on the St. Croix and Penobscot Rivers. A hard-worker in a few years he rose to the position of boss hand. He married at Bangor in 1837 and attended school at Wesleyan Seminary, now Kents School, and in 1839 became a minister and moved to Massachusetts where he preached for seven years.

In 1847 he began collecting the material for his book, Forest Life and Forest Trees, which chronicled the lumbering activities of the Maine Woods. Thoreau's Maine Woods and Springer's book are often quoted as the two mainstays of the Maine woods literature.

This story, set on the frontier towns of the upper Kennebec, is the only one in which ice skating, a rather new sport in the mid eighteen hundreds, is featured. The other half of the story shows how the towns were ever in fear of the savage wolf, which could plunder their livestock once the cold winter froze the rivers.

During the winter of 1844, being engaged in the northern part of Maine, I had much leisure to devote to the wild sports of a new country. To none of these was I more passionately addicted than that of skating. The deep and sequestered lakes of this northern state, frozen by intense cold, present a wide field to the lovers of this pastime. Often would I bind on my rusty skates, glide away up the glittering river, wind among each streamlet that flowed on toward the parent ocean, and feel my pulse bound with joyous exercise. It was during one of these excursions that I met an adventure which, even at this period of my life, I remember with wonder and astonishment.

"I had left my friend's house one evening, just before dusk, with the intention of skating a short distance up the noble Kennebeck, which glided directly before the door. The evening was fine and clear. The new moon peered from her lofty seat, and cast her rays on the frosty pines that skirted the shore, until they seemed the realization of a fairy scene. All Nature lay in a quiet which she sometimes chooses to assume, while water, earth, and air seemed to have sunken into repose.

"I had gone up the river nearly two miles, when, coming to a little stream which emptied the larger, I turned in to explore its course. Fir and hemlock of a century's growth, met overhead, and formed an evergreen archway, radiant with frost-work. All was dark within; but I was young and fearless, and as I peered into the unbroken forest that reared itself to the borders of the stream, I laughed in very joyousness. My wild hurra rang through the woods, and I stood listening to the echo that reverberated again and again, until all was hushed. Occasionally a night-bird would flap its wings from some tall oak.

"The mighty lords of the forest stood as if naught but time could bow them. I thought how oft the Indian hunter concealed himself behind these very trees-how oft the arrow had pierced the deer by this very stream, and how oft his wild halloo had rung for his victory. I watched the owls as they fluttered by, until I almost fancied myself one of them, and held my breath to listen to their distant hooting.

"All of a sudden a sound arose; it seemed from the very ice beneath my feet. It was loud and tremendous at first, until it ended in one long yell. I was appalled. Never before had such a noise met my ears. I thought it more than mortal-so fierce, and amid such an unbroken solitude, that it seemed a fiend from hell had blown a blast from an infernal trumpet. Presently I heard the twigs on the shore snap as if from the tread of some animal, and the blood rushed back to my forehead with a bound that made my skin burn; I felt relieved that I had to contend with things of earthly and not spiritual mold, as I first had fancied. My energies returned, and I looked around me for some means of defense. The moon shone through the opening by which I had entered the forest, and considered this the best means of escape, I darted toward it like an arrow.

It was hardly a hundred yards distant, and the swallow could hardly excel my desperate flight; yet, as I turned my eyes to the shore, I could see two dark objects dashing through the underbrush at a pace nearly double that of my own. By their great speed, and the short yells which they occasionally gave, I knew at once that they were the much-dreaded gray wolf.

"I had never met with these animals, but, from the description given of them, I had but little pleasure in making their acquaintance. Their untamable fierceness, and the untiring strength which seems to be a part of their nature, render them objects of dread to every benighted traveler.

> With their long gallop, which can tire
> The hound's deep hate, the hunter's fire,

they pursue their prey, and naught but death can separate them. The bushes that skirted the shore flew past with the velocity of light as I dashed on in my flight. The outlet was nearly gained; one second more, and I would be comparatively safe, when my pursuers appeared on the bank directly above me, which rose to the height of some ten feet. There was not time for thought; I bent my head and dashed wildly forward. The wolves sprang, but, miscalculating my speed, sprang behind, while their intended prey glided out into the river.

"Nature turned me toward home. The light flakes of snow spun from the iron of my skates, and I was now some distance from my pursuers, when their fierce howl told me that I was again the fugitive. I did not look back; I did not feel sorry or glad; one thought of home, of the bright faces awaiting my return, of their tears if they should never see me, and then every energy of mind and body was exerted for my escape. I was perfectly at home on the ice. Many were the days I spent on my skates, never thinking that at one time they would be my only means of safety. Every half minute an alternate yelp from my pursuers made me but too certain they were close at my heels. Nearer and nearer they came; I heard their feet pattering on the ice nearer still, until I fancied I could hear their deep breathing. Every nerve and muscle in my frame was stretched to the utmost tension.

"The trees along the shore seemed to dance in the uncertain light, and my brain turned with my own breathless speed; yet still they seemed to hiss forth with a sound truly horrible, when an involuntary motion on my part turned me out of my course. The wolves close behind, unable to stop and as unable to turn, slipped, and fell, still going on far ahead, their tongues lolling out, their white teeth gleaning from their bloody mouths, and their dark, shaggy breasts freckled with foam. As they passed me their eyes glared, and they howled with rage and fury. The thought flashed on my mind that by this means I could avoid them, viz., by turning aside whenever they came too near; for they, by the formation of their feet, are unable to run on ice except on a right line.

"I immediately acted on this plan. The wolves, having regained their feet, sprang directly toward me. The race was renewed for twenty yards up the stream; they were already close on my back, when I glided round and dashed past my pursuers. A fierce growl greeted my evolution, and the wolves slipped upon their haunches and sailed onward, presenting a perfect picture of helplessness and baffled rage. Thus I gained nearly a hundred yards each turning. This was repeated two or three times, every moment the wolves getting more excited and baffled, until coming opposite the house, a couple of stag-hounds, aroused by the noise, bayed furiously from their kennels. The wolves, taking the hint, stopped in their mad career, and after a moment's consideration turned and fled. I watched them till their dusky forms disappeared over a neighboring hill, then taking off my skates, I wended my way to the house, with feelings better imagined than described."

MASSACHUSETTS BOG

By Heber Bishop, from *Guide Book to the Megantic, Spider and Upper Dead River Regions*, 1887

Dr. Heber Bishop

Heber Reginald Bishop (1840-1902), of Medford, Mass. began as a clerk in the counting house of Burgess & Company in Boston and three years later was sent as their representative to Cuba. But in 1861 he started his own sugar company, which he operated for seventeen years and amassed a fortune. When the Cuban market fell, Bishop dissolved his company in 1876 and returned to New York City where he began investing in iron, gas, utilities and railroads, further building a vast personal empire.

Bishop's greatest achievement was in the world of art. He was a trustee of the American Museum of Natural History to which he donated over 1,000 artifacts of the Pacific Northwest tribes and the Metropolitan Museum of Art, to whom he gave a precious collection of jade stones and gems. An avid canoeist, Bishop traveled extensively and produced several travel books of his adventures. He became secretary of the newly formed Megantic Club, a private fishing and hunting club of men primarily from New York. The club purchased vast tracts of land in the region of Lake Megantic, Quebec and the Seven Ponds region of western Maine, where they set up lodges and camps. As secretary of the club, Bishop produced a guidebook to help the members find the best fishing spots and to promote its lodges to prospective members and guests.

Between three and four miles north of Big Northwest Pond, the most remote of the Seven Ponds group, and between it and Arnold Pond, lies a dilatation of the Gore Stream (a branch of the Dead River) and named Massachusetts Bog. Its original name --Caribou Bog-- was given it by Mr. Kennedy Smith; but it was changed to its present name by a party of sportsmen from Boston, who, on account of its wonderful and almost inexhaustible supply of speckled trout, honored it with the name of their native State. It is a question whether the palm belongs to this or Northwest

Pond for the best fishing in the region. Presumably, Massachusetts Bog contains a larger number, but the fish will average larger in Northwest Pond. Both waters are upon the township leased by the Club from Messrs. Hazeltine, Knowlton, and Hall, of Belfast, Me., the same lease also comprising Grant, Northwest, and the South Boundary Ponds.

The bog lies at the base of the Boundary Mountains upon the Maine side, and, running in a winding course parallel to them, is over a mile and a half long, but at no place over three hundred feet wide. During the summer months there is only a narrow channel in places not covered with lily-pads, and it is in these clear places, where there is an opportunity to cast a fly, that the trout rise so well. This bog is widely known for it excellent fishing, the trout rising all through the season and at any time of the day. One is always assured of good sport at Massachusetts Bog. The trout are not large, but will average in the best season of the year half a pound, while an occasional trout weighing as high as a pound and a half or two pounds is taken. Four pound trout have been caught here.

There is little doubt that the bog still contains large trout, although it has been the writer's' misfortune to find them average smaller than other report. The following very interesting letter from our Vice-President Mr. Woodruff, of New York, shows what fish have been taken out, and within the last three years. The story of his success has often been told in the region as a "fish story"; but, being a little incredulous, the writer asked Mr. Woodruff for the facts of the case, and lately received the following letter, dated New York, July 16, 1887:--

My dear Doctor,--Absence from the city for a few days has prevented an earlier reply to your last. You say that you have heard some tall tales from Mose and Joe Noel about a certain day's fishing I had on Massachusetts Bog, and ask me to give you my account of it. You are very careful, however, I notice, not to say what the tenor and "size" of these stories are; hence, as guides are proverbial at drawing the long bow or--should I say in this case--making a long cast, I will simply give you a plain, unvarnished tale.

We had our camp that season, you will remember, at Point of Pines, on Arnold Pond. For three weeks we had whipped Beaver Brook, Arnold, Horseshoe, Rock, Upper and Lower Hathan, Cranberry and even tried Mud Pond, with but fair success, while our ears were constantly being filled with the tales of the big trout in Massachusetts Bog and the monsters taken out of there through the ice the previous winter. But, whenever we spoke of going there, we were told of the white cedar swamps, three hours to get there, too far to go and return the same day, no camp there, and so on, until every tale was taken *cum grano salis;* and most of our party left on the first of September without having essayed the bog, leaving only my brother, nephew, and myself in camp. The next day, happening to be on the top of Black Mountain with Mose, he called my attention to a little patch of water, about as large as your two palms, two miles off, as the crow flies, which he said was Massachusetts Bog. One glance at the lay of the land, and all fear of white cedar swamps vanished from my mind; and the next morning I started with him for the much-talked of spot. Going directly across from the Point of Pines, I took the ridge on the left of the brook until it ran into the swamp, which we crossed at a spot only a few hundred feet wide, and then took the hard wood ridge again on the right, much to the disgust of Mose, who wanted to follow the "blaze" made in the winter, on snow-shoes, through the swamp the whole way. I think he predicted that, if I kept on my course, I would come out at Northwest Pond. However, when I left the ridge at right angles and turning to the left, plunged down into the valley, my good luck was again with me, and we struck the bog just where the brook enters it, thus placing myself as high in the estimation of Mose for my knowledge of woodcraft as my lucky shot that first season at a buck forever perched me on the highest pinnacle of Joe's estimation as a crack rifle shot.

I had my rod and little Stevens's rifle, while Mose had only his inseparable axe and a small parcel of grub. It was now three in the afternoon, and our first thought was to find the boat, which Mose had cached that spring, and which he said was essential in order to get any trout. After an hour's fruitless search, Mose "remembered" that the Indian--What was his name,--the one who had the cow moose?--had been told where the boat was; and, as he had been there a few weeks before, *ergo* the boat must be at the "other end." The quickest way to get to the "other end" was to make a bee line through the white cedar swamp, Mose said. Leaving coats and rod where we *intended* to spend the night, taking only the little rifle and axe, Mose took the lead through the swamp. If you have never been through that bit of white cedar in a wet season, then I can only give you *Punch's* famous advice, "Don't,"--words fail me even at this length of time to do justice to it. It was after six when we got to that "other end," wet through to the skin, half fresh and half salt water. By seven o'clock we had decided that the boat was not at the "other end." It was too late to go back to camp, it was rapidly growing cold, for you know how cold the nights often are up there early in September, and there was nothing for us to do but build a fire, dry our garments, and lie down on the bare ground, with the leaves, for our bedspread, the stars for our canopy, and empty stomachs for an early rising alarm clock. We had even left three partridges at the camp, which I had shot on the way over. I recall how Mose complained only at his not having put a handful of tea in his pocket. Between the water from below and the perspiration from above, it would have been in a fine condition, though, doubtless, he would have no fault with it, and I question if I should have "made a fuss over such a trifle." But the fun began after dark. Mose made a roaring fire on the edge of the bluff, and we steamed and scorched one side while we slapped the other to keep it from congealing until we were partially dry. Then lying down on our arms we waited for the stars to roll around. About midnight all the bears in the State of Maine seemed to have congregated on the mountain back of us, and the roaring, grunting, and squealing I ever heard equaled in any menagerie. Sleep under any circumstances would have been difficult in our case, with that infernal racket, it was impossible. With every fresh outburst Mose would jump to his feet, mutter something about "dam bear," throw more wood on the fire, until the flames leaped twenty feet in the air, and then chop away until he had replenished his pile for the next stoking, keeping it up until the thing became ludicrous to me. Every little while there would be stamp, snort, and indignant whistle, on the opposite shore, of some deer kept from wetting the aforesaid whistle by the bright light of our protective fire. But all disagreeable as well as good things finally come to an end, and the first clear gleam of daylight saw us wending our way back, this time on the ridge, even Mose having had enough of the swamp. After demolishing all the grub we had brought with us, and soothing our injured feelings, with several pipes, I took a nap while Mose hunted up the boat. About ten o'clock we met, he saying he saw the boat adrift on the tamarack swamp side of the bog. Taking my rod, I went about one hundred yards down the bog, where there was a grassy bank, and proceeded to "limber up," to be in readiness when Mose came with the boat. But Mose, who could never get over the mystery of putting a rod together, stayed to see the operation. I had that heavy English rod--pole, it should almost be called--and the famous blue silk line, both of which you probably remember. Having adjusted my leader, I let the flies fall in the water at my feet, where it was not more than a foot deep. As I stepped back to take hold of the butt of my rod, z-z-z-z-i-p-p-p went the reel, and a few moments later Mose was taking off a fourteen-inch trout, which had had the impudence to take a fly within a foot of the bank. With three flies on, the first cast hooked two beauties, and the next cast gave me one on each fly. Nothing but the toughness of that heavy old rod and the strength of the silk line enabled me to land the whole party. I then took off two of the flies, and at every cast, standing in full sight of the bank, five to ten trout would throw themselves completely out of the water, and I had such tough fishing as I never even dreamed of. Mose, standing in the water up to his knees, would land them, and take them off the hook, and toss them into a little pool back of him. I had no idea of the time, never having to make a second cast for a fish, but striking a big fellow every time, until Mose said, "How much feesh you want, Monsieur Vood?" As I looked around, the pool was filled to overflowing with such a pile of golden beauties as Fulton Market never knew. There was not a fish under fourteen inches in length, and from that up to twenty-two inches for the longest. But such misshapen fellows as some of them were, the under jaw projecting far over the upper,--regular beaks; others with a corporation on then which would have done honor to a member of the Fat Men's Club. Upon looking at my watch, it was a quarter past twelve. I had been fishing for about two hours. On counting the catch, we had one hundred and thirty-seven trout. My heart smote me for taking so many, but we had carried them up to camp before counting them and it was too late to put any of them back then. So we did the best we could to prevent willful waste, by gutting them, building a smoke house, and giving what we did not eat that day a smoking all that afternoon, night and until noon the next day, when we started back to Arnold. Mose had all the 'pack' he wanted, and said he had fully seventy-five pounds in weight. On showing them to my brother, I was pleasantly greeted with the announcement that one rod could not have caught all that quantity in the short time stated, and asked how large a *net* Mose had. Two days later my brother and nephew went over to Massachusetts with me, reaching there about noon. All that afternoon the rods were whipping the bog from one end to the other, from the shore and from the boat, and not a single rise could any of us obtain. *Nets* of all kinds were the staple of conversation around the campfire that night. Needless to say that Mose and I took no interest or part in the conversation. But the next morning, before the others were up, I slipped down to the spot where I had caught all the first lot, and the first cast gave me a stunner, tipping the scales at four and one-quarter pounds. I woke the others up by flapping the cold tail in their faces. Inside of half an hour they took back all they had said about nets, and they only ceased catching the big fellows, which seem to be the only kind in the bog, because we did not know what we should do with them. As it was, we sent in or rather took in with us to Montreal, as we broke up camp the next day, close on to one hundred pounds of half-smoked trout, which were a great treat to our friends there, but who wondered why we did not seem to care much for them.

Such is my experience at Massachusetts Bog. If you want to know why, the afternoon of the first day my brother was there, we could not get a single rise, I can only say that trout, like some woman, are "queer critters." I have heard since the most contradictory stories about this spot, some parties praising it in the most extravagant manner, while others will declare that there is not a single trout in the bog. Of one thing I am certain, there are not small trout there, and the question is, what will we do when all these big ones are yanked out? Another thing, I did not see a single dark colored trout taken from the bog, all of them being the handsome golden striped trout, with flesh of an unusually dark pink tint.

Now let me know how my plain, ungarnished tale compares with what you heard from Mose and Joe Noel. I expect to be with the boys next month, when I shake off the dust of the city, for a month in the greenwood and, if they have said anything to stagger my reputation, I want to know it in time to get even with them.

Trusting to meet you at White Birch Camp some time next month, and…I am

Very truly yours, I. O. WOODRUFF

A CARIBOU HUNT IN MAINE

By Forest, from *Shooting and Hunting,* February 13, 1890

(From the Maine Sportsman, Nov 1894)

LIVERMORE FALLS, ME., FEB. 4

I am about to relate an account of a hunting trip for the benefit of those who have (and also those who have not) been fortunate enough to shoot and carry home with them a specimen of the large game of Maine, happily so numerous and rapidly increasing in this and other game districts in our State. The open season has, in most sections, been quite unfavorable for still hunting, as our first snows were followed by rain, the resulting crust making it a little noisy, especially for still hunting our favorite, the caribou, which roam in large herds.* There are two distinct species of the game, the smaller a light grey and red in color, often spotted, with well rounded bodies, and the antlers of the bulls varying much in shape, and having the prongs a little flatish. The other and perhaps rarer variety are much larger and taller, some weighing from 700 to 800 pounds. They are dark grey, with white bellies, square built, short-pointed tail and white band, fine strong limbs of dark color, and large spreading antlers. The does of this species also wear this beautiful head appendage, but in their case it is of finer dimensions.

Both species feed on the same kind of food, chiefly mosses off rocks and black growth, which is in great abundance in these mountain forests. Large herds of each species seem often to mingle together, making well worn paths for miles, but soon separate are seldom found together by sportsmen, especially after snow has fallen.

With this brief description of the game, I will give you an account of a hunting trip in December 1889. Our party proceeded by rail to Phillips, Me., thence by teams to the home of Mr. John W. Shepard, one the best guides in Franklin County. After spending the night there, we continued our journey as far as we could with teams, about ten miles from Phillips. There we proceeded on foot to the camp in Caribou valley, reaching it after an easy tramp of about two miles.

The ring of the tin dippers, and the plates of pork and beans was music indeed; and soon packs, rifles, snowshoes and blankets, distributed about the camp, showed that we had taken possession. In the afternoon we put on our snowshoes and took a stroll, soon coming upon tracks of herds varying from 5 to 20, but as the snow of about 10 inches was crusted by recent rain it was useless to follow. We returned to camp, content to wait until some friendly snow should come to cover up the old tracks and deaden the sound of our steps.

The next day, Tuesday, opened fine, but cold and again we strolled into the forest, Shepard, the guide, taking the party under his care. Fresh tracks had crossed ours during the night, and we were eager to sight the game. Once on the trail we followed it around the mountains, and soon came to a spring, which was evidently the favorite watering place of that section of the range, as most of the water is often frozen. The snow for acres around was completely trodden down with tracks, coming in and leading out, and so recently had the animals been there that the water was roily. We soon found the path taken by the last visitors, but as it was beginning to snow and growing dark, we thought it best to follow our own track back to the camp. A jolly party did justice to our camp supper that night; mirth and song were in order, and not until a late hour were we rolled in our blankets on the soft boughs.

Friday morning at six o'clock we were drinking our dippers of smoking coffee, and soon a joyous party filed out of camp; four inches of snow had fallen during the night; a morning made to order could not have been better for our purpose. Knowing as we did that the game we had left over night would not go far in such stormy weather, the programme was drawn up quickly, and under the command of our trusty guide we were soon on the war path, and by a short route, reached the spring from which, to our joy, we found where eight caribou had laid down during the night. We crept along and in short time came upon three (of the darker species), feeding among some fallen spruce tops. The recent storm had rendered them easy of a near approach; at a signal from Shepard, the still mountain woods echoed with the report of our Winchesters and three forest beauties lay stretched upon the snow. They proved to be two does, and one large buck with large antlers. He tried hard to get away, but we soon despatched him and after removing the entrails, left the carcasses where they fell, returned and spent another pleasant night in camp.

The next morning, Saturday, with a hunter's sled and lots of help, we brought them all out to the camp and then teamed from there to Phillips, where a pleasant Sunday was spent at the home of the guide, large numbers of people coming to see the game. Our party was unanimous in declaring Caribou valley the finest hunting ground for caribou they ever visited, being of easy access (only ten mile's ride by team and a short tramp to camp), and having also the other still greater advantage of allowing the game to be taken out whole (the hunting grounds being so near the settlement) instead of forcing the hunter to be contented with a single head or set of antlers, as in some sections his very season.

– FOREST

*Our correspondent is in error; the only caribou that is ever found in Maine, or indeed anywhere south of the northern part of Labrador, is the woodland caribou. It varies much in appearance and weight, and the calves are dappled (which may have deceived our correspondent). He is equally mistaken about the weight of the animals mentioned. 700 pounds is an utterly impossible weight for a caribou to attain to. The largest ever reported from Newfoundland (where they are notoriously larger than anywhere on the mainland), only tipped the bean at 480 pounds, and out of dozens which we have seen from the Provinces and Maine, none ever exceeded 350 pounds.---ED.

A MOOSE HUNT IN KIBBY VALLEY

By C. B. Parker, from *Forest and Stream*, January 15, 1891

For two seasons I have not only explored but made many inquiries and corresponded with sportsmen in different parts of this country upon the subject of moose and caribou. Generally I received favorable answers from every point, which is often the case; but the game is seldom realized at the season of the year I wish to hunt.

Last summer while on a fishing trip, but principally on the lookout for moose signs, I was convinced that I had at last found my hunting ground, as well as guides and teamsters, who knew the country and game to be found in it probably as well or better than any one else at the present day. Before leaving for home I had made all arrangements with my guides for a still hunt as soon as there should be snow enough, they to send for me and have everything in readiness on my arrival, so as to save time, as at that season of the year it was inconvenient to leave business for any length of time. Packing a few things as hurriedly as possible, for the word had arrived to come by first train, we leave New York by Fall River line in the evening and Boston at 8:30 the next morning by Maine Central, arriving at Kingfield, Maine at seven in the evening, this being the terminus of railroad travel.

The next morning we are flying along behind a pair of bays, the merry jingle of the bells keeping time with the rushing waters of the Carrabassett, along whose bank we ride for fifteen miles with constantly changing mountain scenery on either side. A change of horses here and we are off again, and in two hours arrive in Eustis some twenty-eight miles from the start. Here we find a typical Maine frontier village, the jumping-off place, as it were, of civilization, for the public road ends at the saw mill. The residents numbered between fifty and sixty, and most all were born and reared there, and depend principally on logging in winter, hunting, trapping and guiding sportsmen in season. Eustis is the last of civilization we see, for the forest begins here. At this place I was met by my guides, Gus Douglass and Otis Witham, Gus being the son of the famous old moose and bear hunter, Andrew Douglass, who took the boy Gus into the woods hunting and trapping when he was only eight years of age. He is never so tired when night comes, but what he is always ready with a song or a good story.

In starting from Eustis we cross the Dead River; and up in the mountains for ten miles, one half the way through burnt timber, which now affords splendid feeding ground for moose and deer, the unmistakable signs of deer were seen, as the ground was covered with snow. We could tell every few minutes where one or more had crossed or fed around among the bushes that were now growing up since the fire.

Three hours time brings us to the Kibby Stream Camps, built by my guides, a favorite resort for fishermen, and a hunter's paradise. Here it was we made ready for the hunt, each one provided with a good heavy blanket, and provisions calculated to last from six to eight days. The cooking utensils were composed of one four-quart pail for tea and coffee, one frying pan, and a drinking cup for each. A small tin plate and spoon were provided for me, that I might better indulge with the luxuries. One great feature of a trip of this kind is to reduce the camp kit and provisions to a minimum, as it must all be carried on the back, and the lightest pack gets heavy enough before night. Our provisions comprised of prepared flour, rice, pork, tea, coffee, butter and sugar, and nearly every day we shot a partridge or two, which made our larder quite complete. In starting out we found the snow about two feet deep, and as we had to go on snowshoes, it was no easy task for me to keep pace with my guides the first day, as they were following my instructions, to push along as fast as possible. As several yards of moose had been located before I arrived, we lost no time in going directly to where the hunt was to commence. We stopped to camp for the night about a mile from a certain yard, so as not to frighten them by the noise of the ax, or smoke from the camp fire. After supper we were soon rolled up in our blankets before a good fire, and had a very comfortable night's rest considering the weather, as it was storming hard and had been all the day before.

Breakfast was soon disposed of, and while waiting for daylight to appear our pipes were smoked and plans all talked over, even estimating the spread of the antlers we should have hanging up before sunset. As soon as it was light enough we were off, going right up the mountain, for the yard was on the very top, reaching over and down on the north side, for the supposed reason that experience or instinct has taught the crafty animal that snow warmed by southern exposure soon forms a crust, in which they cannot easily "work" or protect themselves by escape, as in the softer snow lying on the colder side.

A yard is where moose or deer congregate in early winter, among the firs and spruces, where there is a plentiful supply of small growth and moose wood, the bark and tender branches of which they feed on while there is deep snow. A yard may cover over fifty or a hundred acres, possibly more, according to the number of animals herding together, and is covered with paths running in every direction where the game feeds from bush to bush. If not molested, and their feed holds out, they will remain all winter. In about an hour or so we came upon signs of moose, the principal indications being places where the bushes and small trees had been browsed and girdled, looking as though it had been done a day or so before. But we knew it was longer than that as there were no tracks in the snow. However, the guides were satisfied that the game was not far away; and it was here that the hunt began in earnest. The direction of wind was noticed and we kept to the leeward of the signs (for it must be remembered that the moose is the keenest scented animal of the forest), for fear they would get our scent, and that would end all chances of getting a shot in the yard.

Continuing on, we soon saw signs in the snow, although covered with about six or eight inches of light snow of the day and night before. This was at once brushed away, that the tracks might be examined to learn the direction the moose were going, as we wished to do the surprise instead of being the ones surprised. We had not gone far when a peculiar hiss from one of the guides gave us the warning, and instantly we were like statues. Looking directly in front of us, we saw a fine cow moose (much to our surprise) coming in our direction, browsing as she passed slowly along, retracing the steps of the day before. What was to be done passed through the minds of each of us. We dare not move nor shoot, as it was a bull moose or nothing that I wanted. Presently she saw us, and painful were the few moments that passed while she was looking, not knowing really whether we were stumps or human beings, as she could not at first get our scent; but when she did, she gave the alarm that was unmistakable, a sound similar to that of the deer, only ten times as loud. As one of the guides express it. "The jig is up now, for every moose within half a mile is on the run."

Now, the first thing to do was to pick out the tracks of a bull, if there was one in the yard. So we proceeded for a short distance only, when the experienced eyes of my guides detected what they thought to be the track of a bull. We found that two had left the yard together, one of them supposed to be a bull on account of the large size of tracks and long strides, showing it to be an animal of unusual size. We went but a short distance, when it was discovered that one of them had gone through a thicket and the other had gone around. This looked encouraging, so we took the larger track that went around only to find that the other had joined company a little further on. The story was told for certain when they came to another thicket, where both were obliged to go through, thus betraying the bull and spread of his antlers by marks on the trees. Now began our work in earnest, for we must walk him down, which usually takes from four to six days of steady walking from daylight until dark, stopping to cook dinner and camping on his track wherever night overtakes us.

As a rule when a moose is followed he never eats, but keeps steadily plodding along until he is completely exhausted, then lies down to rest. The moose has slept only, with nothing to eat, while we have had a good breakfast. But before we found his bed he had heard us and gone. The second day was about the repetition of the first. The third day we found where he had stopped occasionally, and rested a few moments, and at the same time listening to hear us if possible. The fourth and fifth days the guides could easily read the condition of the old fellow by the number of times he would lie down to rest, and on the fifth especially, when he began some of his sharp practice on us, by traveling in circles trying to get us to the leeward and behind us, thinking, I suppose, we would go on and leave him. But on the morning of the sixth day the old monarch of the forest decided that he would go no further, and as he arose from his bed, about 50yds. away, with mane standing straight up, and looking the picture of defiance, Gus remarked that it was just about the right time to do the work, and in one minute two balls from my Winchester had told the story, His weight as he fell was estimated, and has since proved quite correct, to have been over a 1,000lbs. His head and antlers weighed 102lbs., and spreading a little over 4ft. 8in. The blades of the horns are 12 ½ in. wide; the horns are evenly balanced, each containing eleven perfect prongs. It is considered a very fine specimen, and pronounced by very good authority to bag as large as any on record. Feeling very well satisfied with the work done in Maine, I shall leave the rest of it to the well-known taxidermist, Mr. Akhurst, of this city.

– C. B. PARKER., BROOKLYN, N. Y.

JOB BARTLETT'S THANKSGIVING

By Frederick Howard, from *Shooting and Fishing,* November 26, 1891

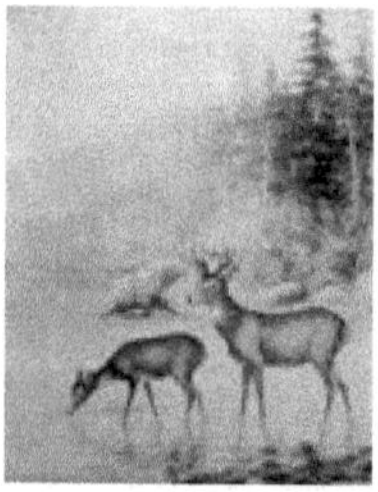

The outlines of old Bigelow's range of snow-capped peaks were but dimly discerned into the rather uncertain light of the cold gray November dawn, as a stalwart hunter emerged from the porch door of a long, low farmhouse, which blended so with the dun hillside pasture, sloping up from under its very eaves, that its unpainted sides and mossgrown roof were seldom noticed from the stage as it crept over the "hight o' land" on the Eustis highway.

Sometimes, when he had a stranger aboard, the driver, as he pointed out the points of local history, would introduce it as the home of Job Bartlett, "that quarest cuss in the hull Dead river valley. He's er lived by hisself ever since that sister o' his'n left 'n married Ned Richards over tew the forks. Job he never tuk tew the young chap, 'n when Mollie married him, that settled it. He packed off her half o' the household stuff, and paid her for the share o' the farm. Now Ned's a cripple nigh onter six years, and she's got three young 'uns ter look arter, with her money all gone, and ther little farm all run down ter nuthing but thistles and stuns. Bless ye, no, Job he don't go nigh 'em; says it's a jedgement agin her fur taking up with a wuthless scamp. Lord knows he's plenty to spare and not feel it. He sells the most and spends the least o' anyone on the range." Having vented his feelings by a vicious snap of the whip at the leader's ears, the narrator would relapse into silence and await the comment of his hearers.

Job Bartlett walked briskly along the lane that led from his barn to the upper pasture. His rifle lay on his forearm and his hands thrust deep in to the pockets of his coon skin jacket, for Thanksgiving never came over the Bigelow Range unheralded by winter's chill. The fields lay covered with a frost that left the hunter's tracks as visible a trail behind him as in the remnant of the first snow which still lay along the north sides of the walls and edges of the woods, away from the wasting power of the Indian summer that was now over. The slim white trunks of the birches wreathed in the hazy network of their branches, stood in sharp relief against the sombre shadows of the firs on the ridge above. Job passed on up the narrow path through the woods, the brittle leaves crackling under his quick tread, and the frost covered twigs of the birches snapping their hold on the parent tree as they came in contact with is swiftly moving form. When he reached the little blueberry knoll on "Bear's Head," he halted and gazed long and steadily at the distant pond below the clearing at the foot of "The Nose." Apparently satisfied, he located the direction of the wind as blowing down the range, and then resumed his march in a wide detour to the south of the mountain.

It is seldom that Job Bartlett was found on Thanksgiving anywhere save his logging camp up on Spencer stream. He always went in the Monday before, and his crew, having spent Thanksgiving with their families at the settlement, would begin their work with him the following week.

As Job had no family which to spend the day of feasting, he averred that it made no odds where he spent the day; but his men, with sly winks to each other, would recall that on Thanksgiving day old Parson Thompson made his annual rounds to receive from his parishioners such funds as they could spare to support the little church at the plains, and never yet had he found Job Bartlett at home. On this day, however, Job had been unable to get located up on Spencer. His supplies for the "wagin" had not arrived; therefore he left his house at break of dawn to try for a shot at a deer over on the famous runway from Flagstaff to Beaver Bog.

Job prided himself on his accuracy with the rifle. At turkey shoots when a lad and in later years at targets in camps he had excelled all opponents, and for a snap shot at a jumped deer he "do say, if I must say it myself, thar aint many as can come up to me fur a reg'lar sure drop on a buck streaking it along a run like a log down a sluiceway." He was, moreover, proud that his skill was a natural instinct in him from the long line of dead and gone Bartletts who had been the most famous hunters north of the lakes, ever since their ancestor had settled her in the valley after that memorable march of Arnold's men toward Quebec. One of the survivors of that ill-fated campaign, the original Bartlett, had, with scarce more than his rifle and axe, laid the foundation of the sturdy success of the following generations. The modest fame of the name was now perpetuated clear to the boundary range. Upper and Lower Bartlett were much heralded ponds to the trout fisher, closely seconded by the virtues of Bartlett Brook, while "Bartlett's Carry" was the only blazed trail over to Spencers.

Job's thoughts, as he pushed his way along the mountain side, dwelled much on these reminiscences of the past. He thought of his great empty, cheerless home, and of former days when a great strong lad he used to carry his little sister to and from the winter's school a mile away, and how she would listen in silent admiration to his stories of the bears in the woods on old Bigelow, and cling tighter to the neck of her big brother. "Ef she'd only a married well, but thar aint one worthy of a Bartlett in the hull lot," he repeated almost aloud as he seated himself behind the roots of an upturned tree to the leeward of the well defined deer run, in readiness for the first victim which should venture from the lake to the feeding ground at the bog.

Job had a long wait that morning. He sat so still and so long that the chickadees stared inquisitively into his bearded face, and a silent moose bird perched over his head, awaiting events that with patient curiosity so indicative of the corvinae race, flew away thinking that he had made a mistake in that silent form. Once a great white rabbit bounded from his cover behind him with so much force in the thumps of his sturdy forelegs on the frozen earth, as to make the hunter start in expectation.

At last he can just make out through the hemlocks a magnificent buck coming slowly up the run. With no knowledge of the hunter's proximity, the noble animal turns his head from side to side to nip at the tender twigs of moosewood, or the moss that adheres to the rough bark of the hemlock. Now is the time, as a fair sight is obtained between the scaly hemlock trunks, and the rifle speaks out sharply on the frosty air. A sudden bound, followed by a distinct thud, as all four feet strike the earth together, and the buck goes flying up the runway. "Missed a walking deer, by thunder, for the first time," Job testily grumbled to himself as he came out on the trail into which he had hardly struck when the sharp report of a rifle was heard up beyond the bend of the run. Job gave a sudden exclamation as he heard the shot, and started rapidly forward to learn the success of his rival.

Just beyond the bend he came on to the buck lying dead in the run, and standing by his side, the slayer, an overgrown lad of about a dozen years. Dressed in a well patched suit which he outgrew years before, and encased in a huge army overcoat, the boy presented a strange figure with an old pattern Kentucky rifle as tall as himself.

"Say, bub, ye didn't shoot this ere deer all by yerself, did yer?" was Job's salutation, deeply chagrined at this own unlucky shot, but full of admiration for the skill of the other."

"Er course I did," was the reply, as the boy endeavored to warm his blue-veined hands in his breath, plainly visible in the frosty air. "When ther greeny down below fired he just socked it right up on the run ser fast I c'ud hardly see him, but I jes aimed at this nose and let er go."

Job winced at the allusion to his own part in the proceedings, but refrained from any excuses. "Dy'e think ye kin do it agin, bub?"

"Why er course; didn't I shoot one over to the carry last week, and cu'ld a got anuther ef I cu'ld a loaded the blamed ol gun."

Job gazed at the boy with growing admiration. Here was one worthy to be a Bartlett. "What's yer name, bub?"

"Job, that's what they allers call me."

The elder hunter was getting more and more interested. "What's yer father a thinking on that he lets yer cum out alone; don't he know ye can't lug the quarters back home?"

A tear shone in each eye of the quaint overcoated figure. "Father he got struck by a tree that swing the wrong way, and can't get out o' his chair, and--and--ma'm and me try ter run the farm. It's Thanksgiving to-day, ye know, mister, 'n I wanted to have a square dinner. Say, if ye'l help me with this I'll give ye half on it."

"Sartinly," Job secretly cursed himself for not offering to assist, and set to work to skin and quarter the deer. "Say, bub," he continued, as he plied the shining blade of his big hunting knife, "Ain't ye got any folks ter help ye? Ye seem to be hoeing an all-fired hard row."

The overcoat stood silently erect and the voice came hard in reply, "Thar's an uncle or suthin that lives somewhat over the range; I never seen him 'n I don't want to fur he'd never help us. So ma says. I jest hate him."

Job grew indignant. A boy like this was worthy of a better uncle. He would find out who the flinty hearted relative was and bring him to a sense of the justice and mercy due to a sister and his nephew. If this boy were a Bartlett, they were always the best hunters in the range, but now there were none to perpetuate their fame after him. With these thoughts running through his mind, Job worked away at the buck until he stood with the haunches wrapped in the skin and thrown across his sinewy shoulders. "Naow, bub, ef you'l take both guns and lead ther way, I'll take this Thanksgiving dinner o' yourn nearer the pot."

Thus they went down the east side of the range, the overcoat grasping a rifle in either hand, nearly lost to view in the turned-over sleeve of the garment and following in its wake the sturdy form of the hunter bending under his load. Out from the shade of the hemlocks, through the birches and poplars into the straggling cedars of the pastures; over tumble-down stone walls and weedy fields until Job was vaguely conscious, though his soft felt hat crushed down by the weight on his shoulders nearly blinded him, of an approach to a house. A cursory glance under the brim convinced him of the poverty of its occupants. Not until he had stumbled over the stone step and broken threshhold, and heard the voice of his guide proclaiming his success to his mother did Job lay down his heavy burden. Then his rapid glance took in the desolate picture - the emaciated form of the crippled father; the bare room not as comfortable as a logging hut, scarce warmed by a feeble brush fire on a broken hearth. Suddenly a pair of arms were thrown around his neck, and a weak voice sobbed on his shoulder, "Job, brother, have you come to forgive us at last."

When old Parson Thompson arrived home late that afternoon from his round of Thanksgiving visits he seriously alarmed his good wife by his lack of appetite for the dinner long kept waiting for him. Her fears were speedily quieted, but a sensation of surprise and wonder shook her rotund figure when at a season he informed her that he had just partaken of a hearty dinner at Job Bartlett's. "They had dinner rather late, for Job said it took considerable time to get things ready and the family together."

– FREDERICK HOWARD

MAINE BEAR TRAPPERS

By J. B. Burnham, from *Forest and Stream,* August 26,1899

Capt. Cliff Wing (1872-1962), one of Flagstaff's greatest hunters and outdoorsman, spent many years hunting and trapping bears and other animals in the Dead River Region. In the early 1900's he opened up his house as a sporting camp, from which he guided sportsmen on hunting and fishing trips for many years.

"Four years ago," said Mr. Wing, "I made $120 in ten days' time trapping bears. I got four old bears and two cubs. One of the cubs was alive. On this trip I got a bear every other time I looked my traps over.

"I started from home and went into my camp on Pray Hill in the northeast corner of the town. It was about the 1st of May. I went out and sot four traps and then went home again. In about a week's time I went back to look at my traps. The first trap I came to was gone. I hunted for it for two hours and couldn't find it. The trail was an old one, and it rained since it was made, and I couldn't follow it good.

"I was looking off through the woods uncertain which way the trail went, when I happened to see a bear's head cocked up looking at me. I knew well enough the bear was in my trap, and I walked right up to it to get a good shot. I saw a couple of small animals that I took to be rabbits run off in the bush, but I didn't pay much attention to them, being so hard upon the bear. I got where I wanted, and knocked my bear over, and sot to skin her. When I turned her over I see she was suckling cubs, and that reminded me of the small animals I had seen run off, and I knew well enough then what they were.

"After I took the old lady's hide off I spent the best part of an hour looking for the cubs, but I didn't find them, and I had to give it up as I had the other traps to look over.

"The next trap I visited was gone, too, but the bear had got into it since the rain, and left a good trail, and I soon found him.

"The bear kept head on and would not give me just the shot I wanted, so I gave him one through the head and knocked him down. When I worked the gun for a new cartridge there was nothing there. For some reason or other my magazine was empty, and I could find no more cartridges in my pockets. About the time I found this out, the bear rolled over and got on his feet and stood there looking at me to see what I was going to do next. It was kind of aggravating, and I says to myself, 'Your hide's going back with me to Flagstaff, Mister Bear, some way or 'nother.'

"You can bet I wasn't going to lose my bear just because I had run out of ammunition.

"I looked around for something to kill the bear with, but couldn't find anything till I got clear back where the trap had been set, a matter of a couple of hundred yards or so. There I go a chunk of wood 6ft. long and 3in. through that I'd used setting the trap. It was heavy rock maple, and I says to myself, 'This is good enough for a cartridge, and it won't play out.'

"When I got back to the bear he set there winking and blinking and showing his teeth, telling me he didn't like me trying no more experiments on him. I crept up behind, and swung my club, and the very first clip I drove the skull right in, and after that I had no more trouble taking off the pelt. The rifle ball had hit him in the nose and missed the brain, and only stunned the bear temporarily.

"I generally figure to get a side shot on the skull between the eye and ear. I look the bear in the eye, and after awhile he turns his head and looks away, and that gives me my chance.

"The next day I thought I'd see what I could do to get the cubs, so I took my boy with me and went back to where the old bear lay. When we got near to the carcass we saw two cubs going up a big spruce tree, snake fashion, circling round and round the tree as they went up. I brought my rifle up and took a quick shot and put a ball right through the head of one of the cubs, and that was the end of him.

"Then I thought of catching the other one. I asked the boy if he thought he could climb the next tree to the big one, for that had no limbs. He said he believed he could skin it, and started for the tree.

"Hold on,' I said; 'I want to rig you out.'

"I went and cut a crotched pole 10ft. long and fastened the crotch to his belt so he could climb with hands and feet, and told him to go ahead and skin up the tree.

"He got up 30ft. or so, carrying the pole with him and then he was on an even height with the cub in the other tree, and only about 10ft. off. I told him to take the pole and put the crotch on the bear and shove it off the limb it was sitting on.

"The boy gave the bear a punch and knocked him off the limb, but he hung on underneath. 'Now," I says, 'you give him a good big punch and knock him off anyway.'

"The boy gave him a good punch and knocked him off. The cub made himself round like a bat-ball coming through the air, and he struck on his rump right at my feet. I grabbed him by the nape of the neck and back and he turned like a flash and began scratching like a bag full of cats.

"I sang out to the boy to hurry up and come down or I'd have no flesh left on my hands, and when he got down had him tie the forward feet with a piece of string and help me get the little devil under control.

"All this time the cub was making the most unearthly noise, and I thought to myself if there were any old bears around I should have company. I kept the bear till he was six months old and then sold him. When I got him he weighed 5lbs., and when I sold him he weighed 50.

"I had put the old she bear in for bait, and about a week after I got the cubs I went back to the trap and caught another old one, and a little after that I got my fourth grown bear in the trap where I had knocked the bear over with a club.

"Bear meat makes as good bait as anything. The secret in catching bears is to select the right spot for setting the trap. One man may set a trap in one place and never catch anything, and another man may go fifty or a hundred rods to one side and get a bear right off the first thing.

"Some bears are mighty smart. I tried three years for one, and had the blacksmith make me a special heavy trap. He was a monstrous big bear, and you could follow him through the woods by his track just as easy as you could an axe. I put out a dead horse weighing 1,000lbs. for him and he hung around till he ate him all up, and it didn't take a great while either. I covered the horse with brush and hid the trap in different places, but he'd paw the brush away till he'd located the trap before he'd take a bite of the horse. I've known bears to walk round and round a trap till they'd worn a regular ring in the ground. At last I took bee's honey and smoked herrings and that was too much of a temptation for him to go by, and I got the old fellow.

"As a rule bears, when they get in a trap, they fight themselves and get het up so they choke themselves. If one gets in a stream or pond, where he can keep cool, he'll live for quite a spell."

TWO WEEKS IN THE MAINE WOODS

By F.E.B., from *Forest and Stream,* July 7, 1900

On the Moose River

Our party consisted of four. This being our second season in the woods together, we have organized ourselves into a club, which we call the "Big Indian Gun Club," taken from the location of our camp in the fall of '98, which was on Big Island Pond. We left civilization the morning of Nov. 8, and met at White River Junction, Vt. From there we went to Lenoxville, P.Q., where we took the Canadian Pacific R. R. through to Lowelltown, Me., leaving the train at Skinner's Station, where we arrived about 2:30 A.M. Nov. 9 with Mr. Frink and party from Montpelier, Vt., who were out for a two week's hunt. Mr. Skinner was soon up and arranging sleeping accommodations for us. We got a few hours' rest, and after having breakfast at Hotel de Skinner finished our plans for getting into camp, which we decided to make at a logging camp on Dead Stream, about two and a half miles from Skinner's Station. I was left at the station to get our provisions together. Mr. Skinner has a store here well-stocked with everything one could wish for. A post office has recently been established here and is located in one corner of the store. The rest of the party started for camp with a part of our outfit, and were coming back for dinner, when we were all to go in for good.

After I had all our provisions together, had mailed a letter home, and everything was ready for camp, I had one hour before dinner. I loaded my Winchester and started out for a walk. I had not been out over thirty minutes, and was not over half a mile from the store on a branch of the Moose River, when I shot my first buck. I bled him, and I as I did not have any hatchet with me I decided to let him lie and wait until the boys came back before hanging him up, and get points from Joe, who, by the way, was our guide, and one of the best hunters in the Maine woods. I had considerable sport "jollying" them, and got them in nearly to where the deer lay, before telling them I had shot one. They had sport with me later to pay for this. After dressing and hanging up the buck under Joe's directions, we went to the mill and got our dinner; then started for camp, where we arrived just before dark.

The next day it rained nearly all day. We passed the time gathering wood and repairing camp. Two of the boys went out and brought in two partridges, which, with the heart and liver of the buck, which we brought in with us, made quite an addition to our bill of fare. They also reported a big buck with a fine point of antlers as a result of the afternoon's hunt. This big buck, however, proved to be the smallest buck fawn, but I did not discover the joke until after I had made a trip out to the mill and told them all about the big buck we had hung up in the woods. This was to pay for my fun with them a few days before. We had no snow until Sunday, Nov. 12, when it snowed all day. The hunting was good after that.

George and myself started out one morning for a day's hunt in the burnt land. We separated, and soon after I saw a buck about 125 yards from me walking slowly. He stopped a moment near an old top. I fired, and he started on the run in the direction of a swamp, and I after him. I had not followed far, when I saw a drop of blood. I shouted to George to come on; then the chase began.

I came up to him once, and had just time to give him a parting shot as he went over the brow of a hill. He had been lying down, but we did not give him a chance to do so again. We were now well warmed up, and pressed him hard. He soon knew we were on his trail, and began playing fox with us through the swamps and lily-wags. He would jump off to one side, and then come back again and circle around us, and do his best to throw us off his trail. We kept this up as late as we dared to, then held a council of council of war to determine where we were. The signs of blood had disappeared, so we decided he was not wounded seriously, but we would take up the trail in the morning and follow him. We had not much idea where we were, but started in the direction that we thought camp was, and soon were on familiar ground and not far from where we had started on his trail. If it had all been in a straight course we would have been obliged to lay out that night.

We took the trail the next morning, and followed it until nearly noon, when we left it on the edge of the burnt land, where he had found another deer and gone off in company. We hung up once more this day. It is needless to say that we were enjoying every moment of our outing. We had some hard tramps, but generally we found the days not long enough.

A Frenchman came into our camp one day bewailing his misfortune. It seems he was employed by the railroad company; had obtained permission to be off duty for the day, and had borrowed and old gun and started out in the expectation of taking home a deer for family use. He said, "I met with one big misfortune, to bad, to bad!" Joe was alone in camp, and he thought the man had shot some one, and asked him what was the trouble. "Oh, he big fellow; awful big one - too bad. I loose him. Don't see how I could miss him; very bad misfortune," and so on. Joe went out with him and found the tracks of a doe and a big buck close by the camp. The Frenchman had shot at them both and missed; no signs of blood could be found. He had an old gun, which had not been shot for a long time; it would have been a chance shot if he had brought one of them down. This was a case that is often repeated of parties going into the woods with strange guns, and oftentimes with the sights out of order. We had five hung up the first week, and during the second week we spent more time exploring the country and gathering gum. Two weeks of camp life in these woods is worth more than the services of a physician for a whole year. We dread to think of the day when our time is up and we have to break camp and start for home. We had all the partridges we can eat. They sit still just long enough to lose their heads by a rifle ball. There are some mink and otter around us. Joe is making figure 4 traps for them. A white weasel has been holding high carnival in our camp; he carries off our meal and anything he can get hold of, and keeps us awake nights chasing the little deer mice over the camp. He got out of our trap twice, and finally George got a bead on him with the shotgun outside of camp. We now have his pelt for a souvenir. A red squirrel got into the cabin one morning. We were all suddenly awakened by his trill. On opening our eyes, there he was on the opposite side of the camp clinging to a log, looking at us, as much as to say, "It is time you were up."

Our time was growing rapidly short. Monday morning we broke camp. Saturday we brought in our largest buck, which had been hung up about two miles from camp. We strapped him to a pole and carried him out of the burnt land; then we tied a long rope to his horns; and one with the rope over his shoulders and under the arms acted as leader, while two more took hold of the horns - one on each side. In this manner we dragged him to camp over the snow. We had seven deer at this time; one more would give us two apiece, all the law allows; but it looked doubtful if we could get it. However, there were five hours left before dark, and we might get a shot on our way out Monday morning. Saturday at 8:30 P.M. we had all been hunting hard since noon except Joe, who stayed in camp until late, when a feeling suddenly came over him that if he went out he could shoot a deer. He took his rifle down and started, and in a short time brought down the finest buck we have seen since coming into the woods. It would weigh nearly 200 lbs. I came into camp soon after Joe had started out. In about thirty minutes I hear someone coming and then George shouted. "Hurry, and come out here; man hurt!" I started thoroughly frightened, thinking some one was injured. It was growing quite dark, but I could see them coming dragging something between them, which proved to be Joe's big buck. Now we had as fine a string of game as you often see.

The next day found us on our journey home. The Big Indian Gun Club voted a first-class outing at Camp W. F. Hunt and all promised to meet again next fall if possible for a two week's hunting in the Maine woods.

– F.E.B.

TRAPPING A BEAR

By Joseph Knowles, from *Alone in the Wilderness*, 1913

Joe Knowles

In the early part of the 1900s American Society was showing a lot of interest in physical health and survival. Many wondered if man had become too "civilized" to survive in the wilds. Spurred on by the publication of the Tarzan series, the Boston Globe chose Joe Knowles (1869-1942), a middle-aged Maine Guide and amateur artist, for a grand experiment.

On Aug 4, 1913, Knowles arrived at King and Bartlett Camps and there, surrounded by reporters and photographers, he stepped into the woods, wearing only a loincloth. Leaving birch bark notes in a hollow tree, info about his survival was continually published by the paper, each episode portraying the drama of survival in the forest. In October he emerged from the woods in Quebec and was brought back to Boston, where he was honored with a grand parade and made a celebrity.

However the critics could not be quieted and called the whole experiment a fraud. To appease them Knowles wrote a book about his two-month adventure and told where he had stashed food. Local guides and hunters later found the stashes, somewhat proving that he had survived just as he detailed in his book. After the hullabaloo subsided, Knowles retired to California to continue his artwork.

The following story from his book occurred early in his ventures, providing him with food and a robe to keep him warm.

That night it was colder than usual. I began to realize that, sooner or later, I would be forced to break the game laws and get some sort of skins for protection.

During the day, while I was on the move, I really didn't need anything on my body. In fact, through the entire trip, even up to the very last day, I went around the forest, rain or shine, absolutely naked. But at night I did need something for a covering.

It was also time for me to be thinking about what I should wear when I came back to civilization. I could scarcely return to the world naked! I thought of the deer I had obtained and then lost.

In my wanderings I had seen many signs of bears. Once, in the burnt lands, I saw three feeding on the berries, shortly after the deer episode.

A bearskin would mean much to me. Then, too, I could utilize the sinew and meat to good advantage.

A man little dreams what he can accomplish until he is put to the test. I fully believe that necessity, coupled with determination and confidence, makes failure impossible.

From the first moment the idea of getting a bear came into my head I felt confident I could trap one. I carefully went over in my mind various ways I might make the attempt, and when morning came I had my plan all mapped out.

I didn't even wait that day to see if any friends, the red deer and white fawn, would come to the spring. I was all bear now, and was anxious to get to work constructing a trap.

For over an hour, I walked about searching for a suitable spot and finally found the right place. A deadfall was impractical, so my plan was to build a combination pit and deadfall, much after the plan of the Indian way of trapping grizzly bears in the west.

Digging a pit meant a lot of work. I started in by loosening the ground with sharp pointed stones and hornbeam sticks. It was slow work, but I made some progress, scooping the earth out with flat shale from ledges. I worked for several hours that day, returning to my partially excavated hole the next day and again setting to work.

I don't know how many hours I worked on that pit; it might have been ten or fifteen during the two or three days I kept at it. Once during the digging I thought I should have to give up that spot, for I came across some heavy rock and buried, petrified wood. It took the most arduous labor to dislodge that rock and chip my way through the wood until I found earth again.

At last the hole was large enough to hold a bear, being about three and a half or four feet deep. I bedded two logs--one on each side--in the earth I had scooped from the hole. I next made a kind of deadfall over the pit with logs and sticks, covering this with rocks I had taken out of the hole. Then I set a spindle trip, with the figure four, under the deadfall. This spindle I baited with stale fish.

I arranged the bait quite high up so that the bear would have to stand on his hind legs to get it. The trap was done at last, and I was pleased with it.

The covering leaded with rocks fitted securely just inside the bed logs. This would make it impossible to move the top from side to side, when once it was down.

I didn't get a bear that night, but the next night as I passed by the pit I thought I heard a rustle as if some animal were moving away from the trap. I didn't go any nearer, because through the trees I could just make out the slant of the roof. It hadn't been sprung yet.

The next night I "looked over" the trap and found a bear in it. While I had been confident all along that I would be able to land a bear, there was more or less surprise attached to the capture of this one.

Coming up to the side of the pit, I saw, through the roof-cover, a young bear, making every effort to get out. "This is great luck," I said to myself. "Everything is coming my way." There would be the skin, and the meat, and I began to think of everything about the animal I could use.

I made up my mind that he must not get away from me. I can't describe to you my feelings just then. I imagine they were something like those of a miser when there is a possibility of his losing his gold. At that time the bear was worth more to me than all the gold in the world.

Considering the situation carefully I found that I would have to break away some of the lashing in order to get at the animal. But I had to be careful not to break away too much, so I made an aperture just big enough for him to stick his head out. Before doing this I got a hornbeam club, which I held in readiness.

Presently out came the nose of the bear. I made a vicious swing and missed him. My presence so enraged the animal that he struggled around trying frantically to escape. Again his head came up through the torn place in the cover, and this time I landed squarely on top of it! But you can't kill a bear by hitting him over the head. You must strike him on the nose. I knew that, and just waited my chance.

As I looked down at him a feeling of pity came over me at the method I was forced to use. But how else could I do it? Pretty soon he stuck out his front paws. I swung and hit them. With a cry of pain he pulled them back.

Keeping my eyes on the bear every minute I backed away to a tree and broke off a small limb covered with leaves. Returning to the trap I tore away another lashing. With my left hand I began to dangle the leaves on the end of the branch in his face, to divert his attention so that I could deliver a blow with the club.

In his anger a good part of his nose came out. I swung my club, landing on the side of the bear's nose. The animal toppled over in the pit and lay perfectly still.

Knowing bears of old I did not take any chances even then. I prodded him with the stick. There was no question about it---he was dead!

It had been pretty strenuous work, so I decided to put off the task of skinning the creature until the next day. I knew what that would mean without any knife! It would take me hours to complete the work.

Catching that bear was the biggest thing I had yet accomplished in the forest. I think every man who has accomplished something a bit bigger than the ordinary things of his daily routine has a right to feel proud. It is a part of his reward. However, there was a great deal of luck attached to my catching the bear. Anyway I had him, and I was pleased beyond measure.

The red deer and the little white fawn came up to my spring the next morning.

By seven o'clock I was at the trap again. On the way I picked up the sharpest-edged rocks I could find, throwing away those I had as I came across better ones. These rocks are surprisingly sharp, and abound everywhere in this region.

I was ready for a hard day's work.

Pulling away the covering, I broke down the side of the pit and forced a couple of logs under the body of the bear, raising him slightly. I should estimate that he weighed close to two hundred pounds. By getting a good hold and tugging and hauling I managed to drag him up the side of the pit I had just broken down. Then I rolled him over on his back. I would have given anything for a knife just then! In its place I took one of the sharp rocks and began sawing back and forth on the inside of one of his hind legs. After a seemingly endless time the hair began to curl up under the rock. It worked hard at first, but my putting all my muscle back of it I finally broke the skin.

Not until later had I worked down the hind legs, up the stomach, and then up and down the inside of the front legs. While it was a crude piece of work, the skin was now ready to be taken off. I was tired after finishing this stunt. A few moment's rest and I was at work again. Then for hours I tugged and pulled at that skin trying to remove it from the carcass. Alternately working and resting for short periods, I took hold of the skin with one hand while I ripped it away from the flesh by scraping between the two with the sharpest stones I had.

Of course, quantities of meat came off with the skin, but that didn't bother me for I know I could scrape it off later. Not until late in the afternoon---judging by the sun---did I finally pull that skin entirely off. And I had started to work about seven that morning!

As Lost Pond was not very far from where I had made the trap I decided to go there, and afterwards to my first lean-to, which was in that vicinity. First I sawed off with my rock a large portion of the bear meat for food, gathering the sinew. Slinging the meat and skin over my shoulder, I started for camp.

I confess I was pretty much "all in" when I arrived at the pond. My hands were cramped and stretched, and every muscle in my back and arms ached. Throwing the skin and meat down on the shore I plunged into the water. The bath was very refreshing; it made a new man out of me. After I came out I lay down in the sun to rest.

The beavers were busy over on the dam, and I watched them a long time. With visions of an early bed I went back into the woods in the direction of my lean-to, where I built a new fire and ate a supper of dried berries and smoked trout, which I had previously stored away for just such an emergency.

I slept soundly that night. In the morning the first thing I determined to do was to get that skin into some form of condition. I laid it out on some cedar logs and fleshed it clean, by scraping it off with rocks and pulling it over the logs.

Next I took a sheet of birch bark and made a water-tight dish. Filling this with water, I threw in some small pieces of rotted wood, and began to steep it over the fire. A birch-bark dish will never burn below the water line. When the mixture had steeped enough I spread the bear-hide flat on the ground, with the hair side down, and poured the liquid from the birch-bark dish upon it. By repeating this process several times the skin became tanned to a certain extent.

A thorough drying was needed now. I singled out two saplings about the proper distance apart, and, stretching the skin as much as I could, I laced it to the slender trunks with cedar bark. I had yet to work the skin and make it pliable and soft. Off and on I worked on that hide for about three days. During those days I walked back to the trap and brought the remainder of the meat to my camp.

Tearing the grain, I ripped the meat into strips with my hands, roasting some for immediate use, and putting the rest in the smoke hole. I used quantities of dirty wood in this smoking process, as I could get up a lot of smoke that way. This smoked meat wasn't particularly pleasing to look at, but it would keep and was nourishing.

While this was not the first time I had ever trapped a bear in my life, it was the first time I had eaten any of the meat. In my years of experience as a guide I had hunted and trapped all kinds of game--animals and birds. But I had never eaten a pound of wild meat in my life, because I never liked it particularly. In fact, I had never eaten much fresh meat.

Now I was compelled to eat it. I didn't relish it a bit; but, after I devoured some, I always felt stronger, and knew that it was just what I needed. Aside from the comfort of having that bearskin to throw over me at night, and the supply of food I had obtained, I had secured in the sinews of that creature a lasting cord for my fire-kindler. The inner lining bark of the cedar, while it had answered the purpose after a fashion, is not the best thing for sawing back and forth. It wore out too quickly.

With the sinew string I would not have to use any care for fear of its breaking. I could work the bow with all my strength and the cord would not be affected in any way, producing the friction in much less time. There is no known substance for sinew that can equal its toughness and lasting qualities. The Indians have a way of chewing it and stripping it into thin fibers, which they use as thread to sew moccasins and rawhide. I hadn't reached the sewing stage just yet.

Since I had trapped the bear something had been prowling around my camp at night. I could tell by the sound that it wasn't a very large animal, but as it kept coming I became curious to see what it might be. First I thought that the meat in my lean-to might have attracted a wild-cat. Then the idea of a bear cub came into my mind.

Anyway, I was bound to find out just what it was, so one night, just before getting ready to turn in, I let my fire burn pretty low and sat up watching for some signs of the visitor. On the other nights the sound of crackling twigs had always come just after my fire had burned out.

Scarcely had the last glimmer of my fire flickered away then, off in the darkness to my right, came the expected sound. I had almost dozed off as I sat there, but I woke up quickly and listened. Straining my eyes in the direction of the noise I could barely make out the outline of some animal. It was impossible to tell what it was, but I knew it was dark colored.

As if suddenly switched on by an unseen electric current, two balls of light flashed in the darkness. The creature was looking at me too! The fire was between us, and as a lazy flame sputtered a moment before fading away I could see the reflection of the firelight in those eyes! Presently the eyes disappeared. I seized a smoldering brand, and, fanning it into flame, rushed toward the spot.

I was on the right track, sure enough, for I nearly fell over whatever it was. It was so slow in getting away that I managed to get it between the fire and me.

I was now convinced that the animal was a bear cub by the way it acted. Through the dim light my brand, which was already burning low again, I saw that the creature was black. I couldn't see clearly enough to determine the head and hind; but I felt sure that my company was a clumsy young bear.

My first thought was to catch him alive.

The little fellow made a sudden turn and almost dodged past me, but I hurled the brand at him and drove him back toward the fire. He was literally between two fires. As the brand struck the ground it went out. With that the animal turned and ran directly toward me. Again he tried to rush by me, but I jumped in front of him and stopped him with my legs.

Then I jumped again, but in a different direction! My supposed bear cub had turned out to be a hedgehog, and for some moments I was fully occupied removing quills from my legs. My bark chaps were ample protection against briers and brush, but not against quills of hedgehogs.

My third week in the wilderness was already drawing to a close. Physically I was perfectly well. I had plenty of food and a comfortable bearskin. But mentally I was suffering.

It was terribly lonesome!

Chapter 4

MOOSEHEAD LAKE AND PISCATAQUIS REGION

Moosehead Lake, the largest lake in Maine, is one of Maine's greatest treasures. Along with the Rangeley Lakes, it was one of the most frequented areas by sportsmen in the nineteenth century. The Piscataquis region, which stretches from Monson to Millinocket, includes many mountains and ponds and was the home of many sporting camps.

Halfway up the lake is an isthmus that projects out from the eastern shore and has a promontory, which rises over 700 feet above the lake and is known as Mount Kineo. Historically the Penobscot and other nations visited Kineo annually for the flint-like rock, from which they could form tools and weapons. Our earliest written description of Moosehead Lake comes from the journal of British Col. Montressor, who canoed down the Moose River, down the lake and then down the Kennebec River in 1767. About 1804 John Ellis, a hunter and guide, visited the lake when he was a young man, remained there trapping, hunting and fishing, supplying the hotels with venison, moose-meat and partridge. He became the most popular guide for many years.

Greenville, located at the foot of the lake, was settled about 1827 and with its several hotels, became the starting point and base for supplies for lumbermen, tourists and sportsmen. The Kineo House, first built as a tavern and store, mostly served the lumbermen who were coming in and out of the woods, and what few sportsmen who ventured by on their way to the West Branch. This hotel burned down several times and was rebuilt until it boasted over one hundred rooms. It finally closed in the 1960's, but the golf course remains and it is the starting point for people who come over by boat or ferry to climb the mountain. It formerly had a fire tower, which has been converted into a viewing platform, affording one of the best views in the entire State. In years past there were also several hotels located at the top of the lake, known as Northeast Carry.

Starting in the 1840', several sportsmen, including Thoreau, paddled in the Moosehead region and wrote accounts of their adventures. John Way of Boston created a small guide and map of Moosehead in 1874. This was followed by more extensive guidebooks by A. J. Farrar and Lucius Hubbard. Besides the colorful Old Ellis, who told wonderful stories, one of Moosehead's most famous sons was Chief Henry Red Eagle, who starred in western films and wrote many articles about the history of the region.

Due to its difficult access, the Piscataquis region was mostly frequented by lumbermen, but in 1882 Charlie Randall and his son opened sporting camps at Little Lyford Pond and West Branch Pond. After this sporting camps flourished on many of the ponds, including Sebec Lake, Lake Onawa, Horseshoe Pond, Long Pond, Third Roach Pond, Yoke Pond, Houston Pond and Second Roach Pond. Camps were also located on the many ponds whose waters flow into the West Branch of the Penobscot.

Katahdin Iron Works flourished in the mid nineteenth century a hotel was built on Silver Lake, eventually being accessed by railroad. Further up the West Branch of the Pleasant River is Gulf Hagas, a deep ravine which is often called "The Little Grand Canyon of the East." The wildest and most remote section of the entire Appalachian Trail, known as the Hundred Mile Wilderness," traverses across this region.

Recently there has been a lot effort to conserve this region, with large holdings purchased and maintained by the Appalachian Mountain Club, the Nature Conservancy, Elliotsville Plantation and the State of Maine.

THE SPECULATOR

By Seba Smith, from *'Way Down East'*, 1852

Seba Smith

Seba Smith (1792-1868), graduated from Bowdoin College in 1818, and soon began contributing political articles in the local newspapers of Portland. He soon became editor of the "Portland Daily Gazette" and through this he created his fictitious but famous Jack Downing, a character he used to satirize the administration of Andrew Jackson. His character, considered the first political satire in the country, became nationally known and admired, spawning other such characters as Mr. Dooley and Sam Slick. Unfortunately, he did not patent Downing and others used the name and he lost a lucrative income. Fortunately his wife, Elizabeth Oakes Smith, was a successful poet in her own right and was able to provide for their needs.

This story, set in the Monson area, is one of many stories Smith produced.

In the autumn of 1836, while travelling through a portion of the interior of the State of Maine, I stopped at a small new village, between the Kennebec and Penobscot rivers, nearly a hundred miles from the sea-board, for the purpose of giving my horse a little rest and provender, before proceeding some ten miles farther that evening. It was just after sunset; I was walking on the piazza, in front of the neat new tavern, admiring the wildness of the surrounding country, and watching the gathering shadows of the grey twilight, as it fell upon the valleys, and crept softly up the hills, when a light one-horse wagon, with a single gentleman, drove rapidly into the yard, and stopped at the stable door.

"Tom," said the gentleman to the other as he jumped from his wagon, "take my mare out, rub her down well, and give her four quarts of oats. Be spry, now, Tom; you needn't give her any water, for she sweats like fury. I'll give her a little when I am ready to start."

Tom sprang with uncommon alacrity to obey the orders he had received, and the stranger walked toward the house. He was a tall, middle-aged gentleman, rather thin, but well proportioned, and well dressed. It was the season of the year when the weather began to grow chilly, and the evenings cold; and the frock-coat of the stranger, trimmed with fur, and buttoned to the throat, while it insured comfort, served also to exhibit his fine elastic form to the best advantage. His little wagon, too, had a marked air of comfort about it; there were the spring-seat, the stuffed cushions, and buffalo robes; all seemed to indicate a gentleman of ease and leisure; while, on the other hand, his rapid movements and prompt manner, betokened the man of business. As he stepped on to the piazza, with his long and handsome driving-whip in his hand, the tavern-keeper, who was a brisk young man, and well understood his business, met him with a hearty shake of the hand, and a familiar "How are you, Colonel? Come, walk in."

There was something about the stranger that strongly attracted my attention, and I followed him into the bar-room. He stepped up to the bar, laid his whip on the counter, and called for a glass of brandy and water, with some small crackers and cheese.

"But not going to stop to supper, Colonel? Going farther to-night?" inquired the landlord, as he pushed forward the brandy bottle.

"Can't stop more than ten minutes," replied the stranger; "just long enough to let the mare eat her oats."

"Is that the same mare," asked the host, "that you had when you were here last?"

"Yes," answered the colonel; "I've drove her thirty miles since dinner, and am going forty miles farther, before I stop."

"But you'll kill that mare, colonel, as sure as rates," said the landlord; "she's too likely a beast to drive to death."

"No, no," was the reply; "she's tough as a pitch-knot; I feed her well; she'll stand it, I guess. I go to Norridgewock before I sleep to-night."

With a few more brief remarks, the stranger finished his brandy, and crackers and cheese; he threw down some change on the counter, ordered his carriage brought to the door, and bidding his landlord good night, jumped into his wagon, cracked his whip and was off like a bird. After he was gone, I ventured to exercise the Yankee privilege of asking "who he might be."

"That's Colonel Kingston," said the landlord; "a queer sort of a chap, he is, too; a real go-ahead sort of a fellow as ever I was met with; does more business in one day than some folks would do in a year. He's a right good customer; always full of money and pays well."

"What business or profession does he follow?" I asked.

"Why, not any particular business," replied the landlord; "he kind o' speculates round, and such like."

"But," said I, "I thought the speculation in timberland is over' I didn't know that a single person could be found, now, to purchase lands."

"Oh, it isn't exactly that kind of speculation," said the landlord; "he's got a knack of buying out folks' farms; land, house, barn, live stock, hay and provisions, all in the lump."

"Where does he live?" said I.

"Oh, he's lived round in a number of places, since he's been in these parts. He's been round in these towns only a year or two, and it's astonishing to see how much property he's accumulated. He stays in Monson most of the time, now. That's where he came from this afternoon. They say he's got a number of excellent farms in Monson, and I'll warrant he's got some deeds of some more of 'em with him, now, that he's going to carry to Norridgewock to-night, to put on record."

I bade the landlord good evening, and proceeded on my journey. What I had seen and heard of Colonel Kingston, had made an unwonted impression on my mind; and as Monson lay in my route, and I was expecting to stop there a few days, my curiosity was naturally a little excited, to learn something more of his history. The next day I reached Monson; and as I rode over its many hills, and along it fine ridges of arable land, I was struck with the number of fine farms which I passed, and the evidence of thrift and good husbandry that surround me. As this town was at that time almost on the verge of the settlements in that part of the state, I was surprised to find it so well settled, and under such good cultivation.

My surprise was increased, on arriving at the centre of the town, to find a flourishing and bright-looking village, with two or three stores, a variety of mechanics' shops, a school-house, and a neat little church, painted white, with green blinds, and surmounted by a bell. A little to the westward of the village, was on of those clear and beautiful ponds, that greet the eye of the traveller in almost every hour's ride in that section of the country; and on its outlet, which ran through the village, stood a mill, and some small manufacturing establishments, that served to fill up the picture.

"Happy town!" thought I, "that has such a delightful village for its centre of attraction, and happy village that is supported by surrounding farmers of such thrift and industry as those of Monson!" All this, too, I had found within a dozen or fifteen miles of Moosehead Lake, the noblest and most extensive sheet of water in New England, which I had hitherto considered so far embosomed in the deep, trackless forest, as to be almost unapproachable, save by the wild Indian or the daring hunter. A new light seemed to burst upon me; and it was a pleasant thought that led me to look forward but a few years, when the rugged and wild shores of the great Moosehead should resound with the hum and the song of the husbandman, and on every side rich farms and lively villages should be reflected on its bosom.

I had been quietly seated in the village inn but a short time, in a room, that served both for bar and sitting room, when a small man, with a flapped hat and old brown "wrapper," a leather strap buckled around his waist, and holding a goad-stick in his hand, entered the room, and took a set on a bench in the corner. His bright, restless eye glanced round the room, and then seemed to be bent thoughtfully toward the fire, while in the arch expression of his countenance I thought I beheld the prelude to some important piece of intelligence, struggling for utterance. At last, said he, addressing the landlord, "I guess the colonel ain't about home to-day, is he?"

"No," replied Boniface, "he's been gone since yesterday morning; he said he was going up into your neighborhood. Haven't you seen anything of him?"

"Yes," said the little man with the goad-stick, "I see him yesterday afternoon about two o'clock, starting off like a streak, to go to Norridgewock."

"Gone to Norridgewock!" said the landlord; "what for! He didn't say nothing about going when he went away."

"More deeds, I guess," said the little teamster. "He's worried Deacon Stone out of *his* farm, at last."

"He *hasn't* got Deacon Stone's farm, has he?" exclaimed the landlord.

"Deacon Stone's farm!" reiterated an elderly, sober-looking man, drawing a long pipe from his mouth, which had until now been quietly smoking in the opposite corner.

"Deacon Stone's farm!" uttered the landlady with upraised hands, as she entered the room just in season to hear the announcement.

"Deacon Stone's farm!" exclaimed three or four others, in different parts of the room, all turning an eager look toward the little man with the goad-stick. As soon as there was a sufficient pause in these exclamations, to allow the teamster to put in another word, he repeated:

"Yes, he's worried the deacon out, at last, and got hold of his farm, as slick as a whistle. He's been kind o' edging round the deacon there three weeks, a little at a time; jest enough to find out how to get the right side of him; for the deacon was a good deal offish, and yesterday morning the colonel was up there by the time the deacon had done breakfast; and he got them into the deacon's fore room, and shut the door; and there they staid till dinner was ready, and had waited for them an hour, before they would come out. And when they had come out, the job was all done; and the deed was signed, sealed and delivered. I'd been there about eleven o'clock, and the deacon's wife and the gals were in terrible fidgets for fear of what was going on in t'other room. They started to go in, two or three times, but the door was fastened, so they had to keep out. After dinner I went over again, and got there just before they were out of the fore room. The deacon asked the colonel to stop for dinner, but I guess the colonel see so many sour looks about the house, that he was afraid of a storm abrewing; so he only ketched a piece of bread and cheese, and said he must be a-goin'. He jumped into his wagon, and give his mare a cut, and was out of sight in two minutes."

"How did poor Mrs. Stone feel?" asked the landlady; "I should thought she would a-died."

"She looked as if she'd turn milk sour quicker than a thunder-shower," said the teamster; "and Jane went into the bedroom, and cried as if her heart would break. I believe they didn't any of 'em make out to eat any dinner, and I thought the deacon felt about as bad as any of 'em, after all; for I never see him look so kind o' riled in my life. 'Now Mrs. Stone,' said he to his wife, 'you think I've done wrong; but after talking along with Colonel Kingston, I made up my mind it would be for the best.' She didn't make him any answer, but began to cry, and went out of the room. The deacon looked as if he would sink into the 'arth. He stood a minute or two, as if he wasn't looking at nothing, and then he took down his pipe off the mantel, and sat down in the corner, and went to smoking as hard as he could smoke.

"After a while, he turned round to me, and says he, 'Neighbor, I don't know but I've done wrong.' 'Well,' says I, 'in my opinion that depends upon what sort of bargain you've made. If you've got a good bargain out of the colonel, I don't see why his money isn't worth as much as anybody's, or why another farm as good as your'n isn't worth as much.' 'Yes,' said the deacon, 'so it seems to me. I've got a good bargain, I know; it's more than the farm is worth. I never considered it worth more that two thousand dollars, stock, and hay, and all; and he takes the whole jest as 'tis and gives me three thousand dollars.' 'Is it pay down?' says I. 'Yes,' says he, 'it's all pay down. He gives me three hundred dollars in cash; I've got it in my pocket; and then he gives me an order on Saunder's store for two hundred dollars; that's as good as money, you know; for we are always wanting one thing or another out of his store. Then he gives me a deed of five hundred acres, of land, in the upper part of Vermont, at five dollars an acre. That makes up three thousand dollars. But that isn't all; he say this land is richly worth seven dollars an acre; well timbered, and a good chance to get the timber down; and he showed me certificates of several respectable men, that had been all over it, and they said it was well worth seven dollars. That gives me two dollars clear profit on an acre, which on five hundred acres make two thousand dollars. So that instead of three thousand dollars, I s'pose I've really got four thousand for the farm. But then it seems to work up the feelings of the women folks so, to think of leaving it, after we've got it well under way, that I don't know but I've done wrong.' And his feelings came over him so, that he begun to smoke away again as hard as he could draw. I didn't know what to say to him, for I didn't believe he would ever get five hundred dollars for his five hundred acres of land, so I got up and went home."

As my little goad-stick teamster made a pause here, the elderly man in the opposite corner, who had sat all this time knocking his pipe-bowl on the thumbnail of his left hand, took up the thread of discourse.

"I'm afraid," says he, looking up at the landlord, "I'm afraid Deacon Stone had got tricked out of his farm for a mere song. That Colonel Kingston, in my opinion, is a dangerous man, and ought to be looked after."

"Well, I declare!" said the landlord, "I'd no idea he would get hold of Deacon Stone's farm. That's one of the best farms in the town."

"Yes," replied the man with the pipe, "and that makes seven of the best farms in town that he's got hold of already; and what'll be the end of it, I don't know; but I think something ought to be done about it."

"Well, there," said the landlady, "I *do* pity Mrs. Stone from the bottom of my heart; she'll never get over it the longest day she lives."

Here the little man with the goad-stick, looking out the window, saw his team starting off up the road, and flew out of the door, screaming "Hush! Whoa! Hush!" And that was the last I saw of him. But my curiosity was now too much excited, with regard to Colonel Kingston's mysterious operations, and my sympathies for good Deacon Stone, and his fellow-sufferers, were too thoroughly awakened, to allow me to rest with further inquiries.

During the days that I remained in the neighborhood, I learned that he came from Vermont; that he had visited Monson several times within a year or two, and had made it his home there for the last few months. During that time he had exercised an influence over some of the honest and sober-minded farmers of Monson that was perfectly unaccountable. He was supposed to be a man of wealth, for he never seemed to lack money for any operation he chose to undertake. He had a bold, dashing air, and rather fascinating manners, and his power over those with whom he conversed had become so conspicuous, that it was regarded as an inevitable consequence in Monson, if a farmer chanced to get shut up in a room with Colonel Kingston, he was a "gone goose," and sure to come out well stripped of his feathers. He had actually got possession of seven or eight of the best farms in the town, for about one quarter part of their real value.

It may be thought unaccountable, that thriving, sensible farmers could in so many instances be duped; but there were some extraneous circumstances that helped to produce the result. The wild spirit of speculation which had raged throughout the country for two or three years, pervaded almost every mind and rendered it restless and desirous of change. And then the seasons, for a few years past, had been cold and unfavorable. The farmer had sowed and had not reaped, and he was discouraged. If he could sell, he would go to a warmer climate. These influences, added to his own powers of adroitness and skill in making "the worse appear the better reason," had enabled Colonel Kingston to inveigle the farmers of Monson out of their hard-earned property, and turn them, houseless and poor, upon the world.

The public mind had become much excited upon the subject, and the case of Deacon Stone added fresh fuel to the fire. It was in this state of affairs that I left Monson, and heard no more of Colonel Kingston until the following summer, when another journey called me into that neighborhood, and I learned the sequel to his fortunes. The colonel made but few more conquests, after his victory over Deacon Stone; and the experience of a cold and cheerless winter, which soon overtook them, brought the deluded farmers to their senses. The trifling sums of money which they received in hand were soon exhausted in providing necessary supplies for their families; and the property which they had obtained, as principal payment for their farms, turned out to be of little value, or was so situated that they could turn it to no profitable account. Day after day, through the winter, the excitement increased, and spread, and waxed more intense, as the unfortunate condition of the sufferers became more generally known. "Colonel Kingston" was the great and absorbing topic of discussion, at the stores, at the tavern, at evening parties, and sleigh-rides, and even during intermission at church, on the Sabbath.

The indignation of the people had reached that pitch which usually leads to acts of violence. Colonel Kingston was now regarded as a monster, preying upon the peace and happiness of society, and various were the expedients proposed to rid the town of him. The schoolboys, in the several districts, discussed the matter, and resolved to form a grand company, to snowball him out of town, and only waited a nod of approbation from some of their parents or teachers, to carry their resolutions into effect. Some reckless young men were for seizing him, and giving him a public horse-whipping, in front of the tavern at mid-day, and in presence of the whole village. Others, equally violent but less daring, proposed catching him out, some dark evening, riding him out of town on a rail. But the older, more experienced, and sober-minded men, shook their heads at these rash projects, and said: "It is a bad plan for people to take the law into their own hands; as long as we live under good laws, it is best to be governed by them. Such kind of squabbles as you young folks want to get into, most always turn out bad in the end."

So reasoned the old folks; but they were nevertheless as eager and as determined to get rid of Colonel Kingston, as were the young ones, though more cautious and circumspect as to the means. At last, after many consultations and much perplexity, Deacon Stone declared one day, with much earnestness, to his neighbors and townsmen, who were assembled at the village, that "For his part, he believed it was best to appeal at once to the laws of the land; and if *they* wouldn't give protection to the citizen, he didn't know what would. For himself, he verily believed Colonel Kingston might be charged with swindling, and if a complaint was to be made to the Grand Jury he didn't believe but they would have him indicted and tried in Court, and give back the people their farms again." The deacon spoke *feelingly*, on the subject, and his words found a ready response in the hearts of all present. It was at once agreed to present Colonel Kingston to the Grand Jury, when the Court should next be in session in Norridgewock. Accordingly, when the next Court was held, Monson was duly represented before the grand inquest for the county of Somerset, and such an array of facts and evidence was exhibited, that the Jury, without hesitation, found a bill against the colonel for swindling, and a warrant was immediately issued for his apprehension.

The crisis had been some months maturing, and the warm summer had now commenced. The forest trees were now in leaf; and though the ground was yet wet and muddy, the days began to be hot and uncomfortable. It was a warm moonlight evening, when the officer arrived in Monson with the warrant. He had taken two assistants with him, mounted on fleet horses, and about a dozen stout young men of the village were in his train as volunteers. They approached the tavern where Colonel Kingston boarded, and just as they were turning from the road to the house, the form of a tall, slim person was seen in the bright moonlight, gliding from the backdoor, and crossing the garden.

"There he goes!" exclaimed a dozen Monson voices at once; "that's he! ---there he goes!"

And sure enough, it was he! Whether he had been notified of his danger, by some traitor, or had seen from the window the approach of the party, and suspected mischief was at hand, was never known. But the moment he heard these exclamations, he sprang from the ground as if a bullet had pierced his heart. He darted across the garden, leaped the fence at a bound, and flew over the adjacent pasture with the speed of a race-horse. In a moment the whole party were in full pursuit; and in five minutes more, a hundred men and boys, of all ages, roused by the cry that now rang through the village, were out, and joining in the race. The fields were rough, and in some places quite wet, so that running across them was rather a difficult and hazardous business. The direction which Kingston at first seemed inclined to take, would lead them into the main road, beyond the corner, nearly a half a mile off. But those who were mounted put spurs to their horses, and reaching the spot before him, headed off in another direction. He now flew from field to field, leaping fence after fence, and apparently aiming for the deep forest, on the eastern part of the town. Many of his pursuers were athletic young men, and they gave him a hot chase. Even Deacon Stone, who had come to the village that evening to await the arrival of the officer---even the deacon, now in the sixty-first year of his age, ran like a boy. He kept among the foremost of the pursuers, and once getting within a dozen rods of the fugitive, his zeal burst forth into words, and he cried out, in a tremulous voice: "Stop! You infernal villain! --stop!" This was the nearest approach he had made to profanity for forty years; and when the sound of the words he had uttered fell full on his ear, his nerves received such a shock that his legs trembled and he was no longer able to sustain his former speed.

The colonel, however, so far from obeying the emphatic injunction of the deacon, rather seemed to be inspired by it to new efforts of flight. Over log, bog and brook, stumps, stones and fences, he flew like a wild deer; and after a race of some two miles, during which he was at no time more than twenty rods from some of his pursuers, he plunged into a thick dark forest. Bearing his adversaries close upon him, after he had entered the wood, and being almost entirely exhausted, he threw himself under the side of a large fallen tree, where he was darkly sheltered by a thick clump of alders. His pursuers rushed furiously on, many of them within his hearing, and some of them passing over the very tree under which he lay. After scouring the forest for a mile round, without finding any traces of the fugitive, they began to retreat to the opening, and Kingston heard enough of their remarks, on their return, to learn that his retreat from the woods that night would be well guarded against, and that the next day Monson would pour out all its force "to hunt him to the ends of the 'arth, but that they would have him!"

Under this comfortable assurance, he was little disposed to take much of a night's rest, where he would be sure to be discovered and overtaken in the morning. But what course to take, and what measures to adopt, was a difficult question for him to answer. To return to Monson opening, he well knew would be to throw himself into the hands of his enemies; and if he remained in the woods till next day, he foresaw there would be but a small chance of escape from the hundreds on every side, who would be on the alert to take him. North of him was the new town of Elliotsville, containing some fifteen or twenty families, and to the south, lay Guilford, a well-settled farming town; but he know he would be no more safe in either of those settlements than he would in Monson. East of him lay an unsettled and unincorporated wild township, near the centre of which, and some three or miles to the eastward of there he now lay, dwelt a solitary individual by the name of Johnson, a singular being, who, from some unknown cause, had forsake social life, and had lived a hermit in that secluded spot for seven or eight years. He had a little opening in a fine interval, on the banks of Wilson River, where he raised his corn and potatoes, and had constructed a rude hovel for a dwelling. Johnson had made his appearance occasionally at the village, with a string of fine trout, a bear-skin, or some other trophy of his Nimrod propensities, which he would exchange at the stores for "a little rum, and little tobacco, and little tea, and a jack-knife, and a little more rum," when he would plunge into the forest again, return to his hermitage, and be seen no more for months.

After casting his thoughts about in vain for any other refuge, Kingston resolved to throw himself upon the protection of Johnson. Accordingly, as soon as he was a little rested, and his pursuers were well out of hearing, he crept from his hiding-place, and taking his direction by the moon, made the best of his way eastward, through the rough and thick wood. It did no easy matter to penetrate such a forest in the daytime; and in the night, nothing but extreme desperation could drive a man through it. Here pressing his way through dark and thick underbrush, that constantly required both hands to guard his eyes; there climbing over huge windfalls, wading a bog, or leaping a brook; and anon working his way, for a quarter of a mile, through a dismal tangled cedar-swamp, where a thousand dry and pointed limbs, shooting out on every side, clear to the very ground, tear his clothes from his back, and could wound him at every step. Under these impediments, and in this condition, Kingston spent the night in pressing on toward Johnson's camp; and after a period of extreme toil and suffering, just at daylight, he came out to the opening. But here another barrier was before him. The Wilson River, a wild and rapid stream, and now swollen by a recent freshet, was between him and Johnson's dwelling, and he had no means of crossing. But cross he must, and he was reluctant to lose time in deliberation. He selected the spot that looked most likely to admit of fording, and waded into the river. He staggered along from rock to rock, and fought against the current, until he reached nearly the middle of the stream, when the water deepened and took him from his feet! He was but an indifferent swimmer, and the force of the current carried him rapidly down the stream. At last, however, after severe struggles, and not without imminent peril of his life, he made out to reach the bank, so much exhausted, that it was with difficulty he could walk to Johnson's camp. When he reached it, he found its lonely inmate yet asleep. He roused him, made his case known to him, and begged his protection.

Johnson was naturally benevolent, and the forlorn, exhausted, ragged, and altogether wretched appearance of the fugitive, at once touched his heart. There was now--

> "NO SPECULATION in those eyes
> Which he did glare withal,"

but fear and trembling blanched his countenance, and palsied his limbs. Possibly the hermit's benevolence might have been quickened by a portion of the contents of the colonel's purse; but be that as it may, he was soon administering to the comfort of his guest. In a few minutes he had a good fire, and the exhausted wanderer took off his clothes and dried them, and tried to fasten some of the flying pieces that had been torn loose by the hatchel-teeth limbs in the cedar-swamps. In the meantime Johnson had provided some roasted potatoes, and a bit of fried bear-meat, which he served up, with a tin dipper of strong tea, and Kingston ate and drank, and was greatly refreshed.

They now set themselves earnestly to work to devise means of retreat and security against the pursuit of the enraged Monsonites, "who," Kingston said, "he was sure would visit the camp before noon." Under a part of the floor, was a small excavation in the earth, which his host called his potato-hole, since, being near the fire, it served in winter to keep his potatoes from freezing. This portion of the floor was now entirely covered over with two or three barrels, a water-pail, a bench, and sundry articles of iron and tin-ware. It was Johnson's advice, that the colonel should be secreted in this potato-hole. He was afraid, however, that they would search so close as to discover his retreat. Yet the only alternative seemed between the plan proposed and betaking himself again to the woods, exposed to toil and starvation, and the chance of arrest by some of the hundreds who would be scouring the woods that day, eager as bloodhounds for their prey. Something must be done immediately, for he was expecting every hour to hear the cry of his pursuers; and relying on Johnson's ingenuity and skill to send them off on another scent should they come to his camp, he concluded to retreat to the potato-hole.

Accordingly, the superincumbent articles were hastily removed, a board was taken up from the floor, and the gallant colonel descended to his new quarters. They were small to be sure, but under the circumstances very acceptable. The cell was barely deep enough to receive him in a sitting posture, with his neck a little bent, while under him was a little straw, upon which he could stretch his limbs to rest. Johnson replaced all the articles with such that no one would have supposed they had been removed for months.

This labour had just been completed, when he heard shouts from a distance, and beheld ten or a dozen people rushing out of the woods, and making toward his camp. He was prepared for them; and when they came in, they found him seated quietly on his bench, mending his clothes.

"Have you seen anything of Colonel Kingston?' inquired the foremost of the company with panting eagerness.

"Colonel Kingston!" asked Johnson, looking up with a sort of vacant, honest stare.

"Yes--he's run for't," replied the other, "and we are after him. The Grand Jury had indicted him, and the Sheriff's got a warrant, and all Monson, and one half of Guilford, is out a hunting for him. Last night, just as they were going to take him, he ran into the woods this way. Ha'n't you seen nothin' of him!"

Johnson sat with his mouth wide open, and listened with such an inquiring look that any one would have sworn it was all news to him. At last he exclaimed with the earnestness inspired by a new thought, "Well, there! I'll bet that was what my dog was barking at, an hour ago! I heard him barking as fierce as a tiger, about half a mile down the river. I was busy mending my trowsers, or I should have gone down to see what he'd got track of."

The company unanimously agreed that it must have been Kingston the dog was after; and in the hope of getting upon his track, they hurried off in the direction indicated, leaving Johnson as busily engaged as if, like

"Brian O'Linn, he'd no breeches to wear,"

until he finished repairing his tattered inexpressibles.

The fugitive now breathed freely again; but while his pursuers were talking with his host, his respiration had hardly been sufficient to sustain life, and "cold drops of sweat stood on his trembling flesh." He did not venture to leave his retreat for two days; for during that day and most of the next, the woods were scoured from one end of the township to the other, and several parties successfully visited the camp, who were all again successively dispatched to the woods by the adroitness of its occupant.

After two days the pursuers principally left the woods and contented themselves with posting sentinels at short intervals on the roads that surrounded the forest, and in the neighboring towns, hoping to arrest their victim, when hunger should drive him forth to some of the settlements. Kingston felt that it was unsafe for him to remain any longer under the protection of Johnson, and he knew it would be exceedingly difficult to make his escape through any of the settlements of Maine. Upon due reflection, he concluded that the only chance left for him was to endeavor to make his way to Canada.

He was now a dozen or fifteen miles from the foot of Moosehead Lake. There was a foot-path to Elliotsville, where there were a few inhabitants. Through this settlement he thought he might venture to pass in the night; and he could then go a few miles to the westward, and meet the road leading from Monson to the lake. Once across or around the foot of the lake, he believed he could make his way into the Canada road, and escape with safety. Having matured his plan he communicated it to Johnson, who aided it in the best manner he could by providing him with a pack of potatoes and fried bear-meat, accompanied with an extra Indian "Johnny-cake," a jack-knife, and a flint and tinder for striking fire.

It was late in the night, when all things were prepared for the journey, and Kingston bade an affectionate adieu to his host, declaring that he should never forget him, and adding, with much originality of thought and expression, that "a friend in need was a friend indeed." He had nearly a mile to go through the woods, before reaching Elliotsville; and when he passed the Elliotsville settlement the day began to dawn. A stirring young man, who was out at the early hour, saw him cross the road at a distance and strike into the woods. Satisfied at once who he was, and suspecting his object, he hastened to rouse his two or three neighbors, and then started toward Monson village with all the speed his legs could give him. Kingston, observing this movement from a hill-top in the wood, was convinced that he should be pursued, and redoubled his exertions to reach the lake.

When the messenger reached Monson and communicated his intelligence, the whole village was roused like an encamped army at the battle-call; and in twenty minutes every horse in the village was mounted and the riders spurring with all speed toward the lake, and Deacon Stone among the foremost. As they came in sight of the Moosehead, the sun, which was about an hour high, was pouring a flood of warm rays across the calm, still waters, and soon half a mile from land, they beheld a tall, slim man, alone in a canoe, paddling toward the opposite shore.

For a moment the party stood speechless, and then vent was given to such oaths and execrations as have had made familiar. Something was even swelling in Deacon Stone's throat, well-nigh as sinful as he had uttered in a former occasion, but he coughed, and checked it before it found utterance. They looked around and ran on every side, to see if another boat, or any other means of crossing the lake could be found; but all in vain. The only skiff on that arm of the lake had been seized by the colonel in his flight. His pursuers were completely baffled. Some were for crossing the woods, and going round the southwest bay of the lake over the head waters of the Kennebec River, and so into the great wilderness on the western side of the lake. But others said, "No; it's no use; if he once gets over among them swamps and mountains, you might as well look for a needle in a haystack!"

This sentiment accorded with the better judgment of the party, and they turned about and rode quietly back to Monson---Deacon Stone consoling himself on the way by occasionally remarking: "Well, if the heathen is driven out of the land, thanks be a kind Providence, he hasn't carried the land with him!"

THE TRAPPER'S STORY

By Daniel P. Thompson, from *Gaut Gurley, the Trappers of Umbagog; A Tale of Border Life.* 1857

In his novel, Thompson told us how two hunters sat by a campfire one night and competed in a story contest, trying to be the better storyteller. The first hunter told of an exciting panther and bear fight; the second hunter related a fantastic beaver story...

"My story," commenced the trapper, who was next to be called on for his promised contribution to the entertainment of the evening, "my story is of a different character from the one you have just heard. It don't run so much to the great and terrible as the small and curious. It may appear to you perhaps a little queer, in some parts; but which, after the modest drafts that have been made of my credulity, you will, of course, have the good manners to believe. It relates to an adventure in beaver-hunting, which I met with, many years ago, on Moosehead Lake, where I served my apprenticeship at trapping. I had established myself in camp, the last of August, about the time the beavers, after having collected in communities, and established their never-failing democratic government, generally get fairly at work on their dams and dwelling-houses, for the ensuing cold months, in places along the small streams, which they have looked out and decided on for the purpose. I was thus early on the ground, in order to have time, before I went to other hunting, to look up the localities of the different societies, so that I need not blunder on them and disturb them, in the chase for other animals, and so that I should know where to find them, when their fur got thick enough to warrant the onslaught upon them which I designed to make.

"In hunting for these localities in the vicinity around me, I soon unexpectedly discovered marks of what must be a very promising one, situated on a small stream, not over half a mile in a bee-line over the hills from my camp. When I discovered the place, --- as

I did from encountering, at short intervals in the woods, two wolverines, always the great enemy and generally prowling attendant of assembled beavers, ---these curious creatures had just begun to lay the foundations of their dam. And the place being so near, and the nights moonlight, I concluded I would go over occasionally evenings, --- the night being the only time when they can be seen engaged on their work, ---and see if I could gain some covert near the bank, where, unperceived, I might watch their operations, and obtain some new knowledge of their habits, of which I might thereafter avail myself, when the season for them arrived. Accordingly, I went over that very evening, in the twilight, secured a favorable lookout, and laid in wait for the appearance of the beavers. Presently I was startled by a loud rap, as of a small paddle flatwise on the water, then another, and another, in quick succession. It was the signal of the master workman, for all the workers to leave their hiding-places in the banks, and repair to their labors in making the dam. The next moment the whole stream seemed to be alive with the numbers in motion. I could hear them, sousing and plunging in the water, in every direction, --- then swimming and puffing across or up and down the stream, --- then scrambling up the banks, --- then the auger-like sound of their sharp teeth, at work on the small trees, -- then soon the falling of the trees, --- the rustling and tugging of the creatures, in getting the fallen trees out of the water, --- and finally, the surging and splashing with which they came swimming towards the groundwork of the dam, with the butt end of those trees in their mouths. The line of the dam they had begun, passed with a curve up stream in the middle, so as to give it more strength to resist the current; across the low-water bed of the river some five rods; and extended up over the first low bank, about as much farther, to a second and higher bank, which must have bounded the water at the greater floods. They had already cut, drawn on, and put down, a double layer of trees with their butts brought up evenly to the central line, and their tops pointing up, and those of the other, down stream. Among and under this line of butts had been worked in an extra quantity of limbs, old wood, and short bushes, so as to give the centre an elevation of a foot or two, over the lowest part of the sides, which, of course, fell off considerably each way in the lessening of the tops of the trees, thus put down. Over all these they had plastered mud, mixed in with stones, grass, and moss, so thick as not only to hold down securely the bodies of the trees, but nearly conceal them from sight.

"Scarcely had I time to glance over these works, which I had not approached near enough to inspect much, before the beavers from below, and above, came tugging along, by dozens on a side to the lower edges of their embankment, with the loads or rafts of trees which they had respectively drawn to the spot. Lodging these on the solid ground, with the ends just out of water, they relinquished their holds, mounted the slopes, paused a minute to take breath, and then, seizing these ends again, drew them, with the seeming strength of horses, out of the water and up to the central line on top; laid the stems or bodies of the trees parallel, and as near together as they could be got; and adjusted the butt ends, as I have stated they did with the foundation layers, so as to bring them to a sort of joint on the top. Then they all went off for new loads, with the exception of a small squad, a part of which were still holding their trees in a small place in the dam, where the current had not been checked, and the other part bringing stones, till they had confined the trees down to the bottom, so that they would not be swept away. This task of filling the gap, however, after some severe struggling with the current, was before long accomplished; when those engaged upon it joined in the common work, in which they steadily persevered till this second double layer of trees, with the large quantity of short bushes which they brought and wove into the chinks, near the top, was completed, through the length of their dam. They then collected along on the top of the dam, and seemed to hold a sort of consultation, after which they scattered for the banks of the stream, but soon returned, walking on their hind legs, and bringing a load of mud or stones, held between his fore paws and throat. These loads were successively deposited, as they came up, among the stems and interlacing branches of the trees and bushes they had just laid down, giving each deposited pile, as they turned to go back, a smart blow with the flat of their broad thick tails; producing the same sound as the one I have mentioned as the signal-raps for calling them out to work, only far less loud and sharp, since the former raps were struck on water, and latter on mud or rubbish. Thus they continued to work, --- and work, too, with a will, if any creatures ever did, __ till I had seen nearly the whole of the last layers plastered over.

"Thinking now I had seen all that would be new and useful to me, I noiselessly crept away and returned to camp, to lay awake half the night, in my excitement, and to dream, the other half, about this magnificent society of beavers, whose numbers I could not make less than three dozen. I did go to steal another view of the place for nearly a week, and then went in the daytime, there now being no moon, till late, --- when, to my surprise, I found the dam finished, and the river flowed into a pond of several acres, while on each side, ranged along, one after another, stood three family dwellings in different states of progress; some of them only rising to the surface of the water, showing the nature of the structure, which, you know is build up with short, small logs, and mud, in a squarish form, of about the size of a large chimney; while others, having been built up a foot or two above the water, and the windows fashioned, had been arched over with mud and sticks, and were already nearly finished.

"Knowing that the establishment was now so nearly completed that the beavers would not relinquish it without being disturbed by the presence of a human foe, --- which they will sometimes detect, I think, at nearly a quarter mile distance, --- I concluded to keep entirely away from them till the time of my contemplated onslaught, which I finally decided to begin on one of the first days of the coming November.

"Well, what with hunting deer, bear, and so on, for food, and lynx, otter, and sable, for furs, the next two months passed away, and the long anticipated November at length arrived; when, one dark, cloudy day, having cut a lot of bits of green wood for bait, got out my vial of castor to scent them with, and got my steel traps in order, with these equipments and my rifle I set off, for the purpose of commencing operations, of some kind, on my community of beavers. On reaching the spot, I crept to my old covert with the same precautions I had used on my former visits, thinking it likely enough that, on so dark a day, some of the beavers might be out; and wishing to know how this was, before proceeding only along the banks to look out the right places to set my traps, I listened awhile, but could hear no splashing about the pond, or detect any other sounds indicating that the creatures were astir; but, on peering out, I saw a large, old beaver perched in a window of one of the beaver-houses on the opposite shore. I instinctively drew up my rifle, --- for it was a fair shot, and I knew I could draw him, --- but I forbore, and contented myself with watching his motions. I might have lain there ten minutes, perhaps, when this leader, or judge in the beaver Israel, as he soon showed himself to be, quietly slid out into the water, swam into a central part of the pond, and, after swimming twice or three time round in a small circle, lifted his tail on high, and slowly and deliberately gave three of those same old loud and startling raps on the water. He then swam back to his cabin, and ascended an open flat on the bank, where all the underbrush had been cut and cleared off in building the dam. In a few minutes more, a large number of beavers might be seen hastening to the spot, where they ranged themselves in a sort of circle, so as just to enclose the old beaver which came first, and which had now taken his stand on a little moss hillock, on the farther side of the little opening, to which he had thus called them, and, evidently, for some important public purpose. Soon another small band of the creatures made their appearance on the bank above, seeming to have in custody two great, lubberly, cowed-down looking beavers that they were hunching and driving along, as legal officers sometimes have to do with their prisoners, when taking them to some dreaded punishment. When this last band reached the place, with these two culprit-looking fellows, they pushed them forward in front of the judge, as we call him, and then fell into the ranks, so as to close up the circle.

There was then a long, solemn pause in which they all kept still in their places round the prisoners, which had crouched sneaking down, without stirring an inch from the places where they had been put. Soon, however, a great, fierce, gruff-appearing beaver left the ranks, and, advancing a few steps within them, reared himself up on his haunches, and began to sputter and gibber away at a great rate, making his fore-paws go like the hands of some over-heated orator; now motioning towards the judge, and now spitefully towards the prisoners, as if he was making bitter accusations, and demanding judgment against them. After this old fellow had gotten through, two or three others, in turn, came forward, and appeared also to be holding forth about the matter, but in a far milder manner than the other, which I now began much to dislike for his spitefulness, and in the same proportion to pity the two poor objects of his evident malice. There was then another long and silent pause, after which he proceeded to utter what appeared to be his sentence; and, having brought it to a conclusion, he gave a rap with his tail on the ground. At this signal, the beavers in the ranks advanced, one after another, in rapid succession towards the prisoners, and circling round them once, turned and gave each one of them a tremendous blow with their tails over the head and shoulders; and so the heavy blows rapidly fell, whack, whack, whack, till every beaver had taken his part in the punishment, and till the poor prisoners keeled over, and lay nearly or quite dead on the ground. The judge beaver then quietly left his stand and went off; and, following his example, all the rest scattered and disappeared, except the spiteful old fellow that had raised my dislike, by the rancor he displayed in pressing his accusations, and, afterwards, by giving the culprits and extra blow, when it came his turn to strike them. He now remained on the ground till all the rest were out of sight, when, --- as if to make sure of finishing what little remains of life the others, in their compunction, might have left in their victims, so as to give them, if they were not quite killed by the terrible bastinadoing they had received, a chance to revive and crawl off, ---he ran up, and began to belabor them with the greatest fury over the head. This mean and malicious addition to the old fellow's previously unfair conduct was too much for me to witness, and I instantly drew my rifle and laid him dead beside the bodies he was so rancorously beating. Wading the stream below the dam, I hastened to my prizes, finished their last struggles with a stick, seized them by their tails, and dragged them to the spot I had just left; and then, after concealing my traps, with the view of waiting a few days before I set them, so as to give the society a chance to get settled, I tugged the game I had so strangely come by, home to camp, where a more particular examination showed them to be the three largest and best-furred beavers I had ever taken.

"This brings me to the end of the unaccountable affair, and all I can say in explanation of it; for how these creatures, ingenious and knowing as they are, should have the intelligence to make law, --- as this case seems to pre-suppose, ---get up a regular court, try, sentence, and execute offenders; what these offenders had done, -- whether they were thievish interlopers from some other society, or whether they had committed some crime, such as burglary, bigamy, or adultery, or high treason, or whether they had been dishonest office-holders in the society and plundered the common treasury, is a mystery which you can solve as well as I. Certainly you cannot be more puzzled than I have always been, in giving the matter a satisfactory explanation.

"And now, in conclusion, if you wish to know how I afterwards succeeded in taking more of this notable society of beavers, I have only to say, that, having soon commenced operations anew, I took, before I quit the ground that fall, by rifle, by traps, by digging or hooking them out of their hiding places in the banks, and, finally by breaking up their dwelling-houses, twenty-one beavers in all; making the best lot which I ever had the pleasure of carrying out of the woods, and for which, a month or two after, I was paid, in market, one hundred and sixty eight hard dollars."

MOOSEHEAD LAKE AND VICINITY TWENTY-FIVE YEARS AGO

By Zoophilus, from *Forest and Stream*, August 10, 1876

"Moosehead is Beautiful Even in a Storm" (from Maine Sportsman June 1906. Courtesy of Ernst Mayr Library, Harvard)

It was at midnight following an August day a quarter of a century ago, that the writer, with two friends, ended a boat journey across Moosehead Lake, and leaped upon the wharf at Kineo. A low, unpretending structure stood upon a position of the site now covered by the great hotel. After a few sounding knocks, Barrows, the landlord, made appearance, and having been ushered into comfortable rooms, we soon joined the rest of the inmates in the realm of Somnus.

Next morning bright and early found us up and outside, anxious to take a look at our surroundings by daylight. The view was the same (with perhaps the exception of one or two small clearings) that meets the eye of the traveller at the present day. Forests covered the hill and shores in every direction, while behind the house, towered Mt. Kineo with its precipitous sides, dwarfing all objects in its vicinity. As I strolled down towards the lake I noticed, standing by the water, a man who will take a prominent part in the remainder of this narrative. Rather short in stature, hair well streaked with gray, quick in his movements, with an eye at once restless and piercing, with a complexion bronzed by exposure, and a form sinewy though slight, he was the personification of the toughened, experienced woodsman.

How the time rolls back, until it seems but yesterday as I thus recall the appearance of Uncle Ellis as he stood before me on that morning, and doubtless many of those who have visited Kineo in later years will remember this famous old moose hunter. I at once entered into conversation with him, and our talk soon turned to the great deer that were so numerous about the lake, for I was very desirous of meeting with my first moose.

"It is a good time now for moose?" I asked. "Well, it's getting on to the right time," he answered. "They still come down to the water at night to feed on the lily pads and grass, and its likely enough I can find one. And pretty soon the moon's bulls'll begin to run and then we can call 'em down to the shore and git a good shot at 'em. But now the moon's full and the nights still warm, and it's a good chance to kill one up Tom Heegan." "Do you think we can get one to night?" I asked, eager to start. "I think I can show you one, mebby," was the cautious reply. "We can start towards the evening, and paddle up Tom Heegan, and look about us there, and like enough see one of the critters. Have you ever been much in a birch?" I was obliged to confess my utter ignorance of that lively craft, as those lying upon the shore were the first I had seen outside a museum. "You're got to keep plenty quiet in them things," he said, with a merry twinkle of his eye "and your tongue right in the middle of your mouth, or you'll get spilled out before you know where you are," and then looking at me all over, he continued, "but I guess you'll manage it; leastwise, we'll try it anyhow." And so it was agreed forthwith that I should make my first attempt that night at moose hunting, introduced by Uncle Ellis, that whom as I afterwards learned, I could have had no better sponsor.

How long that day seemed! And as the afternoon wore on my impatience increased to be off. I was new to the woods, and knew nothing of the things requisite to make one comfortable during a night in the woods. About sunset the old man said it was time for us to be off. The birch, as it lay upon the water, seemed only waiting for me to step in order to throw me into the lake, as the least touch swayed it about in a very ominous manner; but Uncle Ellis drew the stern on shore and sat astride of it, thus holding the frail thing quite steady, while I crawled along to the bow, where I ensconced myself in a doubled-up posture, like a tailor on a beach. The gun was then passed to me, and the birch was shoved off. For a moment while Uncle Ellis was setting himself in his place, I expected to take a header for the bottom, but when I found the thing kept right side up, and moreover, began to move rapidly and easily over the water, my courage returned, and I gradually shifted myself into a more comfortable position. We soon passed around the rocky point is front of Kineo, and the great lake lay all before us, the way up to the carry over the Penobscot. That was so distant however that the shore was merely indicated by a line of forest that seemed to grow out of the water. We were gradually approaching the opposite side of the lake, and in a short time the birch was brought to the shore at the mouth of a small stream. "This here," whispered Uncle Ellis, "is the Tom Heegan, and after we start up it you mus'nt say nothing. Like enough you'll hear the moose if we git nigh nary a one splashing in the water, but when I hear 'em I'll just shake the birch a little, and then tell you when to shoot. Here we go now," and with that the birch's bow turned away from the shore and the boat glided up the stream, seemingly of its own volition, for no sound of the paddle was heard. The stillness was so profound that the plunge of a musk-rat or the sound made by a trout fairly startled me, and so weird-like were our surroundings that I felt I must be under the guidance of the dweller in the Dismal Swamp, as

> "All night long by the fire-fly lamp
> He padded his light canoe."

Occasionally the boat would stop, and we would listen attentively for the splash of a moose as he walked in the water along shore, but although I heard many curious sounds my inexperienced ears refused to discriminate between the plunge of a musk-rat and the walk of a deer. After having gone about half way up the stream the birch halted once more. My heart this time was thumping like a trip-hammer, and I felt sure if there was a moose anywhere about he must certainly hear it and be off, and as I was projecting how I must shoot to stop him in his wild career, I felt the boat shake, and a low "hist" came from the stern. I won't assert it for a fact, but my impression is my cap rose six inches above my head and remained immovably fixed in that position, as each hair stood rigidly on end, and both my ears curved forward. The boat glided forward and nearer to the shore, and then I caught for the first time the splashing around the wild deer makes as he cautiously walks through the water when feeding. Still the boat shot noiselessly forward. “Shoot,” hissed Uncle Ellis. Shoot what? I thought to myself, for I saw nothing but the black shadows of the shore. However, I put my gun up to my shoulder, and gazed with all my eyes over the barrel, hoping to see something that I might particularly shoot at, but I could distinguish nothing, for although the moon was shining brightly, the stream was narrow and the trees stood closely together, so that everything was buried in shadow. But the splashing became more and more distinct and drew nearer and nearer and at last, with my heart in my mouth, I distinguished a mass blacker than the surrounding shadows moving slowly along near the shore. To cover it with my gun and pull the trigger was the act of a second. A bright sheet of flame shot out in front, effectually blinding me for a moment, a report, startling a thousand echoes that seemed to carry the sound all over this world, was followed by a tremendous commotion in the water in front of me. In the midst of it all I felt the birch backing out into the stream. I soon found my voice, and Uncle Ellis, “Didn’t I hit him, where you going?” “Listen,” he said. “Yes you hit him. I want to hear what he does.” After the first rush of the moose on receiving my shot, all had been still. We now heard the beast cough and splash about a little way from the bank in a marshy spot. “There,” said Uncle Ellis, “do you hear that; he’s down. You shot him through the lungs, and he’s dying. We’ll git him in the morning.” Why wait for the morning,” I said. “I guess not,” he replied, “you don’t catch this child going up to a wounded moose at night. No, we’ll just go below and camp, and come back here and get him in the morning,” and with that he turned the birch around, and a short distance down we both got out, a fire was made, and we sat down to have a quiet smoke before turning in. I felt very anxious about the wounded moose, fearing he would get away, but Uncle Ellis reassured me, at the same time warning me never to go near a wounded moose. He told me one of his own adventures when he was younger and less cautious; wherein a “bull” moose, which he had wounded, and gone near, jumped up, chased him to a tree, and fairly lifted him into it by a toss of its head, the spread of the horns fortunately being so great that their points passed each side of his body. The moose kept him there for two hours and was lost at last. The fire soon began to burn low and we went to sleep.

As the day was breaking I was aroused to go up stream and look for our moose. We got into the birch cautiously, and taking the gun I resumed my place in the bow and we started silently up stream. As we reached the spot where I had shot at the moose, just at a turn of the stream, the bow was headed for the shore, when suddenly the canoe stopped, and Uncle Ellis said, "There's a moose on the other side of the river, close to the bank; I'll paddle you right onto its back." I looked over and saw the great gray mass of a moose standing with its back to us, feeding where the water rose nearly to its belly. The canoe was paddled to within five yards of the animal, and I began to think I really was to be put on its back, when Uncle Ellis said, "Shoot!" So, taking a careful aim, I pulled the trigger. To my intense disgust the cap refused to explode; I cocked and pulled again with the same result. The slight noise caused the moose to look around. It had not scented us, and we were so quiet that the animal showed no alarm. "Put on another cap," was hissed out of the stern. I endeavored to get at them, but on the first movement the moose became uneasy and move towards the forest. It was but a moment gaining the shore, where it stopped for an instant to take a look at us, and then starting at a long swinging trot was soon out of sight among the trees. "Well, that is bad luck enough," I said, "I ought to have put on a fresh cap before we started out this morning." "Yes, it is rough," answered my guide, "but it was only a cow anyway, and we want bulls. I guess we'll go and git the one you shot last night," and so he turned the birch around and paddled across the steam. I felt considerably discouraged, and in a frame of mind not to be surprised on reaching the spot where the moose fell the night before to find that he was not there. "Here's where he was," said Uncle Ellis, "and just see how the grass is all smashed where he struggled, and here's a lot of blood, too; he is desperate hard hit.; he's just gone this way, and so he followed up the track.

Blood was found at intervals, and several places were seen where the animal had laid down, but the track gradually led off into the forest, and it soon became evident that the moose had been able to take himself off during the night. Here was another disappointment, but there was no use waiting, the moose had evidently gone away, and we obliged reluctantly to give up the search. “It does happen so sometimes,” Uncle Ellis said, as he paddled towards Kineo. “A moose is a might powerful critter, and it will happen occasionally, when they’ve gone to their death, that they’ll drag themselves off into the woods where you can’t find ‘em and just die there; and sometimes, when des’prate hard hit, they just gits away in spite ‘ov yer, and arter a while gits over it and comes out all right agin.”

DAT MEK ME TINK

By Bajeese, from *Shooting and Fishing*, August 21, 1890

When Fish Laugh

The writer of prolific Sunapee says in his delightful article "the fish will not just now bite, no matter how seductive the lure." "That reminds me (my compliments to the originator of the expression) of one of my early experiences with the late notorious Peter R. ---a former resident of Greenville, Maine, a pretty little town at the foot of Moosehead Lake. Peter was short in stature, small-nosed, weasel-eyed, and hardly more than half-eared, but what he lacked in these respects he more than fully made up in having a never-filled stomach---as far as "bug juice" went. His present address I am unable to give; but when I remember his unquenchable longings for liquid fire--the hotter it was, the better it suited him---I can easily imagine that his present camp needs no fire other than the natural heat afforded by the place. There! I've cremated poor Peter before hearing his defense!

The scene of action was the Wilson Ponds, about three miles east of Greenvllle. A number of visits to these ponds had given me considerable knowledge about the more likely places to fish. The weather being hot and the fish in deep water, fly-fishing was not considered. In consequence of the presence of Peter, I had no voice in the matter of location, and Peter took us wherever he pleased---generally along the shore where the water was quiet and the rowing, of a necessity, easier.

Well, we went through all the ceremonies of fishing, including Peter's frequent assaults on the "pistol," as he called his bottle, for luck. I wonder if the expression "pretty well shot" originated from such a source? The fish did not bite, and in reply to questions upon the non-biting, Peter would say: "Ah, dunno, ah'll carn' tell why'se no bait. Dat mek me tink, ah'll bin fishin' dese pon mor'n tirty yere'n days allus tam wen trouts no bait yes lak disl. Lemme see!

Tree yere 'go ah'll com wid coppul minister on der oppar Wilson 'n bejeese we ketch mor'n two hundred poun', 'n bajeese how dat prichers dey'll drink rum! Ah bin wid mor'n tree hundred tousan party but dis fellers beat it all." And in this way Peter would have gladly earned his three dollars a day had I not objected. Peter's loquacity had made him thirsty, and as a result his "pistol" was empty. "Now, Peter," said I, "we've five hours more for fishing and I propose to take back twenty trout, understand?" "Bajeese, ah'll fired we don't git it." "Never mind, Peter, pull up for the 'narrows," and drop anchor when I say the word." The narrows connects the upper and middle ponds and the gut is filled with large boulders, some of which, in low water, come nearly to or above the surface and are unpleasant things on which to ground a boat, especially on a dark night, as I well know by experience.

We dropped the stone about twenty rods beyond the narrows and began operations in thirty feet of water. The bottom was evidently of gravel and the water quite cold, as evidenced by the temperature of the fish we caught. An hour's fishing brought us only four or five half-pounders, and I concluded to try what had proved successful in other waters. Baiting a hook with two or three good sized worms, I reeled off at least thirty yards of line and made a hand cast. The sinker would run out what I could not send by the cast and the bait would soon rest on the bottom.

The line would then be very slowly reeled in, occasionally giving it a little jerk or allowing it to rest a few moments. Not more than ten feet had been reeled in when that delightful sensation, "a bite," seized me and very quickly a two-and-a-half-pound square tail was under the moss. Peter simply said "dat's er good un." Soon a larger one came in and the occupant of the stern seat tried the same manner of fishing and his efforts met with success. Peter kept on the off side as long as he could, and when he could hold on no longer, he too, voted the straight ticket, and his vote proved to be the needed one, for his big fish weighed three and a half pounds. The fish were surely there, but would take the bait only upon the bottom as it was slowly moved along over the pebbles.

Our catch was thirteen (how unlucky!) trout, the total weight being twenty-six and one-half pounds. No doubt some of the scientific (?) fly-fishermen would have scorned the idea of bait-fishing in such an unsportsmanlike manner. Let him who elevates his nose try the place during some hot spell, when the fish lie close upon the bottom, and will not come up to anything else. His tune would soon accommodate itself to a different key. This is surely a more honorable and sportsmanlike way of fishing than the contemptible cuss who dammed a small stream, making a small pond, beat a good many trout into it, drew off the water and scooped them out. On his return to the Lake House, Greenville, he said: "That's my afternoon's catch all on the fly." This man lives in Connecticut, visits Moosehead every year, and I know he is guilty of the above act. Sportsman, indeed!

Before leaving the Wilson's, I suggested a climb up Rum Mountain. This made Peter tremble, but he sulkily accepted the order, and we began to tramp up the path. This path is very unlike a concrete or brick sidewalk, notwithstanding the fact of its being well-carpeted with moss. The mountain is composed of much the same formation as Mount Kineo---a sort of flint---and there are many crevices, of all sizes, which cross the path, the smaller ones being filled with leaves and moss, and a quick step into one means a barked shin. Half way up the climb Peter called our attention to an old pine stub, saying: "Ah s'pose ah'll mek de bigges shot at er bar you ever see right'n dis pless. Me 'nodder fellers been up Rum Pon', 'n we's com down wid big string fish, w'en pooty soon ah'll smell som't'ing, and ah'll hear grunt. It was poot dark, 'n ah can see notting er' well. W'en ah'll gone rat in one dese big crack, 'n spill whole darn load rat on ma head. Ah'll hear nodder growl 'n see som't'ing black, 'n ah'll know dat was bar. Bajeese! Ah was skard, offul! Todder fellers com 'long, 'n git mos' down ter pond, 'n ah was allone in date hole wid tingo pile all over me, so's ah couldn't do notting. Ah mannige to git ma ha' on ma pistol; he's big, ole-fashin oine, 'n mek offul noise, 'n ah tink mebbe ah'll skar der bar. Wall, seh, ah'll p'int her most anywhar, 'n pull der trig', n' what you'll s'pose ah done! Ah hit 'im rat in der eye, 'n, bajeese! Dat was er big shot, don't it? "N dot mek me tink of big carbou dat ah'll see down by der outlet---bigges' one ever was been roun' here---'n ah'll been go down"--- His words suited the action, and down he did go all in a heap. The effect of the downfall was wonderful, and Peter devoted his whole attention to his shins, with an accompaniment of words, the general drift of which can easily be imagined.

We took eleven pretty black trout from the dark water of Rum Pond, and our day's catch was 36 ½ pounds. Peter was apparently done for; his tongue responded but feebly, and his little black eyes had lost much of their twinkle. I feared some unpleasant consequences from his fall, and asked him if he was badly hurt. "No, ah'll been feel shame maself for fall down lok baby." Comparative silence reigned on the way home, until we passed some fine looking cows, one of which carried an enormous bag. In reply to my remark about it, Peter said, "Dat's notting. Dat mek me tink wen ah was boy in Canada, my fadder had cow date bigger bag as dat, 'n sometime de milk run out his bag cause it git so full, 'n when dat' cow know dat, he'll go pooty quick for de pail what we give it water in, 'n he'll stan' rot over dot pail 'n let milk run in, so's it won't git waste. Ah spose dat cow know more as any cow 's ever live."

Peter---but there! He has "ketched" his last trout, shot his last bear, and gone---where?

– BAJEESE

THE PHANTOM OF NAHMAKANTA

By Willis H. Colby, from *Forest and Stream*, November 13, 1890

Born in Limerick, Willis H. Colby soon moved to Bangor with his family, growing up amongst the excitement of Bangor's lumber mills, shipping and busy waterfront. As a young man Colby went to work as a clerk among the bustling firms on State Street, Bangor's business center. Working in a printing house, he read all the wonderful stories printed in Forest and Stream and after returning from a trip to Nahmakanta Lake, wrote this wonderful account of a trip he had taken a few years prior. Later in life he moved to the bustling city of Detroit, Michigan, where he opened up his own printing shop.

Twilight in the Wilds (From Paddle & Portage, by Thomas S. Steele, p. 57)

No lovelier spot in which to take an outing can be found than one of the picturesque mountain-girt lakes that stud the rugged surface of Maine. It was my good fortune a few summers ago to have the necessary leisure to allow me to visit this charming region.

It was one of those mild September days when all nature seemed to be decked in her best, filling the air with sweet fragrance and imparting a feeling of ecstasy and happiness. The trees spread out their branches covered with crimson drapery; the voices of the forest sent forth sweet songs that seemed to come from some enchanted land, lulling into that dreaminess of mind where life for the hour is an absorption into the glory of the world around.

As we paddled down the Penobscot on such a day as this, the birch canoes gliding silently along, propelled by the swift strokes of the Indian guides, I gave myself up to the fascination of the hour. On either side of the river, which is here little more than a stream, the rich foliage overhanging from the banks, kissed the water as it glided past. Here and there a tall pine raised its majestic head, towering above the surrounding forests like some kingly giant. The sun shone from the clear, blue sky with rare brilliancy. The stream occasionally broke into little falls or "rips," through which we sped, passing great rocks and boulders, over which the water foamed and hissed in petty fury.

The day previous we had left Chesuncook, and paddling across the northern end of Pamedumcook Lake, and from thence westward through a small stream, we reached Nahmakanta Lake, where we had been informed fish were abundant. We entered this lake late in the afternoon, as the sun was sinking in the west, leaving faint streaks of gold and red to mark the course of its decline, and illuminated that placid sheet of water and the surrounding forest.

A suitable camping place having been found we landed. While the guides were pitching the tents and conveying our luggage from the canoes we occupied ourselves with cutting fir boughs for our beds. No one who has not tried a couch of this kind can have any conception of the ease and comfort it affords, especially when one has paddled a canoe all day or waded in brooks casting a fly for the wary trout. By the time we had completed our task the guides announced that supper was ready. Our table was a rude structure of boards, while our provision buckets did duty as seats. It was surprising what a quantity of trout, "flapjacks" and molasses we managed to stow away, just how much I would not dare to say.

After supper had been finished the most of the party gathered round the camp-fire, some filling out their journals, while others got their fishing tackle in readiness for the morrow. As for myself, taking one of the guides, I paddled out upon the lake, in the hope of getting a shot at a deer, as they frequently come down to drink and feed upon the lilies about the shores of these lakes.

A light breeze had sprung up from the westward, ruffling the tranquil surface of the lake. A little later the moon rose, piercing the dark canopy. I sat in the bow of the canoe, and as it danced over the little waves I found myself again indulging in reverie. The stars overhead, the swish of the waves on the side of the canoe, and the moon-lit panorama, extending from our camp-fire in the distance to yonder hill, all had a tendency to dispel thoughts of care and the outside world from my mind and let me drift away in dreamland. Suddenly the tranquility was broken by a wailing cry. I started in my seat, nearly overturning the canoe, and grasping my rifle, looked about, expecting to see some strange form come into view. After a moment of silence there was a repetition of the cry; it was a cry as of some one in distress. I felt a chill creep through my body as again that wail rose on the night air. Looking in the direction from which the sound came, I beheld a sight that seemed to transfix me with terror. Even now when my mind goes back to the scene of that night, a feeling of horror steals over me that I cannot describe or suppress. I tried to speak, but could not; the scene held me as one in a trance. I could not move, but sat, gazing spellbound. There, standing on a point of land which jutted out into the lake, in the full light of the moon, stood a figure, draped in a long mantle of white hanging loosely about it. The arms were extended at full length toward the heavens, while the voice was continually to be heard in mournful cries.

At once there came to my mind a thought of the many weird Indian legends repeated and believed even in our enlightened days by nearly all dwellers in these parts. One can imagine my state of mind, impressed and stimulated as I was, by the supernatural calm of the surrounding scenery.

Suddenly the Indian gave a prolonged yell and dashing his paddle into the water, sent the canoe over the lake toward our camp at a tremendous rate of speed. Not a word was spoken by either of us. We were both thinking of what we had just seen. As the bow of the canoe grated on the sandy beach in front of the camp, the Indian leaped ashore, and trembling from head to foot, stood leaning on his paddle, gazing with dilated eyes out upon the lake toward the place where still could be seen the strange and ghostly figure. As we stood there the cry was again repeated, and turning round I saw the Indian sink terrified to his knees.

I must confess that my nerves were not very steady, and calling to the men in the camp to join me, I told them what I had seen.

Although they had heard the cry they laughed at me, saying that I was a "dreamer," but looking toward the neck of land I saw that the apparition had not disappeared altogether and was still dimly to be discerned standing in exactly the same attitude as before, while its thrilling cry, now rising, now falling, floated toward us on the night breeze. For some time we gazed at it in silence and then retraced our steps to camp. Sitting around the fire, the silence was not broken until again the cry rose on the midnight air, when involuntarily every one jumped to his feet; when, as if ashamed of the action, all again became quiet.

No one asked the other why he so silently wrapped himself in his blanket that night, each feeling, though ashamed to own it, a blending of alarm, apprehension and uncertainty.

The rest of more than one was disturbed by dreams, from which the sleeper would spring up, thinking himself contending with some strange phantom, only to see the motionless forms and the flickering light of the campfire. Putting an armful of wood on the smouldering logs, and again seeking the blanket and couch of fir, sleep would quiet the troubled mind.

The camp was astir at an early hour, and after breakfast all, with fixed resolution, set out in the direction in which the strange object of the night before had been seen. When we reached this point of land we got out and carefully examined the place. No signs were to be found of any one having been there during the night. After spending over an hour in the place, we were about to leave it, when Mr. R. called out for us to come where he was standing. As we approached, he pointed to an old birch stump and asked if we could not see in it the phantom of last night. The bark on the lower part of the trunk had been torn aside and lay rolling back, looking like the folds of a loose garment, with two limbs, one on each side, resembled extending arms. This was what we had seen, and the moon shining upon it had given it the appearance of life. But then if this was what we had taken for the strange figure, what had caused these mournful cries? We had heard them and they had filled us with terror. Surely they could not have issued from this queer stump. We spent some time trying to find a clue, but at last had to give it up. We remained three days on the lake, but there was no repetition of the sound, and on the morning of the fourth day we left. Our stay had not been without interest, for besides the adventure of our first night, we had good sport hunting and fishing, and nowhere during our trip did we make such large catches. Our only regret was our inability to solve the mystery.

* * * * * * * *

Two years later I again visited this lake, and during the second night once more heard those mournful cries, and immediately started for the spot from which they seemed to come. There was the same old stump which had so terrified us on that night, and close by, seeming to rise from the earth, came those startling cries. The sensations which I had before felt I again experienced, but upon a closer examination I found my fears to be groundless.

The wailing noise was produced by the wind blowing through a hollow log lying on the ground. The inside was covered with large thin slabs or splinters. One end was much smaller than the other, and when the wind came from the west, blowing through the log, a wailing noise was produced. Thus the mystery connected with the phantom of Nahmakanta was solved.

– WILLIS H. COLBY

IN THE SHADOW OF KATAHDIN

By William H. Avis, from *Forest and Stream*, 1900

Capt. William Henry Avis (1865-1944) was a successful businessman in New Haven, Conn., where his family manufactured gun barrels for the government during the First World War. He resided in the nearby town of Hampden where he served as captain of the Home Guard, helped form the Progressive Party to support Theodore Roosevelt, and was a correspondent for the "New Haven Register."

An avid outdoorsman, he particularly loved fishing and swimming and for many winters took daily plunges in the icy waters at Short Beach on the Long Island Sound. He wrote a number of accounts of his trips, including this story that takes place in the Piscataquis Lakes region.

Maine Sportsman, Sept 1893 (Courtesy of Ernst Mayr Library, Harvard)

After supper all hands gathered around the fireplace. The sparks soared up the chimney from blazing logs, and we smoked and listened to one another's stories.. One yarn ran like this:

"A few winters ago I was employed in a lumber camp. We had worked into logs all the desirable timber in the vicinity, and the stream, which connected with the Penobscot, was badly jammed with logs. So thick was the jam that it was impossible to drive anything through. 'Jim,' said the boss to me one day, 'we're out of dynamite, and some one will have to go to the other camp and get some. We must start these logs moving. How would you like the trip?'

"Now the other camp was twenty miles away, and not a building between, and an old tote road was the only way. I was willing to go, however, and next morning bright and early I was on my way. It took the best part of the day to make the trip, for the thawing weather had melted the snow, and the traveling was bad. I was ready for supper and bed that night, you can bet!

"I had breakfast before daylight next morning and with 20 pounds of dynamite sticks with fuses attached on my back I started on the return trip. With the exception of seeing a few deer, nothing occurred until I was within two miles of the camp. I had been compelled to rest a number of times, and it was getting dark. I had just crossed a strip of burnt land, and was on the point of entering a stretch of the road which ran through a blowdown where the young growth had reached a height of about 20 feet, when, happening to turn my head, I thought I saw an animal moving in the path behind me. 'It's another deer,' said I to myself, and paid no further attention. It was quite dusky in the blowdown, but my tracks of the day before could be seen in the wet snow. Becoming tired, I sat down for a short rest. I had hardly seated myself, when cold chills chased rapidly up and down my spine. Back on my track, and not over 150 feet away, I could see the shadowy outlines of an 'Indian devil.' The animal stood motionless, and was looking straight at me.

"To say that I wasn't scared would be a thundering lie. Some say the 'Indian devil' (Wolverine) is a cowardly sneak, and I might not have feared this one. But to save extra weight I had left my rifle in camp, so was unarmed. I sat there and eyed the animal quite awhile. Finally it sneaked into the timber at the right of the road. 'Good!' thought I. 'He's afraid to tackle me and has gone.' I was mistaken, for I had hardly resumed my journey, when I looked back and there was the beast on my trail again---and closer than before!

"Matters were getting serious, and I cudgeled by brain for a scheme to get rid of my unwelcome follower. Finally I turned and shouted back at him, and you bet I felt good to see that cuss sneak into the timber again. I now hurried as fast as possible, but kept a sharp lookout all the while. Camp was a mile away, and when the shadowy form loomed on my trail again, and I was horrified to see that it was within less than 100 feet. 'What can I do? What can I do? thought I. Suddenly I remembered the dynamite, and like a flash came an idea. I stopped and stood still---so did the 'Indian devil.' Then I pulled off my coat--a heavy reefer--took one of the sticks of dynamite from the bundle, lighted a match and touched the fuse to the flame. It sputtered, and I placed the stick on the ground, hastily threw my coat over it in a manner not to interfere with the fuse, and took to my heels.

"How far I ran before the explosion, I don't know. But I was making the best licks I ever made in my life, when the woods burst into a flame of light, and a report like a cannon shook the earth. I never looked behind, but kept up the pace right into camp, where I arrived bareheaded, coatless and breathless. The camp was aroused, and as soon as my wind came back I told my story. Lanterns, axes, clubs and rifles were hastily procured, and all hands started back with me. We picked up the bundle of dynamite which I had dropped in a hurry within 100 feet of a big hole in the ground. Then pieces of coat, hide, flesh and bones and bunches of hair were found scattered within a radius of 100 feet or more. That 'Indian devil' had stopped to smell the old coat, and the dynamite blew him up all right."

Our narrator knocked the ashes from his pipe into the fireplace, borrowed tobacco and a match from his nearest neighbor, struck a light and resumed smoking; and his eyes seemed to study the moving shadows of circle, which the flames threw on the log walls, and the gyrations of the starlike sparks on their course up the chimney. Then some one yawned, and Wilbert, complacently eyed each face through his glasses, and there was a look on his countenance which eloquently said, "Boys, I've heard liars before, but this chap is the champion of them all."

CARIBOU HUNT IN PISCATAQUIS

By Big Game, from *Forest and Stream*, 1888

Woodland Caribou (The Big Game of North America, by G. O. Shields, 1890)

"Good-by, boys; bring us a roast of venison," was the parting salutation of a dozen or more old friends, as we steamed away from the wharf in Belfast, Me., for the Carritunk region, Piscataquis county, for a week's outing.

There were three of us, the Judge, the Doctor and myself. Our route was by steamer to Bangor, thence by railroad to Blanchard, thence to the camp. We reached Blanchard without let or hindrance at 3 o'clock P.M., where we procured stout horses and a buckboard which had apparently done service before the war; we were a little doubtful about the vehicle, as it seemed loose and rickety in all its parts, but Brown, our driver and man of all work, assured us that that was just the way it was made, and it would carry us safely as far as we could go by team. From Blanchard to Carritunk Township is one perpetual ascent for eight or nine miles. We then came to a strip of table land about one mile wide ending at the base of Mount Bald or Pond Mountain, as it is sometimes called. Here we went into the camp for the night, intending to get an early start in the morning for Harmony Camp, on top of the mountain and about four miles distant. We found comfortable quarters in a lumber camp, and while our guide was making things pleasant for us about the camp, we took our fish tackle to try the trout in Thorn Brook, which was but a short distance from camp. We soon found that we had not misjudged the capacity of the stream. It was nearly dark, but in half an hour or so we were able to count up twenty-three trout, some of them weighing nearly half a pound. We had them fried for supper and enjoyed them immensely. We were up and ready to start the next morning at daylight, and commenced the ascent near where the old Skowhegan road crosses Thorn Brook. The ascent was tiresome. We reached the summit at 9 A.M. and took up quarters in Harmony Camp, situated on the shore of a beautiful lake of about four square miles in extent.

Here for several years Captain Nickerson and a few of his friends have spent a few days during the hunting season, and it was through his kindness that we were invited to occupy this camp. Marvelous stories are related by some of the Captain's friends "of caribou brought down at long range, and of huge antlers that were taken but could not be brought out for certain and various good reasons." Certain it was that we found nailed up over the door of the camp a very fair-sized pair of antlers.

We settled ourselves comfortably, occupying the remainder of the forenoon. After dinner we started out to look for signs; made the circuit of the little pond and found plenty of deer and caribou tracks, and one that the Judge decided to be that of a moose. Returning we took a wide circuit observing landmarks and noting the general lay of the land, in order that we might not lose our bearings when hunting singly, a precaution which it is always safe to take, but in this place it was hardly necessary, as the mountain itself afforded us a conspicuous landmark, and plenty of hard climbing would bring us to camp from any direction. We returned to the camp just at dusk, highly pleased with the outlook and feeling quite certain that we should have a successful hunt on the morrow.

We started out the next morning as soon as it was light enough for us to see our way. The Doctor went to the north, I to the west, the Judge proposed to station himself conveniently near a runway leading to the pond, where to all appearances the game went down to drink and feed upon the lily pads. The morning was most propitious for stalking game, it having rained a little during the night, so that our walking through the brush was almost noiseless. For guns, the Doctor carried a long range Ballard .38-caliber; the judge and myself .44-caliber Marlins. About two hours after leaving camp, I came upon fresh caribou tracks going in the direction of the pond. I followed them without difficulty expecting to see my game on reaching the pond some half a mile distant. My carelessness lost me a favorable shot and taught me when tracking game of this kind to be always on the alert, expecting to see game at any moment and especially in the most unlikely places, for after following the tracks for 40 or 50 rods, a sudden cracking of the brush a few rods in advance, caused me to look ahead just in time to see a large buck bounding away down the mountain and out of sight in a moment.

Deeming it useless to follow him now that he was thoroughly startled, I kept on to the pond, hoping that secreting myself I might during the day get a shot. Selecting a cover on a point running out into the pond far enough to give me a fair view for some distance on both sides, I resolved, as I have often done before, that I would stick to that spot until I saw game at all events. So making myself as comfortable a stand as possible, I began my tiresome waiting. Hour after hour passed by and no game appeared. I had become chilled and cramped, but still resolved to stick as long as I could see to shoot. At last, just as dusk began to settle down upon the lake, I heard the crackling of brush upon the right, which warned me that game was approaching. In a moment the blood was coursing through my veins, and instead of the chill I was hot with excitement. I imagined from the second that the game could be nothing smaller than a moose, and began to speculate on the chances of my stopping him at my first shot. The animal stopped before coming into view in a thicket of birch bushes; this gave time to get my nerves steadied for the fatal shot. Soon the bushes parted and a caribou leisurely walked out into full view about fifteen rods away. I was much disappointed in the size of the animal, but there he stood quietly nipping the twigs that grew in the edge of the water. He was about the size of a large buck deer, and had it not been for his immense head, I should at first glance have considered him a deer and nothing more. I study him for some minutes to determine if possible, what food it is that he seems to relish so much. At last the right chance for a favorable and certain shot presents itself, and at the crack of my rifle the caribou, with one convulsive bound, falls dead to the ground; I hasten to bleed him, and with no small degree of satisfaction contemplate my first caribou.

I hang him up and start for camp, concluding to follow the shore of the pond, as it had now become quite dark. As I drew near the camp I heard my comrades talking over the events of the day, and as I had heard several shots from their rifles during the day I was feeling somewhat disgusted at my stupidity in not getting a telling shot at the game I startled in the early morning. I was not so exultant over my first caribou as I anticipated. Both the Judge and Doctor had shot at and missed the same caribou in the forenoon, and as not more game came in sight of their stands they go tired of waiting and returned to camp. In the afternoon they had amused themselves shooting ducks on the pond; they had secured three and one large loon, and were congratulating themselves that they were high line for that day at least. I related to them the story of the day's hunt and informed them where the game was hanging. They would not be convinced that I was not hoaxing them, and after supper I proposed that we take the canoe and go up and bring the carcass to camp, remarking to them what a breakfast of caribou steak would doubtless inspire them with more perseverance in hunting the next day. We found the caribou as I had left him.

The sky was becoming overcast with every appearance of snow, and on arriving the next morning we found that about two inches had fallen and the weather had moderated sufficiently to dampen it, everything was propitious for a successful hunt. We started early, the Doctor and myself keeping together, the Judge preferring to hunt alone. We hoped to come upon a family of caribou, and after traveling some three miles we found fresh tracks, where at least three had gone along. With the utmost caution we followed the tracks for about two hours, stopping every few minutes to listen (we had taken the precaution to put on our white frocks and caps so as to make as little contrast as possible between the snow-laden trees and ourselves). At last we came upon two caribou, a bull and a cow, both full grown. We cautiously worked our way along toward where they were feeding until near enough for certain shots, the Doctor aiming at the bull, myself at the cow, our cracked simultaneously and both animals bounded out of sight. We heard them crashing through the brush on right and left. The Doctor was nonplussed, thinking he had again missed his game. I felt absolutely certain that I should find mine not far off, and knew from the convulsive spring of the Doctor's that it was hit to kill. I thought that most of the noise was made by other caribou which we had not seen.

On reaching the places where the animals stood we found blood and plenty of it, and I soon heard the Doctor shout that he had come upon his game. I had found mine about ten rods from where he stood, the ball had passed through the neck, severing one carotid artery. The Doctor had hit his in the shoulder and lodged the ball in or near the heart. The game had run some thirty rods before falling. After dressing the animals we made a circuit of the ground and found there must have been at least seven caribou within a few rods of us when we shot, and doubtless, had we brought our game to the ground at once, we might have got shots at others, but the snorts of the wounded ones put the whole family to flight. We were well satisfied, however, with our first four hour's work. While we were considering whether to follow the startled animals or look for other tracks, we heard two shots in rapid succession from the Judge's rifle, and decided to go in that direction, as it took us to the pond and camp, not doubting we should see other game before getting in. We were disappointed, however, although we found the Judge had not returned, but we beheld the largest buck's head we ever saw suspended to a limb in front of the camp, and as our toboggan was gone we concluded the Judge had gone for the carcas.

As the snow was rapidly melting we concluded to go back and bring our game to camp. We found a small horse sled in the hovel where we kept our horses, which, with a little fixing, we thought would do for us. Soliciting the assistance of Brown, we soon had it in readiness, and one of the horses harnessed into it. We followed an old logging road nearly to where we left our caribou, which saved us much hard packing. We judged the combined weight of the two caribou to be about 650lbs. On returning to camp we found the Judge with his game, which consisted of the buck before mentioned and young caribou. The buck could not have weighed less than 275lbs. alive.

We were all completely tired out, but in the best of spirits. It was a weariness that brings no languor. We had already accomplished what we had hope to do, which was to secure five venisons to take home with us. We decided to break camp at once.

The trip, considering the time, had been one of the most successful ones we have ever made. We were the first party on the ground, and the game was more abundant than usual, notwithstanding the fact that numbers of deer and caribou are ruthlessly slaughtered in this region every winter, after the snow becomes deep, to furnish meat for the lumbermen. Were it not for that custom of slaughtering (which should merit the contempt of every respectable citizen of the county) this region would soon become one of the most desirable in the State for hunting moose and caribou.

– BIG GAME

Chapter 5

THE WEST AND EAST BRANCHES OF THE PENOBSCOT RIVER

The Penobscot River watershed encompasses a vast area of central Maine, practically circling Katahdin and its surrounding mountains. The North Branch begins about ten miles north of the St. John Ponds, which are the headwaters of the St. John River and flow south to meet the South Branch near Pittston Farm, the only remaining original lumber supply depot in Maine. The South Branch begins at the Canadian border north of Jackman and flows east through Canada Falls Lake and soon joins the North Branch. This junction becomes the West Branch of the Penobscot, which flows through twelve-mile long Seboomook Lake and Chesuncook Lake, Maine's second longest lake.

At Ripogenus Dam the West Branch flows through a wild gorge with many large waterfalls, which formerly was avoided by canoes and lumbermen, but today is the State's most exciting ride in a whitewater raft. In the past this gorge was the scene of many log jams, which took much bravado, moxie and sometimes dynamite to dislodge. Below are a series of waterfalls, rapids and deadwaters, as the West Branch passes by Katahdin and reaches Abol Bridge. Turning more southeast, the river passes over another series of waterfalls and empties into Ambejejis Lake. Here four lakes – Ambejejis, Pemadumcook, North Twin and South Twin -- are joined into one large body of water, which was formerly a challenge to get the logs across. The West Branch leaves South Twin Lake, passes through Quakish Lake and merges with the South Branch at Medway.

The East Branch of Penobscot starts north of Chamberlain Lake in East Branch Pond and merges with Webster Brook in the northern part of Baxter state Park. In the 1840's this was the scene of a daring engineering project. Lumbermen who cut trees above Chamberlain Lake were forced to send them down the Allagash and St. John, subject to Canadian tolls. To counter this, E. S. Coe found a natural ravine on the southeast side of Telos Lake. He built a high dam at the north end of Chamberlain Lake and forced the water to retreat southward though the ravine and into Webster Stream and the East Branch of the Penobscot. The East Branch then passes through Grand Lake Matagamon and heads south, flowing over four more large waterfalls and joining the West Branch. This merger forms the Penobscot River, which then flows southward to Penobscot Bay.

One of the most revered river drivers on the West Branch was David Ross, who inspired many stories and even songs that were recited in many lumber camps. The "Bangor Tigers," as the West Branch crew was called, were famous all over the country for their daring feats and their ability to get the logs downriver in record time. Henry David Thoreau took several canoe trips in Maine, paddling down both branches of the Penobscot, giving us one of the first and most thorough descriptions of the region.

There were a few sporting camps south of Katahdin at Nesowadnehunk Lake, Kidney Pond, Daicy Pond and Katahdin Lake, Rainbow Lake, Nahamakanta Lake, Debsconeag, Pemadumcook and Middle Jo Mary Lake. Once the railroad was opened up, several hotels and camps were quickly built at Norcross Station at the south end of South Twin Lake, where sportsmen could board a steamboat to take them up the West Branch to their camps. On the East Branch there were several camps on that river's shore, including the Hunt Farm, which serviced lumbermen, as well as hikers who approached Katahdin from the east.

AN EVENING WITH A CATAMOUNT

Anonymous, from *The Farmington Chronicle,* January 5, 1871

"An Up-to-date Explorer," from In the Maine Woods, Bangor and Aroostook Railroad (Courtesy of Boston Public Library)

It was our fifth day in an old logging camp near one of the Katahdin Ponds. Clives had got his cordon of traps set and had gone that afternoon on his first round to visit them, telling me I need not expect him till late. I had been fishing along the shore of the pond for nearly a mile from our camp, when turning into a little nook in the shore, overhung by alders, under which a small brook came in, I espied a raccoon digging in the mud.

The recognition was mutual. He eyed me a moment, with his cunning visage turned askew, then scuttled away among the bushes. Hoping to make him take up a tree, I dropped my pole and gave chase. But there were no trees to his liking very near, and I was about giving up the race, when Mr. Graycoat stopped at the foot of a yellow birch, and looking round at me as if he thought it a more than usually good joke, suddenly disappeared.

Coming up, I found there was a large opening in the trunk near the ground, and looking in, saw that the tree was entirely hollow--a mere shell some three or four feet in diameter, lighted by several other holes and clefts up and down the trunk. I could see the coon up some fifteen or twenty feet, clinging on to the side, and peering curiously down to see what I was about.

I had stopped to pick up a pole to knock the coon down, when there was a cry so chilling and piercing that I involuntarily cried out. On glancing up to the treetops, I saw a large gray creature crouched upon a limb, and about to spring. In an instant there was another shriek, followed by a heavy spring among the leaves that shook the ground. I sped into the tree and scrambled up it like a chimney sweep. I went up with as much alacrity as the coon had done, he meanwhile, going higher, throwing a shower of dirt into my eyes, which were open to the fullest extent. I was scarcely up before the creature was at the hole. Perhaps the dust and dirt blinded him, for he was snuffing and purring at the bottom. I managed to wriggle up some twenty or thirty feet to where a large limb had grown out. Here with a long sliver or shim in my hand, I sat prepared to act upon the defensive.

I did not have long to wait. For the cloud of dust subsided a little, the creature perceived me, and uttering another scream, began climbing after us. The sliver I held was six or seven feet long and sound, though covered with rot and dirt. I got out my pocketknife and quickly sharpened the hard wood down to an acute point. It thus became quite an effective weapon. And as soon as the catamount--for such I judged it to have been--came within reach, I gave him a "jab" in the face with my spear--then another, dealt upon him with all my strength. His claws were occupied in holding on. A new shower of dirt rattled into his eyes.

I redoubled my thrusts. It grew too hot for him, and I had the inexpressible pleasure of seeing him slide to the bottom, growling and snarling with rage. But in a moment he was up on the outside. I heard his claws in the bark, and could see him as he passed the rifts and holes in the old trunk. But the aperture at the top was too small to admit anything but his head or one paw at a time.

Seeing the coon he commenced a series of cries and screeches, and thrusting in first one paw and then the other, tried to reach him. When the catamount's claws came too near he would shrink down a little towards me, keeping an eye on both of us, with a coolness that struck me as rather remarkable under the circumstances. Finding that he couldn't get in at the top, the panther began to descend and coming to the hole just above my head, looked in. Quick as a flash his long paw popped in and clutched up my cap with I don't know how much hair. I had to crouch close to keep my head from following it. Withdrawing his foot, he would eye me a moment, then thrust it in again and strain to reach me. But taking out my knife I gave him such sharp pricks that he soon got sick of that sort of exercise; after glaring at me awhile he went down to the bottom again. Lying stretched out on the ground, he would fix his eyes first on one then on another of the holes along the trunk, and at the least movement, spring up, and in a moment be at the top looking down at the coon, till, finding us all still beyond his reach, he would go back and watch again.

I could see him quite distinctly through my loophole. A long, lithe body--six feet, I thought, with the large cat head, strong legs and broad feet, from which his claws were uneasily protruding and receding, and a long tail to and fro with restless impatience--the very embodiment of strength and ferocity.

How to escape was the next question, after the momentary peril had ceased. Would the catamount go away of his own accord? He didn't act like it. His movements seemed to indicate that he meant to try a siege.

Night had come on--but the moon was rising over the treetops. I looked up at the raccoon; he was reconnoitering through a crevice. Suddenly the idea struck me that if I could force the coon out the panther might seize him, and perhaps be satisfied with one of us. But I confess that it was not without some self-reproach that I began to put this plan into operation. We were companions in danger, and to drive him out to certain death was truly the very climax of selfishness. But the instinct of self-preservation is not to be subjected to moral tests.

Again sharpening my stick, I stood up on my seat, and drove the coon before me. He offered no resistance, though manifesting the greatest reluctance to go out at the top. But I forced him out. The moment he appeared in sight, the catamount leaped up after him.

Poor fellow, he made one frantic attempt to get back into the tree, then turned to battle with the ascending monster. One sharp cry of fear and agony and his lifeblood was feeding our savage besieger. After sucking at his throat for a few moments, the cougar sprung down and ran off into the forest, with the coon in his mouth. I saw him disappear among the shadows, and heard his footsteps die away in the distance.

It was an opportunity not to he neglected. I was not long getting down. Crawling out of the tree, I made a beeline for the camp, in nearly an opposite direction, at about my best paces. It was ten o'clock when I got in. I found Clives wondering at my absence, and considerably alarmed. I told him of my adventure, and the next morning we moved our camp down to the Millinocket Lake. We didn't like the neighborhood. A catamount is not, in my very humble opinion, a very agreeable companion to spend an evening with.

SEARCHING FOR SALMON IN MAINE – THE EAST BRANCH OF THE PENOBSCOT

By Old Isaak, from *American Angler,* March 1892

"Hulling Machine Falls." (From Canoe and Camera, by Thomas S. Steele, 1882)

Our party consisted of three, Julius H. Wheeler, of Mount Clair, Dr. George S. Ward and the writer, all of Newark N. J. We had expressed our provisions and heavy impedimenta to Mattawamkeag a week before our start, in care of Aleck McClain, one of the wardens whom Hon. H. O. Stanley, Fish Commissioner of the State, had kindly recommended as one of the most expert guides in the State, hence we started with only our tackle and light satchels.

"Supper ready boys." It was Clarence who had prepared the meal for us, and we had good appetites for it. We sat on the logs in our rubber suits, for the rain was pouring down pretty lively. A slapjack a half inch thick, and just the size of the frying pan, a slice of ham, a quart of coffee to each of us, and then we lighted our pipes and began to feel a little better natured. Camp-fire yarns and sparks flew about. We told some stories of wood life in the Adirondack and Allegheny mountains, and then called upon McClain to tell us how he got so badly chewed up by that bear.

"Well, you see, boys, I had some traps set not far from my house, about two or three miles and foolishly went to visit them without gun or knife. I found a big bear caught by one paw in the trap. The paw was pretty well skinned by the struggles of the blank, blank brute to get loose, and I was afraid he would get away. I picked up a good, bit stick of hardwood about as big as a fence rail, and let him have it right across his eyes four or five times as hard as I could strike. I've killed a lot of bears, boys, but this was the blank, blank, biggest, and blank, blank, toughest brute I ever saw. The clog was fast between two saplings, but I'm blanked if he didn't drag them saplings down and get loose. I wasn't going to run. I hadn't time. I let him have the club again and skinned one side of his head, but, before I could jump to one side, he had me by the left arm with his blank, blank teeth, and his hind claws stuck into my leg. I jumped back, and the clog, catching between two trees, I tore my arm right out of his blank, blank mouth. That was more than two weeks ago, and it ain't healed up yet, though I can use a paddle and setting pole by resting them on my wrist. You see I can't shut that hand very well, the tendons are so blank bad strained."

Aleck took the bandages off his arm, and while the doctor dressed it, he finished his story.

"I thought I was done for, and that I never should see my folks again, and wondered how long it would be before they would find my body. You see a man thinks awful fast when a big bear has him by the arm. When that clog caught and I tore loose I just tumbled over and laid there. I didn't lose my senses, not by a blank sight, but I got awful riled, for that bear was making desperate efforts to get at me again. I saw that he would likely tear his foot off and get away, so I got up and went to the nearest house. It was only an Indian's hut, but I knew he had a gun. I wanted to shoot the bear the blankest worst kind. I found the Indian at home smoking his pipe. I told him about that bear and his squaw bound up my arm. The squaw wanted to see the bear shot and would go along. I found I could not use my arm at all, so I told the Indian he would have to shoot. We found the bear still fast to the trap, and the clog held by the two saplings.

"Now," said I, "give it to him, quick, for I am afraid he will tear loose."

No, no," said the squaw, "don't shoot yet; I want to see him--he acts so funny."

"The bear was making desperate efforts to tear his foot out of the trap or to get the clog loose. The squaw drew near, laughing and poking a stick at the beast to make him dance about. The Indian drew up his gun, but the squaw got in his way. Just then the desperate struggles of the bear tore his foot from the trap, leaving the skin in it. His rush knocked the woman sprawling against the

Indian, upsetting him, and they both rolled together on the ground, each apparently trying which could kick the highest. The bear went of into the underbrush, and that was the last I saw of him."

"So you did not kill him after all?"

"No, he got clean away; but I'm sure to get him if he don't leave the neighborhood."

"Clarence," said Julius, "have you had a good bear fight?"

"No, Mr. Wheeler; but I've killed a good many. The last one I caught in a trap. I picked up the clog and walked right up to the bear, which backed out as fast as I approached. I had a young friend with me who had never shot a bear. He carried a rifle, while I only had a knife. I got close up to the bear and put my knife twice into him. I called my companion to come quickly, for if he wanted to shoot a bear he must hurry, as this one would be dead in a few minutes. He came up and put a bullet in its head; so he can make his brags that he has shot a bear."

The doctor was getting sleepy, so we retired to our tents, and in a few minutes I was dreaming of bears.

THROUGH THE GAME REGION OF MAINE

By Jonathan Darling, from *Shooting and Fishing,* April 21st and 28th, 1892

Jonathan Darling

Jonathan Darling (1830-1898) known as "Jock" Darling, was born in Enfield, Maine, learning hunting and trapping skills from his father. He became such a proficient hunter that he claimed to have killed over 1,500 moose from 1850 to 1880. Opinionated and obstinate, he was often in trouble with lumbermen, other hunters, and the Game Wardens. He constructed a set of sporting camps at Nicatous Lake, where he would entertain hunters from far away and wrote many stories of his adventures in the sporting journals of that time.

It was his use of dogs in hunting, a practice known as "hounding," which was ill favored by the hunting establishment and later made illegal, that got him in the most trouble. After several attempts, the wardens finally succeeded in capturing Jock, and jailed him with the intention of making him the poster boy of lawlessness, but he made an agreement with the State and became a warden himself, after which all his writings reflected proper hunting techniques and even game conservation.

As it has been sometime since the readers of SHOOTING AND FISHING have heard from me, and as I have been travelling through our best game sections, I will give an account of my adventures. First, I will say that I have never known a winter when game was so plenty and that so few have been killed as has been the past winter. There are several reasons for this: First, the snow in many sections has been shoal, and the crust would hold the animals so that they could protect themselves; another reason, many of the hunters and guides are learning that it is better for them to spare the game, as they can make more out of guiding if they let the game live during the season.

In my travels this winter I came across a hunter and guide, whom I had with party sometime previous. I tried to give him to understand that it was better for him to try to help preserve our moose than it is for him to kill them for the hides, during any part of the year; this is an Indian that I am alluding to, and not long ago I was at his camp; he was trapping, and in the spring he has lots of bear traps to set. I asked him about moose hunting, and he replied, "Well, Jock, I have found that what you told me was true; last fall I got five dollars per day for guiding and my parties got their moose, and in addition to my wages I got several presents. Sportsmen come to me and say, 'John, do you know where you can take me and get a moose? I say, yes. Then the sportsmen says, I will give you three dollars a day to go with me, and if I get a moose, I will give you five dollars a day. I take him where he kills his moose, and I get five dollars a day instead of three; but if we go in winter and kill all the moose, I am liable to get caught and lose 'em all, and may be locked up in jail, and then can't tell sportsmen where I can take them and get moose." This Indian hunter, John, promised if he knew of any hunters killing moose this spring he would tell me about it.

The first thing I did last December was to make a trip through some sections of our moose country. I made the same talk with hunters and guides that I did with John, and I believe the State is well paid in game for the advice I dealt out, as I have been over the ground since the snow was deep, and could not see but little signs of poachers.

My last trip was up on the head waters of the east branch of Penobscot river. At Patten I hired a team to take me to Trout brook, a distance of thirty miles, on a good tote road; I saw where one moose had crossed the road, but here had a snow fall after he had gone and I could not tell whether there were parties following him on snowshoes or not. The next morning I took my snowshoes and pack and started for Third Lake; there were lumber camps there that I wanted to visit. As I went up the Second Lake the snow was so hard that I could not see my own tracks, and when I got near to the head of the lake I saw where three caribou had gone up the lake not many hours in advance of me; their hoofs were so sharp that their tracks could be plainly seen when they trotted and they were trotting at a lively gait, too, as I could see from the distance of their strides. I wondered if they were doing this for fun or practicing for some race course. These animals reach their hind feet past their fore feet, so that the tracks are nearly the same distance apart, and every fourth track shows how far they reach at each step; I paced their strides as I walked along and found that their reaches were nearly twenty feet, as I had to reach out well to get their steps inside of six paces. I followed them to the shores of the lake; here, I found they stopped and fed about the shore awhile before they went into the woods. It was now seven miles in a straight line to the lake. I did not take any road but struck into the woods. I knew there were deer, moose and caribou on my beat, and I wanted to see if the poachers had been there. As soon as I got into the woods and before I was out of sight of the lake I saw the woods was alive with deer, and had hard trodden paths to walk on, but they were not using their paths much as the snow was so stiff they could go on top of it. This yard was some one and a half miles through it, and as I got out of the deer beats I struck a moose beat or yard, and I thought by the signs that there were four moose in the yard. I swung off to the left and got out of their beat. I do not think I started them, for I went several miles in open hard wood ridges and did not see many signs, but saw where a drove of caribou had crossed a ridge. I came to some burnt land that was open; I could see a long distance. Here I saw deer and lynx tracks quite plenty and fresh. I expected every minute to see them bouncing along but did not. I came to the lake and could see teams on the ice, some two miles up the lake; these teams had just come out of the woods with loads of logs. I went up and found the camp which stood near the bank of the lake. The style of building lumber camps, one for the men to stay and sleep in and one for the cooks and for the dining room; there is a shed roof to connect them. The first thing I saw when I came to the shed connecting the two camps was four large Canada lynx skins, two beaver, one otter and several small mink and sable. These animals were caught by the son of the proprietor of the camps, who spent a portion of his time trapping. Hear I learned that some of the

Moosehead district hunters had a trail of line of traps from Chamberlin Lake to the Munsungan Lake on the Aroostook, and that the first camp on these waters was where the Moosehead hunter stopped when they were in that vicinity. I thought perhaps the party that sent out a moose hide that had already seized might be there, and I struck for that camp, some eight miles farther. I got to camp soon after sundown, but no Moosehead Indians were there; they had not been there for several days and the lumbermen could not tell which way they went. It had snowed on their trail so I could not find it, but I will see them when they return to their homes in May or June. I spent the night here. The boss told me when I returned to keep to the left of a mountain and through a valley between two mountains, for by this route I would save some three miles travel. I concluded to go back and follow his directions. I had not gone far before I saw moose tracks, but they were old tracks. I soon came across the tracks of an otter and saw where he had gone each way. I remember that the night before I saw on a brook that emptied into the east branch, where an otter had gone both ways. I know the nature of these animals so well that I was satisfied that it was the same otter. There was just snow enough on the crust to track him and the direction of his trail was the same I wanted to go. It was a cloudy morning and I had to occasionally look at my compass to keep my course. I finally put up my compass and relied on the otter trail. At some places the deer tracks bothered me, but I kept the trail and it brought me to the same place. I saw the track the day before and just where I wanted to strike my own trail. My path was a regular otter carry where these animals went from Aroostook to Penobscot waters. I now made my way to the camp on the shore of Third Lake; here I got a lunch and started for Telos Lake. I took nothing with me to eat, as I expected to reach another lumber camp that night. After travelling some three hours and when within a few miles of Webster Lake, I saw a large moose track with the snowshoe tracks of two hunters or lumbermen after him. The snow was so deep and stiff I was sure the poachers would kill the moose, so I pulled on after them. I followed them some seven miles. I made up my mind that the moose had been started sometime before and was a long distance in advance of his pursuer, but I knew that when they came to his stopping place and started him again they would catch him and I was expecting moose steak for supper. I had a small axe and was expected to camp wherever they killed the moose. I soon came to the Webster brook, but before crossing I came to another moose yard that had the appearance of containing several moose. I noticed as I went through the yard that the tracks were some days older than the one the hunters were following. A short distance after crossing Webster brook, I found the hunters had given up the chase and had started in the direction of the lumber camp. I now saw that the moose steak supper was up, unless I killed the moose myself.

It was now late in the afternoon; I had nothing to eat and Telos camp was out of my reach for that night, but as that was where I wanted to go I started back to the brook and followed it up until I broke through the ice and came near getting a good ducking, but saved myself by grabbing some alder bushes that hung over the bank. I had a hard time getting my snowshoes out of the ice, snow and water, and when I was out all right I saw that it was not safe to follow the stream. About this time it had commenced snowing; I knew that it was not far to an old road that led to Webster and Telos Lakes, but it was not now travelled. I soon struck the road and took it. I very well know that unless I struck some old camps I should have to bed in the show, but at six o'clock I came to an old camp near the road. The weight of the snow had broken the ribs of the camp and the middle of the camp was a mass of timber, cedar splits that the camp had been covered with and the snow. But there was a dry place in one corner; I looked at my watch and then considered my situation, but I was not long making up my mind that it was the best I could get that night. I first made ready for a fire; then I wanted water, for I was very thirsty, having travelled from the Aroostook waters that morning and had been doing considerable sweating during the day. I found a fry pan and cleaned it out as well as I could, and melted snow to quench my thirst. I did not have much trouble in getting wood, for the adjoining camp, which included the cook and dining room, was full of benches and there was plenty of old and dry boughs in the corner of the camp. It was a warm night, but I did not sleep much as I had to watch the fire to keep it from setting the rest of the camp on fire, so kept at work, my mouth watering when I thought of the moose stake I had expected for my supper. When daylight came I quickly put my snow-shoes on and I was soon at Webster Lake. It had snowed during the night about two inches, and the farther I went the less crust there was, and the snow walking grew harder and more tiresome. I could hear logs tumble either on the landing or rolling yard, but they sounded a long way off. I now wished that I had taken something to eat with me the day before; but the idea of being a game warden, to hunt up poachers in our northern wilderness, all alone, would cheer me up amazingly. It soon commenced hailing and later turned to rain, but another hour and a half brought me to the landing. The landing man told me that it was two and a half miles to camp; I asked him if he brought his dinner with him; he told me that he did not, and the team with the next turn brought it to him. I don't know what would have happened if he had brought his dinner and had refused to divide with me; but another hour brought me to camp where I made myself acquainted with the cook.

In my next letter I will give an account of the rest of my trip. I am now busily making arrangements for my camp at Nicatous, and I will say that I have good chance for summer boarders who wish to get into a locality where they can get plenty of fish and see the deer prancing the shores of the lake and streams. I travel all through the State and I don't know of a more quiet and pleasant place for boarders or sportsmen, away from railroad and steamboat whistles.

Before I reached the lumber camp at Telos Lake it commenced to rain, and soon after I got there it grew cold and squally. I went out to take a look at the lake, but the snow blew so that I could not see the opposite side of the lake in any direction. There were some men marking logs at a landing on the shore and they told me that the day before was a warm, pleasant day, and the five caribou came near to them and were in sight on the lake for several hours.

There were some forty men at this camp, and not a gun of any description; this was something unusual for most lumber camps have a good supply of Winchesters. I had a talk with the owners of the camp and they told me that when they could get beef for four to five cents a pound that they should not run any risk of violating the game laws, and I find that many other operators are getting the same opinion.

I was intending to go to St. Johns waters from here, but changed my mind and the next day started for Trout brook. The travelling in the tote road was hard and I wore my snowshoes. I saw several new caribou tracks on my way and some of them in sight of a camp on Trout brook, where I stopped for the night; this was where I made my headquarters in December when I killed my moose and caribou, and the boys all seemed to be glad to see me.

In the morning I started for a shanty that was near the shore of Grand Lake on the east branch of Penobscot river. I saw plenty of caribou tracks along the road. I got dinner at the Trout Brook Farm, and then took a look around to see if I could find any signs of game being killed, but did not see any. I went to some hunter's camp and took a look about; I found some fish but no fresh meat. The owners of the camp were away on their lines of traps. I took some of the fish and dressed it, built a fire and made myself at home; took some slices of pork and fried them and then cooked the fish; it was a fresh water cusk, and as I had not eaten any fresh fish for sometime it tasted good; most any fresh fish or meat will taste good after one gets on a State of Maine forest appetite.

I then went to the shanty kept by Samuel Harvey for the purpose of accommodating travellers of all sorts. There I learned that there were two Frenchmen camping on the Wassataquoik stream and that there were several lumbermen operating there; the distance I would have to go to get there would be some twenty-five miles. There were some lumbermen about half way that were hauling logs into the east branch, some ten or twelve miles below, so I made calculations to get dinner at one of these camps. I had to cross Grand Lake on the start, and soon after the sun rose I was on the lake. It was a nice morning and nice walking on the lake shore; the last snow that had fallen had all blown off. I was soon at the outlet and found a high perpendicular mountain near the shore at my right, and just back of that another longer one, called the Traveller. Here I took the woods following the river's bank, as the river was open. After an hour's walk on the bank I came to a road that led to a lumber camp near to the south end of the old Traveller mountain. I arrived at the camp a little past 2 o'clock. I got my dinner and made some inquiry as to how to go to get to the camps on the Wassataquoik, but no one there could tell me as much as I knew about it myself, although I had not been there for thirty-five years and then went there from another direction. The cook told me that I could not get there that day, but I took out my map and after looking at it a few moments I told him that I should try it anyway, and I started. I had to follow along the side of the mountain some two miles to get to the end of it, and then it was on high ground to the end where I began to descend toward the Wassataquoik. Soon after I started from the camp where I took dinner, I found a logging road that led up the mountain side; it was very steep to haul logs on and there were holes dug by the side of the road all along; these holes were where gravel had been taken out and spread on the road to hold the sleds and loads of logs from shoving the horses too much; but this did not do it always; for several horses had been killed on those roads during the winter by the loads of logs driving them out of the roads against the trees. When I got to the end of the Traveller I saw fresh tracks of some ten or twelve caribou. At this point I struck a track of open burnt land, and soon came to a high point of land where I could look over a country as far as the eye could see. This burnt district looked to be some six miles across. I could make out where the stream run, but I could not see or hear any signs of hunters or lumbermen. I stood for a while calculating where the camps would most likely be; the tote road that went to those camps followed up the brook from its mouth, and I know if I hit the brook and did not find the road I would have to go down to strike it, so I took my course and started. When I found the brook I found snowshoe tracks that led me to the French trappers' camp. I soon came to the camp but no one was there. I could not find any signs of large game being killed, but saw some fur skins and a quantity of spruce gum. I then started down stream to look for the lumber camp. Two miles travel brought me to the road and two more miles brought me to the lumber camp. Just at dark I found that the head man was an acquaintance and friend of mine; he told me that he was in a moose yard the day before, and that he did not know of any animals being killed since last fall; also told me that his crew of men were terribly buggy, which meant they were lousy. I will speak of this camp just to show what a warden has to encounter in northern Maine, if he goes there in the winter. This camp was a low built one, much more so that usual, and the floor was made of round poles, 4 to 6 inches through. The boss told me that there was room in the berths to sleep, but I took the floor and slept a little. The next morning it was snowing and the wind was blowing a gale. This was the end of my journey. I was going back to Grand Lake, but I did not care to start in such a storm. The men all went into the woods to work and I helped the cook keep camp. Another night was spent on the poles. I saw several men get up, light their lanterns, strip, hunt their clothes over and scratch. I saw two scratch their legs and the blood ran down to their heals; there was no little strong language indulged in. There were some forty men in this camp, made up of French, Irish, Americans and Bluenoses, as we call New Brunswick men.

The next day I started for Grand Lake. Some eight inches of snow had fallen and the snowshoeing was heavy and hard. I had some three or four miles of up grade, but I got back to the East Branch Camp in season to take dinner with the occupants. I struck a team here that was going to Trout Brook Farm and I got a ride most of the way, but we had to climb some steep hills or mountains on this tote road. When the teams are hauling supplies to the camps they put chains around both runners and then the horses have hard work to hold ten to twelve hundred pounds. That night I got back to Harvey's shanty, and the next morning I started for Lowell. This ended my snowshoe excursions for this season in northern Maine.

– JONATHAN DARLING

A NIGHT IN THE WOODS

By M. A. P., from *Forest and Stream*, November 3, 1892

(Courtesy of Ernst Mayr Library, Harvard)

One day late in the fall of 1887 just before the first snow fall of winter, I left my husband's lumber camp to return to my home in the settlement, a distance of three miles through the woods, and as the afternoon was well advanced when I started, I knew that I must walk briskly to reach home before nightfall, for as I must ferry myself across the Penobscot River at a point where the water ran very swiftly, and the boat and oars all being well coated with ice, it would be unpleasant and perhaps dangerous to attempt to cross after night had fairly shut down. Realizing this I hurried along the path, over which I had been many times before.

At a distance of a mile and a half from the camp the path ran through a swamp that was now flooded with water from recent rains. At this point I was obliged to leave the path and go through the woods to avoid a slough that was about fifty rods in length. But I stepped boldly into the woods, never dreaming but that I should make connections all right and strike the road at a point below the slough.

After some minutes' rapid walking I found I was diverging from the right direction, but how much I could not tell. I should have reached the path by this time if I had kept the proper course, still I was not uneasy, for I thought surely a few moments more will bring me out to the path, or I shall find some indications of its being near, trusting to chance to guide me aright. I soon found myself in a dense thicket of alder bushes just high enough to reach a couple of feet above my head, and growing as thickly together as the quills on the back of a porcupine. It was impossible to see a rod clearly in any direction. Working my way slowly along, I at last got clear of the alders and found myself on more open ground. I could see off at my left a sharp, narrow ridge which I recognized as a range of small hillocks called the "horse-back" which began on the east bank of the Penobscot, at a point near my home, and terminated ten or twelve miles to the east. I made my way toward this ridge, thinking that I could easily follow along its summit, which was in no place more than 100 ft. across, and so reach home safely. But when I had gained the top of the ridge I found I had not the least idea in which direction to turn. Was the way home toward the right or toward the left? I did not know. My self-confidence now deserted me, and I was obliged to recognize the full grown startling fact that I was lost. Daylight had now entirely faded and the faint light afforded by the stars seemed only to make everything more distinct. There was no wind moving, everything was sombre and still. As I stood there in the weird silence, a feeling of helplessness, hopeless loneliness came over me impossible to describe. It is like no other sensation. It is not exactly fear, but a stupefying, unreasoning, withering dread of you know not what. The fact that it is entirely uncalled for--and as in my case there was no cause for fear--only makes it the more aggravating. I sat down on a fallen tree, resolved to conquer and banish this foolish, helpless feeling, and when I had so far succeeded as to be able to reason clearly, I made up my mind that I must stay in the woods all night sure. I knew no one would think of looking for me until the next day, for my husband would believe me safe at home, while those at home would think that I concluded to stay at camp, as I had often done. So there was nothing for me but to accept the situation with the best grace possible.

I always carry a revolver when walking in the woods, for I will confess to being terribly afraid of a bear. I am sure I don't know why I should be so much afraid of them, for I consider the common black bear quite harmless unless attacked, and the black bear is the only sort found in this vicinity. I have seen them quite frequently in my rambles in the woods and have sometimes been quite near them, but they always seem to be as anxious to increase the distance between us as I was, and that is saying a good deal. In taking my revolver from my pocket to examine and reload it if necessary I found two bunches of matches, placed there for safe keeping by some one while my jacket hung on the wall in the camp. With the revolver and matches in my possession I began to think my situation not so bad after all. I could now build a fire and, I believed, get through the night with some degree of comfort.

I now began to look about for something with which to build my fire and some suitable place in which to build it. Walking along a few rods, I found a pine tree lying on the ground that had evidently been shattered by lightning. It gave a royal heap of kindling wood all ready for a match, which I was not long in applying. After my fire was well under way, and as the moon had now risen, I walked along the top of the ridge. Though determined not to lose sight of my fire, I was not satisfied with my accommodations for the night and still had a faint hope of finding something that would enable me to find my way out. The light from the fire would be visible a long distance, as there was nothing to intercept it. The undergrowth had been burned away years before, leaving here and there a dead tree, with the bark fallen off, standing white and ghostly in the moonlight. As I moved along slowly and cautiously for fear of stumbling, I suddenly heard a sound that fairly froze me. I knew what it was too well, I had often heard it before, but never when I was alone; it was the sound of some animals tearing rotten wood in search of insects. My old fear of a bear returned, reinforced by the hour, the place, and the fact that I was alone and lost in the woods. I could think of no other animal that procured its food in that manner or whose strength enabled him to rent and break wood with such violence.

After I had stood listening for perhaps five minutes, though it seemed five lifetimes, my mind began to take in the situation, and I thought that if I returned to my fire without disturbing this unseen terrorizer, I should be in a shiver of dread all through the night, but if I went near him and frightened him, and I could see him run away as I felt sure he would, then I should have no more fear of him. So, by taking my courage in both hands and telling myself what a miserable coward I was, and how I should despise a man with no more physical ability than I was now displaying, I forced myself to advance steadily toward the sound, which still continued. I walked over softly, for I did not wish to frighten the creature before I had an opportunity to see him. I soon discovered him on the trunk of a leaning rotten stub quietly working away. He did not hear me come up.

The shadows prevented me at first from getting a fair view of him, but presently he slightly changed his position and turned his head and looked at me over his shoulder as I stood about twelve feet distant, and then, thank heaven! I saw it was not a bear. I was so overjoyed to find that it was not my special torment that the brute's round, glistening eyes and gleaming white teeth as he drew his upper lip back with a snarl, looked at me almost pleasant. It was a Canadian lynx. Those who have ever seen one of those cowardly creatures with its ugly, cat-like head, will agree with me when I affirm that this fellow was a scary-looking chap, as he gazed at me without moving a muscle. I was so intensely gratified to find that it was not a bear that had caused me such a wretched fright, that for a moment I stood perfectly still, with no other feeling save that of thankfulness. Then, while the brute continued to gaze into my eyes the thought came to me that if I could shoot him I should have something to tell of, and perhaps it would not be unseemly to brag about it a very little, considering the circumstances. I knew it would be a difficult thing to do, owing to the uncertain light, but I determined to try it at any rate. Slowly moving my hand toward my pocket I drew out my revolver and taking aim as well as I could at the broad forehead of the lynx, I fired. He sprang nearly five feet into the air and fell dead not more than three yards from my feet. The ball had penetrated his head just above the eye. It was a good shot and I was correspondingly elated with it.

Leaving my prize where it lay I retraced my steps a short distance, and, turning to the right, continued to make my way in the same direction in which I was walking when my "bear" drew my attention from all earthly concerns, and held it fixed exclusively on himself. After walking perhaps a mile, for I had little idea of distance and none of time, and I could just see a glimmer of light from the burning pine, I came to a break in my elevated roadway, a notch in the horseback--I knew of several such. Also knew that the lumber men sometimes made use of those natural gateways to pass through the horseback with their teams. And if there should prove on examination to be a path through this one I might yet reach a human habitation and not be obliged to pass the night in the woods. It was worth trying for, anyhow. Clambering down the steep side of the notch I reached the bottom, where it was so dark I could not see a yard before me, but a few stops brought me out into the moonlight, which was still insufficient to allow me to make a close examination of the ground. Lighting a match and holding it near the ground, I saw the prints of horses' hoofs plainly outlined in the soft earth. It being late at night I reasoned that the teams that had made these tracks were the last that had passed, and were on their way homeward, their destination being probably some camp in the vicinity. Lighting a match every few rods to make sure of the hoof prints, I traveled perhaps a mile, when I came in sight of a glimmer of light; drawing nearer I found it came from the window of a camp. I walked up to the front entrance, and, looking through the window, I saw a number of men mending their garments, making axe handles or playing checkers, but none whom I knew. I passed around to the back door, sure of finding the cook in this direction. I was cold, tired and hungry, and glad to find a warm place with people about me once more. I rapped on the door, and it was opened by a stranger. A man who was reading at the table looked up as I came in. To my amazement it was my husband. The man who opened the door was the cook, the men were all known to me, but I was so completely dazed, so lost as it were, that I did not recognize them. The next morning my husband accompanied me home, and then, after a long search, found and brought home my loup cervier, and I hope never again to be lost in the woods at night.

– MAINE, 1892, M. A. P.

A WOMAN'S HUNTING TRIP INTO THE WILDS OF THE BORDERLAND BETWEEN MAINE AND CANADA

By F. W. G., from *Forest and Stream*, May 12, 1894

Maine Sportsman, Oct 1898 (Courtesy of Ernst Mayr Library, Harvard)

Off at last! It was a bright, beautiful autumnal morning of the lst on the which we began our journey, and we even looked to the long day's ride with pleasure, for we were going into what was to us, *terra incognita*. After distributing our belongings and becoming comfortably settled in our chairs we leaned back in the full enjoyment of our surroundings, and of having nothing to do but anticipate, all cares having been left behind as we boarded the train, unless Jerry be excepted, of whom more anon.

The year before I had taken my wife for her first real camping trip. We spent two weeks among the 27,000 islands of Georgian Bay, Ontario, and although the black bass fishing was grand all else was disappointing. It was hot and rainy, the wind was never right, either too much or none at all. The islands were masses of rocks, for the most part without trees, and we found nothing but frogs on which to try the new Marlin. These, however, were good for practice and also for eating, our French boatman and cook presenting them to us as perfectly cooked as though done by a "blue ribbon." The climate, snakes and spiders were tropical; thunderstorms such as we had never experienced about New York were frequent, and we returned much disappointed.

But during the long winter following our trip in retrospect appeared to have been more and more enjoyable, for the disagreeable incidents were gradually forgotten and only the pleasures recalled. The greatest pleasure was then the presence of a little all black cocker, Jerry, who had been loaned us at the village from which we started, and who proved such a sociable companion during the trip that our longing for him after our return home persuaded us to send for him. He arrived during the coldest weather of last winter and ever since has been our companion, joy and comfort, and no doubt was one of the primary causes of our second trip. As the spring approached and brought thoughts of outings, and when Jerry would trot out of doors, turn to the north, raise his nose and draw in long breaths, we would say, "He is trying to smell Penetang, poor fellow," and it would also set us longing for Penetang, or at least, for woods and lakes.

One Thursday in April, when perhaps the longing was something intense, my FOREST AND STREAM contained a letter from Mr. Fred Talcott, of Providence, R. I. He offered to correspond with any reputable person desiring to know of the whereabouts of a "sportsman's paradise." We were the particular ones meant, although unconscious of it all the time. I wrote him and his answer came promptly. I wish I could give it here. His "paradise" was situated on the Maine-Canadian boundary, and was to be entered by leaving the railroad at Jackman, Me. He promised everything--a perfect country; perfect guide; trout faster than one could land them; deer, moose and caribou, ducks, partridge; and last but not least, moderate prices for everything. I wrote again. His replies read like news from a long lost rich uncle. They were awaited with impatience and read with avidity. The correspondence lasted all summer; indeed it has not yet ceased.

I wrote the guide and waited a month for my first answer, and received but little satisfaction beyond his prices. His later letters, however, were more satisfactory, and although he would promise but little, we concluded he was trustworthy, and on the knowledge obtained from Mr. Talcott, we decided to enter his "paradise" and engage his guides.

Then came a busy six weeks of preparation. Bacon and court plaster, flour and bandages, guns and scalpels, fishing tackle and baking powder, 350 assorted cartridges, rifles, shotguns, rods, dozens of flies, ditto hooks, etc., constituted but a fraction of our outfit. Of what we did not already possess we brought enough for half a dozen, and what a pleasure it was with always one more special journey down town to add another leader, more hooks or cartridges for fear we should run short.

Then came the selection of the route with careful consultation of time tables and maps. At least we were ready, our belongings in two strong trunks and a handbag, a package of mackintoshes and wraps, another of guns and rods, and --Jerry.

We left New York about 9 A.M, on the "White Mountain Flyer" of the N.Y. N.H. & H.R.R., our route taking us along the Sound, the Connecticut River, through the Berkshires, and along the edge of the White Mountains, arriving at Wells' River at 5 o'clock. A tramp through that pretty little village, supper, and the north bound train at 7 o'clock brought us to Lennoxville at 11:30 P.M., with an hour to wait for the Canadian Pacific train going east. A little after 5 in the morning we arrived at Jackman an hour late, and a long, mostly pleasant, railroad journey was ended.

We arrived at Jackman cold to the bone and in a pretty state of mind. But a good fire, hot breakfast and cordial greetings from everybody at the Colby House, restored us to warmth and equanimity. A little shopping for things forgotten and at about 8 o'clock we started for a 25 mile drive, Jim and I and Jerry in a buggy, and Llewellyn Rainey with a two-horse buckboard and our trunks.

Fifteen miles from Jackman through a dense woods, always rising, brought us to the top of the Boundary Mountains, 3,000ft. above the sea. A short halt to water the horses and a gradual descent, mostly on a trot over better roads for the ten miles, brought us to hospitable Mrs. Rainey's.

Our journey had been long and wearisome, and after a refreshing bath and a hot dinner, we went to bed and were asleep at 4 o'clock in the afternoon, not waking until sunrise next morning.

Our trunks were searched for our regimentals, and city clothes knew us no more for three weeks. Jim appeared in a short-skirted corduroy hunting suit that had proved so serviceable last year, while I made my debut in knickerbockers, and so comfortable I found them that I shall always wear them upon like excursions hereafter.

The air was crisp that morning and we needed our sweaters during the first hours, for we already felt the effect of the change, and were hungry long before being called to the generous hot breakfast prepared for us. Afterward we met our guides. Robert Elliott, head guide, was a strong, wiry man of 45, active, full of business and exceedingly good-natured and anxious to please. We found him always polite, very even-tempered and a hard worker. Nothing was too much trouble for him if he could add to our comfort or pleasure, and wet to the skin, cold and tired, his heart was as warm and his eyes as twinkling with fun as though he was as comfortable as he had made us. Disagreeable weather and reverses seemed only to bring out good characteristics. He had trapped and hunted winters for twenty-five years and had driven logs in the springs. He was a thorough woodsman and trapper.

Albert Cathcart, the second guide, was a man of 30. He was leaving his two weeks' old son and heir to go with us. He proved strong as an ox, and as kindly, considerate and obligingly good-natured as it is proverbial for strong gentle men ever to be.

Mrs. Rainey and her son, Llewellyn, deserve more than a word. They were the kindliest people we met on our trip. Llewellyn drove us in and out of the woods, and we still hear his cheery voice encouraging the horses at a particularly bad spot, while Mrs. Rainey sent delicacies to us on every occasion, and spent many anxious hours worrying about "that poor little woman off in the woods."

The morning was spent in making the acquaintance of the guides, the family, and the neighbors who came to see the lady who was to go where no white woman had ever been, and carry her own rifle, and shoot it, too. In the afternoon we went out to try our rifles. They were satisfactory except that I could not make mine shoot as straight as Jim's; he beat me, as usual, and rose correspondingly in the estimation of Bob, and from then on I played second fiddle. During our tramp we came to a broad, shallow brook, with pools at intervals. Bob's hat band furnished a 3ft. leader and a fly, and the woods a stick. With this outfit we were soon at work. Bob caught the first trout to show us how, and fishing alternately we soon landed fifteen or twenty trout, averaging about a quarter of a pound. We were both new to trout fishing, and enjoyed it greatly. The fly would no sooner touch the water that a swirl would be a signal for a strike. Several of the larger fish were saved for supper, the others thrown back.

The next morning was cloudy, but we decided to make a start and with our "duffle" packed compactly on two strongly made sledges, each horse drawing about 250 lbs., with Jim riding "Sandwich Island style" on a tall horse led by an officer in one of Her Majesty's cavalry regiments at Quebec, who was a volunteer in our party, we filed out back of Mrs. Rainey's house, across a cleared piece, over a ditch, through a pair of bars, into the woods. When not a hundred yards from the house a fine misty rain began to drizzle down, but there was no turning back, and for the first hour or two, after entering the woods, it was not especially disagreeable, as the trees were so thick the rain did not reach us. Bob had started that morning at daylight with his axe to clear away the windfalls, and we soon came on a specimen of his work--a huge tree cut in two places, the center piece drawn to one side for our passage.

After going about four miles a man appeared coming toward us. It was the U. S. Mail named Armstrong, physically strong-armed. He had made fourteen miles that morning, a Winchester and a haversack containing half a deer and a partridge shot on the way. A few words of greeting, some local news exchanged, and we passed on.

Our first halt was six miles off and we were nearly five hours in reaching it, the rain becoming heavier, also the walking. There had been a heavy storm a few days before our arrival, and mud, water and windfalls were plentiful. I had been over tote roads in the Adirondacks and had read of Mud Pond Carry, but had never imagined that such a collection of stumps and sloughs of despond could be gathered into such a small space as a clearing 12ft. wide and ten miles long, and every one seemed placed where it would most help the others to obstruct our passage. Twenty times one of the other of the sledges would bring up against a stump too large to get over one runner, passing over a boulder, then be itself in a mudhole a little deeper than the driver had anticipated, and over it would go. Under the expert care of the cavalryman, Jim's alternately walking and riding proceeded along beautifully and arrived at our lunch place a little fatigued. Jerry had disappeared after the first mile or two, but caused us little anxiety, for his tracks were plainly visible, and we found him on our arrival, with Bob, each looking wetter than the other, and it continued the rest of the day.

Arriving at the little brook that marked the ending of the first stage, Jim was placed under cover of an uprooted tree, a roaring fire was started and a shelter of rubber blankets was quickly raised. The kettle soon boiled and in spite of the rain we had a jolly cold luncheon with a cup of tea, whole party seeming to think it a regular picnic, and most of all Bob, whom the rain seemed particularly to exhilarate. Perhaps an hour and a half was allowed to bait the horses and we were again on the way. We were now deeper in the woods, on higher ground, and found the roads better and the four miles were soon covered. Then a sudden turn off from the main road, over a brook, up a short rise, and Wilson Pond Camp was in view. It was a long, low camp, built like a double lean-to with no roof over the center, and through the opening the smoke curled, making a welcome sight.

Bob had again preceded us and a roaring fire had already dried the camp a great deal. Many hands make light work, the horses were soon unharnessed, the baggage unloaded and carried under cover and in the experienced hands of the guides; in an hour we were quite at home. Jim and I on one side of the fire sat on our bed made on the ground, in dry clothing, and Bob, Mr. Perkins, and Llewellyn were on the opposite side, standing and sitting, turning first one side and then the other to the fire, but still happy, was busy getting supper. Bob was overhauling the things, estimating the damage, which was trifling, and storing the minor articles among the shingles of the roof. Comfortable, warm, happy and at rest we had nothing to wish for except supper, which came quickly and disappeared with equal rapidity. With pipes and cigarettes, funny stories and the relation of individual experiences of the trip, darkness came all too early, the wet clothing furnished a screen and soon we were comfortably in between the blankets. Jim feared neither spiders nor snakes, lulled into fancied security by Bob's assurance that they did not grow in that part of the country. Neither did she fear bears, wolves nor Indians, for were there not on the opposite side of the great fire in close call and in full view, four stalwart men to defend her. The horses stamped and the rain pattered on the roof, but within the fire crackled and the blaze cheered and soothed us and we slept as though on a bed of down until daylight.

Oh! what a change. The brightest, crispest, sunshiniest morning ever seen! We were soon up. How glorious was the water dipped with a tin basin from the brook! Breakfast was quickly over, and Llewellyn and Mr. Perkins speeded on their return journey. Everything was soon out of camp to dry more thoroughly in the open air. About 10 o'clock, taking our rifles, with Bob leading, we went up to Wilson Pond, half a mile distant, to see it and shoot what we might. Approaching carefully, hoping for a buck, we came to the edge of a pretty little pond, perhaps a quarter of a mile in circumference, a marsh at one end, another at the opposite, and woods on all sides. We sat down on a fallen log, just within cover, keeping very quiet, and in a few moments on the opposite marsh appeared a doe and fawn--the first wild deer Jim had ever seen. A few moments later another doe appeared and they fed slowly along the margin of the pond in full view. With our field glasses we could see them very distinctly, and watched them for half an hour until they vanished into the forest. It was beautiful sight, and we felt amply repaid for all our hardships. We became quite familiar with this sight, for during our week at Wilson Pond we rarely visited it without seeing from one to three deer feeding, always does or fawns, never a buck. The latter were on the ridges at this time, and finding plenty of water, rarely came to the ponds.

On returning to camp about 12 o'clock for dinner, we found Walter Armstrong, the mail man, bound on his journey into the lumber camps. The round trip is made three times a week by him and his brother alternately 23 miles each way, and for this the United States pays them $300 per year, less than $1 a day.

He stayed for dinner, and when he left us, we, thinking of our ten miles of the day before, were rather inclined to pity him with thirteen to fourteen more before him; but from the cheerful manner in which he slung his mail bag on and picked up his rifle and started off, he seemed not to mind it. A short nap over, we started back to the pond with rifle and rods. We had a fair shot at a doe, but as we wanted horns as well as meat we refrained, and went to casting from the shore. We soon landed a dozen trout weighing from ½ to 1lb., then crawling into the bushes we watched for our buck till sundown, but he did not come. There was no wind, the lake was a sheet of glass, and the only sounds heard were the occasional cry of an angry kingfisher, the chattering of ground squirrels, and once in a while the low, booming, penetrating, drumming of a partridge.

Our fish were served for breakfast, and from time we were seldom without trout in the larder. Our morning was spent about camp, while Bob and Albert went to the pond and built a raft from which to fish. The afternoon went quickly on the pond, catching trout about as fast as Bob could take care of them. When the sun sank low in the heavens we stopped, tired of catching fish, and pulling to shore watched for deer.

And thus a happy week passed away all to soon. It rained sometimes, perhaps a good deal, but we did not mind it. We tramped the woods for birds and deer or fished the lake to our heart's content. The extra trout were sent out to Mrs. Rainey by the obliging "U.S. Mail," and also a letter home, written on birch bark, enveloped in the same and sealed with pine pitch. Several times we would know the "mail" had passed by finding one or two partridges hanging on a tree at camp. We shot no deer, but saw numbers, and had one exciting still-hunt for yearlings buck, but frightened him. We had seen fresh caribou tracks several times, but his majesty did not show himself to us. One evening while poling the raft in I shot at a passing duck. Immediately we hear a heavy crash near the foot of the pond. Upon reconnoitering we found our caribou had been down to drink and my shot had sent him off; his tracks were large and deep and the water in them very muddy. Mr. Talcott shot this fellow about three weeks later, and he proved to be a royal animal of twenty-three points.

One morning, on going to the pond to watch for deer, we found a loon in possession, and not a particle of wind. We went back in the afternoon for fishing, carrying plenty of cartridges. The loon was still there and we had some fun with him. Jim's .38 and my .454 rang out alternately and our bullets chased him all over the pond. He did not get one full breath for half an hour; at times he was awfully rattled and once he rattled us. We expected him to rise at a certain point some distance off, but he bobbed up within 10ft. of the raft. It would be hard to say which was the more surprised. We shot and seemed to hit him, but didn't. When we left him his wild cry of triumph and derision followed us half way to camp. Bob declared the loon would get out that night, "if I had to climb a tree." The next morning he was gone.

During the week we grew strong and well. We took longer and longer tramps with less fatigue; we slept like babes and like backwoodsmen, always hungry, with what anxiety we watched the preparation for breakfast, dinner and supper, lest there should not be sufficient food cooked, but the *chef* gauged our appetites well and there was always enough left for Jerry. We made one little side trip, taking tent and provisions and staying over night at a small pond about three miles from the Wilson camp. The shore of the pond was literally embroidered with deer tracks. We watched that night and the next morning, but saw nothing but a little fawn. Albert was with me at one point, Bob and Jim at another, and we were completely hidden by undergrowth. It was about sunset and there was not a sound to disturb the stillness. Suddenly Jim heard a slight crackle as a of twig snapping behind her, and turning found a baby deer staring at her over a fallen log, only 5 or 6ft. away. In a second it turned, showing Bob the tip of its tail as it bounded into the undergrowth. At this little camp we had as visitors a number of jays (moose or meat birds as they are called locally), and we were much interested in them and their peculiar ways, their familiarity on short acquaintance causing much surprise and wonderment.

At length, we felt that we should move along, and so one morning Bob and Albert started with packs as heavy as I could lift to their shoulders and carried six miles to Frost Pond. We went with the second load and half a load more each completed the move, the latter part of which was made in the rain. Our camp at Frost Pond was prettily situated just off the road and within 100yds. of the lake. At one side a picturesque brook flowed, coming from Twin Ponds four miles away to empty into Frost Pond. We were now back in the United States, having crossed the boundary two miles before reaching Frost Pond; there had been a steady rise to that point and from it the descent began. On the one side all waters flowed into the St. Lawrence River, while on the other they went to form the Penobscot and thence to the Atlantic Ocean. We noticed on crossing the line that it was easier walking and not so muddy. A short stop of a day or two and we journeyed on. Bob had brought his canoe up from Dole Pond and was able to take all the luggage down by water. Albert, Jim and I went overland which included a six-mile carry, during which Jerry had a chance to show his untrained skill. We had fair shooting at partridges at our first camp, usually at single birds, but we here struck a covey which Jerry treed very nicely for us and we bagged five out of the lot, Jim shooting three straight. I missed one, Jerry found and brought them to us, and we felt that he had earned the bones he eventually received.

We landed at Dole Pond camp in the rain (we had begun by this time to look for rain whenever we moved), but our tent was rapidly pitched and we were soon under cover. The next day was Sunday and rainy. In the afternoon we had an agreeable call from Mr. Edgerly, manager of a large lumber plant. He was busy establishing new camps and getting ready for the winter's work. He expected to run four camps with crews of forty men each. We found him very entertaining, and on his invitation visited the home camp and took some photographs, including one of the crew, most of whom turned out of bed to have their pictures taken. One man was sharply sent back to put on his trousers, as a lady was present. They were a rough-looking lot, only about half of them being respectable woodsmen, which gave Mr. Edgerly the balance of power, but he needed all his mental and physical strength and all his courage, to manage the rest who came from parts unknown, stayed a few days or weeks and disappeared from camp, to be found scattered along the road toward Jackman, working or beating their way back to railroads and whisky. The rule prohibiting the use of intoxicating liquor is necessarily very strict, and some of the men get fighting drunk. They would be assisted to their bunks, willy nilly, and the next morning if an old hand, and the first offense, he would be forgiven, but if a new hand, he took the road to Jackman. The cook in a lumber camp is next in authority to the foreman of a crew; he has charge of all the supplies, domestic arrangements and the discipline. He is assisted by a "cookee," who is the drawer of water and the hewer of wood, and who also peels the potatoes. Logs for firewood are brought in at night by the returning teams. The food is coarse but wholesome and well cooked, and the men may eat as much as they desire.

Early Monday morning we packed up and were soon under way for Long Pond. Two trips with the canoe carried us and ours across Dole Pond and a two miles' carry brought us to Long Pond. This was the prettiest body of water we had yet seen. It was a lake three miles long by a quarter to three-quarters of a mile wide, surrounded to the water's edge with woods. The water was very high and we knew or chances for deer would be very fair. The carry road had brought us to the outlet of the pond, for we were beginning to swing back around the circle, and we again ascending. Long Pond empties its waters into Dole Pond and is another of the sources of the Penobscot. We paddled up the lake for a mile and a half, and on high ground, a stone's throw from the lake we found a deserted lumber camp which, after some vigorous house cleaning, we made our own; at least that portion of it that had been the kitchen and dining room.

We found the cabin, after a few repairs, dry and tight, and a stove left behind by the lumbermen served us well for cooking and heating purposes. In one corner was the cook's bunk and this, with some dry boughs made a comfortable bed for us. A long shed ran out from the entrance and made us a place to store our supply of dry wood while opposite to the entrance was a large, massive, log-built stable.

The weather was now getting cool, with heavy frost, and we found ice in the basin every morning. We spent pleasantly two or three days here, roaming the woods and looking for a lost pond known only to Bob and one or two others, and at which place Mr. Talcott had shot a caribou the year before. Our next move was to Portage Lake via Penobscot Lake. Bob and Albert carried part of the camp equipage over the four miles to Penobscot Lake the day before and we were able to take everything else on our trip; Bob carrying the canoe. Penobscot Lake is the most beautiful of all and is the largest of the sources of the Penobscot River. The surroundings are primeval--the lumberman had not yet desecrated God's handiwork and we were with nature--pure, grand and beautiful. The trout in this lake are large, plentiful and gamy, but we could not stop to have a try at them. We paddled to the opposite side and after a hasty dinner in the rain, we started over the half-mile carry to Portage Lake, and it was here we found our caribou. We were in usual marching order, Bob first, Jim next, I third and Albert bringing up the rear. It was raining heavily, which may have drowned the noise of our walking somewhat. We had reached a piece of woods more open than usual, when suddenly Bob stepped aside and backward, which brought him to Jim's shoulder, and there appeared before us in the path a magnificent bull caribou. It was a sight worth travelling a thousand miles to see, and sufficiently thrilling to give any one a sever attack of "buck fever." He stood with full face toward us, head elevated and thrown back in proud defiance. Jim had received her instructions, and at a touch from Bob, she raised her rifle, and as she did so the caribou leaped and lightning was not quicker than his movements. A couple of jumps at right angles in our path, into the woods, and he stopped, broadside to, with head again elevated and looked curiously at us. It was fatal to him. The rifle rang out; he plunged forward, partly rose--Bob said "Hit him again," Jim obeyed, another plunge and he was down, never to rise again. We rushed to where he lay and found him dead. Jim burst into tears and the strain and excitement were over. As Jim fired the second shot I brought my .45 into play, and broke his back, but my shot was unnecessary, for Jim had placed both of hers back of the shoulder.

He was a noble animal, and we could not repress a pang at having killed him; but the guide had no such sentimentality, and were soon dissecting the juiciest steaks.

The afternoon was half gone and there was much to be done, but we all worked industriously, and the carry was short. While we lugged the duffle over. Bob crossed the lake in the canoe with a load, and brought back from his camp a large row boat that carried all else remaining, and skirting the shores of Portage Lake for three miles, it was a happy party, though cold and wet, that landed about dusk at Bob's home camp. A good fire soon warmed and dried us and the camp, and caribou steaks were quickly in the pan. After supper we retired, but not before we had "talked it all over again."

The next morning the bright sun showed us the beauties of Portage Lake, the largest of that region. Well wooded, irregular shores, its surface studded with several islands, it is indeed beautiful. Opinions differ as to which is the more beautiful, Portage or Penobscot. They are fortunately close together, and a camp on one or the other is equally convenient, with perhaps the odds in favor of Portage.

We spent several days at Portage eating our caribou, visiting the lakes and points in the vicinity, and fishing, which we found superb. We seldom went without bringing in enough for camp use, and had we been more enthusiastic and diligent could have supplied Fulton Market.

There are thirteen lakes and ponds within a small radius of Portage, and nearly all contain trout of good size and game qualities. Some of these lakes are unknown except to Bob and at all of them one may be sure of the very best sport, as up to the present time they have been but little fished. Bob says June and July he can fill a canoe in short order. He says that sometimes during the summer, when not in the woods, he gets fish hungry, and leaving Mrs.

Rainey's in the early morning he goes to Portage and is back the same night with as many as he can carry.

At last we had to leave, and so Albert was sent out to see his baby and get Llewellyn and the team. They came the next evening and the following morning we started with our belongings on a buckboard with two horses attached, and made the nine miles to Mrs. Rainey's in about five hours. Dinner, a civilized wash and city clothes were resumed. The settling up was rapidly and agreeably accomplished, and by 4 o'clock we were en route for Jackman with sincere regrets that we must ever leave the country and the people. Staying all night in Jackman, the early morning train carried us to Lennoxville and thence home by sleeper, and thus ended the most glorious and satisfactory trip I have ever taken.

In conclusion I would like to say: The trip from New York, compared with that, to say, the Adirondacks, is long and expensive, but the gain more than compensates. The scenery is beautiful. It is as yet a region but little traversed. One can go assured of getting his full share of fish and game. Robert Elliott and the men he employs are truthful, honest, temperate and obliging. They are engaged at Mrs. Rainey's and paid from that time, saving the two or three day's extra pay for guides brought from a distance and the transportation for them and their belongings. They are thoroughly familiar with the country and are first-class woodsmen and hunters. We made a detour of about forty-five miles, as our wish was as much to see the country as to shoot and fish. One can spend the time at his disposal with perfect satisfaction in one camp, and I would recommend that at Portage Lake as preferable, all things considered. If one wishes to travel and explore, there are miles of wilderness to the eastward but little known to sportsmen and full of fish and game.

Every one you meet is anxious that you shall have a good time and will take any amount of trouble to facilitate it. The charges are extremely moderate, and we can pronounce no better recommendation than to declare with enthusiasm that we hope to go there again next year. Mr. Talcott had not employed the language of hyperbole--it is indeed a "Sportsman's Paradise."

– F. W. G.

A WINTER CAMP ON WADLEIGH BROOK

By John Burnham, from *Forest and Stream*, January 20, 1897

John B. Burnham from his biography (Courtesy of Ernst Mayr Library, Harvard)

John Bird Burnham (1869-1939) was born in Delaware, attended a military school and graduated from Trinity College in Hartford, Conn. As a young man he moved to Essex, New York near Lake Champlain, where he obtained a position as a journalist, and from where he would frequently take trips to the Adirondack region, as well as the Maine Woods and would write continuously about his adventures. In 1904 he was appointed as Chief Game Protector for the State of New York and in 1911 became President of the American Game Protection Association, a position he held until 1928. He later retired to his home in Westboro, New York on the shores of Lake Champlain.

The many adventures of this avid sportsman and the account of his involvement in the fledgling conservation movement were chronicled in "John Bird Burnham—Klondiker, Adirondacker and Eminent Conservationist," By Maitland C. De Sormo in 1978.

One day last November a New York doctor himself in need of doctoring, a farmer from that part of Lake Champlain where the Adirondacks and Green Mountains come closest, a business representative of a great fence company manufacturing the one and only elk high, fawn tight and buffalo strong fencing for parks, and lastly a FOREST AND STREAM man, came together by prearranged plan in the waiting room of the Boston & Maine Railroad in Boston, bound for the northern Maine forests.

The doctor, farmer, the fence expert and the newspaper representative dumped in one colossal pile their blankets, rifles and the miscellaneous assortment of boots, moccasins, heavy clothing and camp duffle that figured in their baggage and exchanged greetings, while the omnipresent station loafers debated among themselves whether they were "recruits for Cuby" or "only another lot of North Pole cranks."

It was a cold, raw day--that Nov. 21--and the air had a penetrating chill that suggested snow, resembling in this respect the corresponding day in 1895, when the writer left Boston at the same hour and with the same purpose in view. Then the snow had begun falling a little before noon, before Portland was reached, and continued all the afternoon and evening and well on into the night. History repeats itself and in this case the parallel was striking.

At a corresponding point on the journey before Portland was reached, one of the party looked up from the game of cards we were playing, in which the train boys' cinnamon wafers were utilized as chips, and announced that is was snowing, and when Portland was reached the ground was already white.

Here we had hoped for a chat with Mr. Harris B. Coe, of the Maine Central, who but for the exigencies of a presidential election would have been a member of our party, and who afterward was of invaluable service to us in the recovery of some lost baggage, but fate willed otherwise. North of Portland the snow fell merrily as per schedule, and at Bangor there was already a venturesome sleigh or two on the streets. This was the first snow of the season of any consequence, and we couldn't help feeling that it had been precipitated for our especial benefit.

In only on respect did our journey differ from that of the previous year, in that instead of a cold, cheerless wagon ride from the main line of the Bangor & Aroostook R.R. to Patten, we went this time by train. Otherwise the snow was about the same as last year. We enjoyed equally good hot accommodations at the Patten House, and Herb Brown was on hand with the same intelligent team of black horses to take us back to camp.

Sunday morning dawned bright and cold, with a shrewd wind blowing across the open fields through which the first part of our journey lay, and the road blown bare of snow for long stretches, which necessitated traveling on wheels instead of runners.

At noon we stopped for dinner at Louis Cooper's house, twelve miles from Patten. Mr. Cooper has accommodations for sportsmen both here and at a camp on Sebois Stream, a few miles away, and those who come for deer rarely go away disappointed. In summer there is good fishing in the two Shin Ponds, which are no great distance off. The next cleared land is at Sebois House, ten miles beyond. This is kept by George Cooper, a brother of Louis Cooper, and here we spent the night. Under favorable conditions we might have gone through to Trout Brook Farm, ten miles further, in one day, but we had struck particularly bad traveling. The road had been worn deeply by heavy toting, and in places was full of water covered by ice that, while not strong enough to bear buckboard and team, was sufficiently thick to make it both hard and dangerous work for the horses pulling through.

In this respect the following day saw a condition of affairs still worse. The horses were obliged at times to plunge through mud holes, breaking through viciously tough ice and sinking to their bellies at every jump. Under such conditions it was no wonder that they fell down repeatedly and were badly cut by the ice, and that we were the best part of a day in going ten miles. The remarkable thing was that we got through at all.

That was a cold ride, but in the woods, despite the fact that the thermometer registered 20° below zero, the air did not feel so chill as it had in the open country at the start of our journey.

At Sebois House we met Frank McKinney, who has a camp at Hay Lake in a good moose and deer country, six miles or so south of this point. McKinney is the man who killed a bull moose last fall with a .22cal. Stevens pistol, shooting the short cartridge and a charge of smokeless powder.

He heard the moose calling, and standing behind a tree let him approach within 30ft. before firing. His first bullet went through the moose's heart, but the great animal stood perfectly still, apparently uncertain of his enemy's whereabouts, till McKinney had fired a number of additional shots, all hitting near the same spot. Then he started to run, and the hunter followed, firing at every opportunity, till finally the moose succumbed and fell. The shots varied greatly in penetration, some sticking in the tough skin of the side from which they were fired, while others went completely through the animal.

McKinney has the proud distinction of having killed his moose with the smallest regular cartridge made, and if any one wants to beat his feat he will have to try a BB cap or in air gun; but he is not the only man who has killed this king of the game animals with a pistol. Wm. Cuvrins, the lumberman, a year or two ago shot and killed a large moose with a .32cal. Smith & Wesson hammerless revolver, with a 3 ¼ in. barrel and the coarse factory sights. Cuvrins is a man who travels through the woods a great deal in connection with this business, and he is a first-class shot with either pistol or rifle. He killed this moose at ten rods and only fired one shot. McLain, Jr., at Sourdnahunk Lake, shot and killed a large buck this fall with a .22cal. pistol at a distance that would be a fair rifle shot. This deer was shot through the heart and went no further than if hit by a rifle ball. There is food for reflection in the possibilities of these little weapons in the hands of expert hunters.

Five miles or so after leaving Sebois House we had our first view of the East Branch Grand Lake. This is a beautiful sheet of water, surrounded by hardwood ridges and good hunting country, and also affording a magnificent mountain view south toward Katahdin and the Traveler Range. At the head of the lake is Samuel Harvey's camp, and here we found deer tracks in the clearing right up to within 50yds. of the house, so thick that we thought they had been made by a drove of sheep. Harvey keeps no sheep, however, and his mutton is spelled with a v, except perhaps during the summer months.

Four miles further, having meanwhile crossed the East Branch of the Penobscot above the lake, we swung across the bridge over Trout Brook, were whisked up a hill and down again, and with the customary flourish drew up in front of the hospitable door of Trout Brook Farm, here nestled behind a perpendicular mass of trap rock. This is a favorite point for sportsmen, within striking distance of moose and caribou and surrounded by an unexcelled deer range. On our way out we found at this place two genial Worcester sportsmen, Messrs. J. D. Morton and C. A. Middlemas, who killed three bucks in less than a week.

Here also we found Jock Darling and his grandson, Natey Fogg, whom I doubt if the Pine Tree State produces a better hunter for his years, or a better camp companion. Natey is a chip off the old block and has the same natural aptitude for the woods that characterizes Jock. Like poets and other geniuses, woodsmen are born and not made; also with the woodsman it counts for a good deal to come from the right stock. I suppose Jock is descended direct from Robin Hood, and the strain is the same with Natey.

Jock and Natey had walked across from Sebois Lake, and at the farm secured a river driver's tent, 16ft. long, which was constructed like an Adirondack camp (or half of an A tent cut in two along the ridge) and a number of heavy quilts and blankets, cooking utensils and camp supplies.

We shivered a little at the thought of sleeping out in that tent, which was all front door and the epitome of open-handed hospitality to the elements; but we had a good deal of confidence in Jock and were ready to take his word for it that we would not be uncomfortable. Fortunately we had taken especial precautions before leaving to provide ourselves with an ample stock of heavy clothes and the warmest Jaeger underwear that could be purchased, and plenty of it; so that in the coldest weather we could wear two or three suits at a time. As an actual fact, we were more often too hot than too cold, and the time the mercury went down to 22° below zero the fence man got up in the middle of the night and, standing under the cold, glittering stars, shed a layer or two of his surplus clothes, remarking that the night was so warm he could not sleep comfortably as he was.

That afternoon we all went out for a short hunt, and twenty minutes after leaving the house Dr. Wright got a shot at a deer. They were on the jump, however, when he fired, and he did not score. To the fence man fell the honor of securing the first game. It was the following morning, and we had almost reached the spot selected for our camp on Wadleigh Brook, half a mile in from the tote road, when Hoisington, who was walking ahead of the team, saw some fresh tracks crossing the road. He followed them a short distance to investigate, and presently saw a small buck standing under a tree 50yds. away, looking back over his shoulder. He knew that the deer was likely to take alarm at any instant, as he could hear talking and the noise made by the team behind; so he took a quick aim and fired. Several other deer near by dashed off at the sound of the shot, but the particular one at which he had fired fell within 40ft. of the spot where he first stood. The ball had entered back of the opposite shoulder. It was an ugly wound, and though the bullet had missed the heart, it had killed much more cleanly than the average of such shots, and thus at the very start vindicated the effectiveness of the little 6 ½lb. .30-30 Winchester from which it was fired.

For supper that night we had juicy venison steaks, albeit not so tender as other cuts were later, but vastly preferable to anything else our larder afforded.

The buck was very fat, and I doubt if venison was ever more truly appreciated. We began at the hindquarters, and little by little, through the medium of the frying pan and broiler, converted the various parts to our use, till every shred of flesh had been devoured and only bones remained. It took us a little more than four days to accomplish this result.

Our camp was pitched directly in the old tote road up Wadleigh Brook, and if any future visitor finds a particularly smooth spot 12ft. or so in length in the road he will recognize our bed. Roads in this part of Piscataquis county are nothing to brag on as a rule, but we will back that 12ft. section to be equal to anything in the State, and we know whereof we speak, for we all labored individually for its improvement.

The foundation of our bed was of balsam fir boughs, and over the several sacks of straw were laid on, and on top of all a heavy quilt. The bed was bout 7ft. in width, and the tent roof slanted upward from where it was pinned to the ground at the back to a height of 6ft. or so in front. Opposite and also at one end Jock erected wind breaks of boughs, supported by pole frameworks and slanting in toward the center, and on the fourth side a piece of burlap was stretched as a sort of door.

In the center of the open space between windbreak and tent the fire was built, and on cold nights the camp resembled a miniature volcano, belching a steady stream of fire and sparks from the opening in the top.

In daylight the moosebirds were a constant source of amusement about camp. They made themselves at home from the moment camp was pitched, and investigating our belongings with their characteristic easy familiarity. Soft things that they could swallow seemed to interest them most, and they sampled every such article from Pear's soap to "moccasine." These birds, though their confidence is constantly abused, never seem to learn distrust of man. They perch upon the lumberman's balanced stick just as confidently as they did a hundred years ago, and when this backwoods humorist gives the other end of their seesaw a rap with his axe that shoots them 20ft. into the air that they just as much surprised as ever.

We let the birds eat their fill of the soap, for we had plenty of that, and anyhow soap was not altogether essential to our life in the woods, but it was different with the moccasine. Our boots and moccasins needed constant greasing both to soften them and make them waterproof, and we used it for a thousand other things as well, so our one box of this precious article was carefully guarded.

It was a specific for chapped lips and noses, though it must be acknowledged that it smelled better than it tasted, and this fact prevented our using it as butter when that staple gave out, although the question was seriously considered. It was also proved a good gun grease, and we found it to be a superior lubricant for bullets when we came to reload some of our ammunition with light charges for partridges.

For a day or two we hunted about camp, seeing deer, but for one reason or another not meeting with success. Du Bois, while walking up the main tote road saw two large bucks across Trout Brook, and wounded one very badly. This buck lay down almost immediately, proving the seriousness of his wound, but the approach of night obliged the hunter to leave it, and a snowstorm that followed obliterated the trail before morning.

The first good hunting day, however, all hands, including Jock, who, though in fairly good physical condition, has not since his long confinement in the hospital regained his old hardiness, set out for the burnt land. A mile and a half up Wadleigh Brook from our camp we had our first view of them, and here we jumped a large deer that went bounding off up a hillside fifty rods away.

At this point the party separated. Natey, R. Wright and Du Bois crossed the brook with the intention of working along the north side of the burnt mountain, and then circling back and striking the brook near the upper dam; while Jock, Hosington and myself were to hunt the country nearer the brook and perhaps eventually circle around outside the others.

Shortly after the parties separated we jumped three deer that ran east through the big open. As we watched them disappearing 400 or 600 yds. away, looking for all the world like good-sized rabbits, we suddenly heard a volley of shots, and realized that we had driven them on to the other party.

That night around the camp-fire they did not seem particularly anxious to tell about the occurrence, but they finally acknowledged shooting in self-defense at some deer that tried to run over them. They said they were satisfied to have frightened the deer off and to have escaped the threatened assault, but there was a certain tone of aggravation in their remarks that belied their words. Later, at the station restaurant in Bangor, the Doctor was noticed critically examining some murderous looking clubs carved from birch roots. He said he was thinking of sending one to Natey, but no doubt he was also regretting the fact that he did not have one along himself that day in the burnt lands.

Jock soon gave up the hunt, as the walking was hard and his strength not equal to the task.

Hosington and Natey, while hunting independently, both found fresh tracks of several moose, and in each case a large one was among the number. Both followed their game till dark, and saw signs of recent feeding, but neither got a shot.

None of the rest of us saw moose tracks, but while making my way back to camp late that afternoon I stopped a fair-sized buck with a bullet through the neck.

A warm spell followed our hunt in the burnt lands, and from 20° below zero the thermometer rose to 50° above. Under the influence of the warm air the snow rapidly disappeared, and when freezing weather came again the hunting was very noisy. We had eaten up almost everything in camp and resolved upon a change of base. Accordingly, on Sunday afternoon, Nov. 29, we moved over to the Trout Brook Lumber Camp owned by Messrs. Dudley & Currins, and the following day Jock, the Doctor and myself went on to Sourdnahunk Lake for a few day's sojourn at McLain's camp.

Eight moose had been accounted for at Sourdnahunk Lake this season up to the time of our arrival, two of them having been killed only a few days before by the McLains.

These were large bulls, one having a spread of horns of 55in., and the other 47in. They lay just where they had fallen within a few rods of each other, back on a hardwood ridge no great distance from Thissel Pond. One great bull had careened over backward when hit, but fortunately had not broken his horns.

McLain's camp, which had been but recently opened for sportsmen, is well built of peeled spruce logs set vertically and battened with strips of bark. The roof is of spruce bark, which gives the camp a more picturesque effect than is common.

The McLain's, father and son, are successful trappers, and last year took 112 "sable," besides "black cat" or fisher, mink, fox and otter.

In one corner of the sitting room is a reminiscence of bear, in the shape of a heavy No. 5 Newhouse trap which has one jaw snapped in two and a spring missing as the result of tackling the wrong bear. The bear that wrecked that trap and got away must have been an unusually powerful animal. Near by is a shed moose horn, picked up by Joe Francis that is abnormal in that it has a tine 4 or 5in. long starting from the back edge of the palm and running parallel with it.

At Sourdnahunk I saw a black cat in a tall shrub, but though I tried to prevent its escape the big weasel succeeded in getting out of the tree before I could reach the base. It dropped so quickly that it seemed to go faster than the falling bark dislodged in the scramble.

Another day, while returning from a bog over toward Telos Lake after sunset, a buck deer sprang out of a thicket directly toward me. I was going along at a slashing gait at the time, making plenty of noise, and when the deer appeared he was within 30ft. on the jump. It took him but a second to wheel and disappear, and as my rifle sights were full of snow I did not get a shot. It is an open question whether the deer on hearing my approach thought it was another buck and wanted fight, or whether he got a baffling scent, and ran into me when trying to escape.

The traveling was very noisy during our stay at Sourdnahunk, and though we saw plenty of sign we got no game

Despite the reports from Maine that partridges have been scarce this year, we saw and unusual number. I had loaded some light ammunition for this game, with 5grs. of black powder and the 85gr. S. & W. pistol bullet, and found the charge very accurate and satisfactory except for the fact that it was difficult to seat the ball in the shell without loading tools, as it was a trifle too large. On Dec. 1, as I was returning to camp, I saw six partridges budding in birch trees. They were all close together, and the chances seemed good for killing two with one shot. Accordingly I drew out the cartridge in my rifle barrel and attempted to substitute one of the light charges; but the shell jammed, and do what I would I could not get it in the barrel. I tried in succession half a dozen cartridges, and each one stuck when about two thirds way into the barrel.

It was an extremely cold day, the thermometer being considerably below zero at the time; and the trouble was evidently due not only to the fact that the shells had been expanded by firing, but also to the contraction of the rifle barrel, as I proved afterward by inserting without difficulty all the cartridges when the barrel was warmed. I did not want to use a regular cartridge, as my stock of ammunition was very low, so I left the spot without killing any partridge.

Ten minutes later a spruce partridge flew up from under my feet into a low tree, and sat there stupidly regarding me.

I was still a little mad at losing the others, and I resolved to have this one for revenge, though I nearly did not believe he would be very good eating, being an old bird; so I cut a sapling 10 or 12ft. in length and fastened at the end a noose made from an old moccasin string, and carefully dangled it in front where he could stick his head into it.

The partridge bobbed his head backward and forward and sideways in a self-important way, looking at the noose as if he were critically examining it over the top of a pair of spectacles, and finally stuck his head squarely into it. The same instant I yanked, but as luck would have it the partridge got too far into the loup, and before I could get my hands on him he slipped through and escaped.

That night I related the incident, and was reminded that it was the 1st of December and that the partridge season was over--facts which had not occurred to me before.

Mr. Goodman, the scaler, who was sitting the other side of the stove, slapped his thigh and remarked:

"By George, I know now why it was I missed that partridge to-day when I threw my axe at him. I couldn't break a game law if I tried."

None of the Maine maps give much detail regarding the Trout Brook country. The headwaters of streams which serve to indicate the watersheds are misplaced, while such lakes as Sourdnahunk, which is about three-quarters of a mile in diameter, and Thissel Pond, which measures five-eights of a mile in its greatest dimension, are not set down at all. None of the maps show the deep bay on the north side of Sourdnahunk Lake known as Caribou Cove, and on all I have seen the roads are not given as used at the present time. For instance, the approach to Sourdnahunk Lake at present is by the well-traveled tote road up Trout Brook, but this is not shown on the maps, while Telos lakes down to the lower end of Chesuncook still appears. Of course these tote roads are constantly changing, and it is a difficult matter to keep track from year to year of those which are passable for teams, but with regard to the natural features it is different, and it is surprising that better maps do not exist.

The rough map printed herewith is intended to show some of the features of interest to sportsmen not given elsewhere, and will serve to illustrate the narrative. The dotted squares are six miles across.

In a general way it may be said that the country lying south of Trout Brook and between the stream and the East Branch is a continuous mountain range that finally culminates in Katahdin, 5,250ft. in height. This is the only mountain region of any consequence in Maine and its scenic attractions are noteworthy. From Grand Lake (Matagamon) and the west end of Sourdnahunk Lake the views are particularly impressive.

North of Trout Brook there are no mountains worthy of the name, and the country resembles other parts of the State, with characteristic bogs, ridges, dead water, streams and lakes.

Sourdnahunk Lake lies on a high plateau well up toward Katahdin. By right it should empty into the East Branch waters, but instead it has taken upon itself the vaster more difficult task of discharging its waters into the West Branch of the Penobscot. Its outlet, Sourdnahunk Stream,, has cut a passage through the southern enflanking mountains and rushes down wild gorges in tumultuous fashion, falling hundreds of feet in a few miles. There is nothing like this stream in Maine, and nowhere can such scenes be witnessed as occur there in May, when Messrs. Dudley and Currins start their log drive. The stream at best is the personification of untamed fury, but add the thousands of great spruce logs that go tearing along with it, shooting down over falls like bolts from some great catapult and disappearing in boiling caldrons below or splintering on the adamant rocks that oppose their passage and you have a picture of reckless passion that appalls the beholder.

The lumbermen have three dams with an aggregate head of 36ft. of water behind, and when a jam forms this great wall of water is sent hurling down upon it with a force for smashing and tearing that is absolutely relentless. Under ordinary conditions the water is let run at regular intervals for a few minutes at a time.

Besides their Trout Brook Camp Messrs. Dudley & Currins have two camps on Sourdnahunk Stream, but they have almost finished their operations in this country, and another year will no doubt move elsewhere.

In mentioning the natural features of this region, the burnt lands of Wadleigh Brook should have a prominent place. These lie mostly north and east of the brook from Burnt Mountain on the sough almost to Blunder Pond on the north, and extend in a northeasterly direction pretty well over toward Second Lake. In some places they have been burned over half a dozen times, and are so open that one can see half a mile at a stretch; but as a rule the ground is grown up with small trees, maples and birch and poplar, that effectually prevent an extended outlook. These burnt lands are the natural summer home of moose and other game, but by December everything has moved into the surrounding green timber.

Early in December the caribou begin working down the mountains, and leaving their sprawling trails along the frozen streams and bogs of the Trout Brook country. They had been very abundant on Katahdin during the fall, feeding on the mosses above the timberline, and a lumberman named Rogers, who has camps well up toward the summit, reported that he had seen as many as eighty in one herd.

Caribou are stupid, and their flesh is not highly regarded as food, and it is a noteworthy fact that they are despised by many of the native hunters, who sometimes shoot them down from pure wantonness, piling up their carcasses as long as the animals are in sight or until their ammunition is exhausted.

The morning of Dec. 3rd, Houghton, Du Bois and Natey, who were again in camp on Wadleigh Brook, discussed their plans. Du Bois said: "Natey and I will go across Trout Brook and kill a deer," to which Hosington responded: "Well, I guess I'll go up toward the burnt lands and get a caribou."

Strangely enough, both predictions were fulfilled to the letter. Du Bois got a large doe within a few hours after leaving camp, and even in less time Hosington had killed a caribou.

The thermometer hung on a nearby tree registered 18° below zero at 7:30, when the hunters left camp. Thinking that Wadleigh

Brook would be well frozen, Hosington resolved to go on the ice. There was some thin places on the rapid stream, however, and soon after leaving camp he got his feet wet. He quickened his pace to start the circulation and prevent freezing, and the snow on the ice creaked so loudly in the frosty air that it seemed next to impossible to surprise any game. However, as he rounded a bend in the stream he saw a deer standing on the bank in plain sight looking at him, but before he could fire the deer turned and plunged into the woods. This served as a warning to go more cautiously, and as subsequent events proved was a very lucky occurrence. Game was afoot that wintry morning, and, like the hunter, found that the brook afforded an easy means of travel.

When less than a mile from camp Hoisington suddenly saw the antlered head of a caribou regarding him from the concealment of the tall grass and bushes growing on a point above. The same instant the animal whirled around to run, but just as quickly the little smokeless powder gun spat out its veto, and down he went, shot through the spine just back of the shoulder blades. The caribou tried to rise, but a second shot, fired for safety, pierced his heart, and he was dead when the hunter reached the spot. The caribou was a bull with a very compact and pretty set of horns. The antlers were just ready to drop, and when he fell one loosened and came off. After dressing him Hoisington returned to camp and later went out to drag him in on the ice. This time he had no rifle with him and while sitting on the caribou's body resting he saw a big buck with five points to a side come out on the ice only a few rods away and paw and strut and dare anything to fight him. It was highly aggravating to take the old buck's "sass," but there was no help for it, and finally the buck got tired and went away.

On the 3rd of December Dr. Wright and myself started back for our camp on Wadleigh Brook by a rather round-about way. We crossed little Sourdnahunk Lake on the ice, and by paced measurements made it three-quarters of a mile in diameter. The lake is oval in shape and beautifully situated among hardwood ridges. Half a mile further is Thissell Pond, an equally pretty sheet of water and only slightly smaller. East of both ponds and forming the apex of a triangle drawn from them lies a good caribou bog, which is perhaps a mile long, but so grown up with trees that no extended view can be had. This bog is in the Trout Brook watershed emptying into East Branch waters. Thissel Pond by its outlet flows into Webster Lake, and so into the East Branch, while the waters of Little Sourdnahunk Lake eventually find their way into the West Branch of the Penobscot.

Additional interest attaches to this spot from the fact that a brook that takes its rise a short distance west flows into Telos Lake, formerly on the watershed of the St. John River, but now connected by canal with Webster Lake and the Penobscot.

Beyond Thissel Pond the descent is rapid almost all the way to Webster Lake. Thissel Brook, which we followed, is a tumbling trout stream with steep banks, wooded for long stretches with a beautiful growth of beech, maple, birch and other hardwoods. Along in the afternoon we came out on a bog which extends on both sides of the main stream for a mile or more, and which reaches back also along tributary streams from the east and west. Here we jumped a large buck, who went bounding away over the brown bog grass in plain sight for some distance. Below the dam on Thissel Brook we ran across a moose track which had been made probably within an hour, but it was growing late and we had no time to spare following it.

About sunset we sighted Webster Lake through the trees and took a short cut across on the ice to the dam. Below the dam we found fairly good walking on the old tote road, but the snow was deeper than any we had previously encountered. A mile beyond the dam we sighted some old deserted lumber camps on a hill above the road and thought at first they were Finch's camps, where we expected to spend the night, but soon discovered our mistake.

For a mile further we plodded along in the darkness without any encouragement, but at the end of that distance we struck a recently traveled road and knew we must be near our destination. At this point the road crossed Webster Brook, an angry-looking rapid stream 60ft. in width, and we were uncertain on which side the camp lay.

We decided to try the south side first, and as luck would have it found the camp only a few hundred rods away. And never were weary travelers more glad of shelter. The Doctor's beard and eyebrows were covered with ice, our trousers frozen to board-like stiffness, and our bodies chilled by the arctic cold.

Next morning we got an early start. Finch's Halfway Camp is situated on the outlet to Hudson Pond, and a good road follows the brook up to the pond a distance of about a mile. The pond is half a mile across and contains several rocky islands, on one of which Jock Darling saw a caribou last winter.

He tried to shoot it as it trotted away, but his Bullard refused to go off. How the caribou ever got on the island is a puzzle, as its sides are as steep as a church roof where they are not perpendicular.

It was our intention to cross from Hudson Pond directly to the burnt lands, which are not great distance off to the southeast, without going near the main Blunder Pond (Mr. Finch, who has lumbered in this neighborhood informed us that there are at least three ponds of this name), as the country immediately around the pond is said to be very thick and swampy. Accordingly we lay our course a little east of south along the side of a hardwood ridge where the walking was good. While traveling along this ridge we unexpectedly ran directly on to a large buck coming toward us. We opened fire, and each of us managed to get in a couple of shots before he disappeared. Subsequently we found that three of these shot had hit him, but unfortunately all had gone low. We followed up his trail a short distance, and noting but a little blood decided to leave him alone for a little while and investigate an old moose trail that we happened on. This led us to a thick growth of balsam fir, where we found fresh signs of three other moose.

The moose had evidently gone into winter quarters here, for beds and signs of feeding were on all sides. There was one large bull among them, how large I hesitate to say; but he had refused to go between trees in places where one could almost have driven a team of horses through, and his track, where the snow had thawed out of it, looked like an elephants.

The snow was crusty, and it was a practical impossibility to get up to a moose in such thick growth, so we reluctantly left the yard, hoping to come back the next day if the conditions should be more favorable.

Taking up the buck's trail, we followed very cautiously, and would have succeeded in getting a shot as he rose from the spot where he had lain down had it not been for an untoward incident, which set him off on the jump. Previous to this he had been going west and had carried us within hearing of the groaning ice on Blunder Pond, but now he started directly down wind in an easterly direction. Every step he took in this direction brought him somewhat nearer our camp on Wadleigh Brook; so after consultation we decided to follow him up, knowing that, as he had our wind, he would keep going as long as he could stand. And so we followed along, constantly hopping that he would shape his course more to the south, which would have suited us exactly. Instead, however, he veered if anything more to the north, and led us a long and weary chase. It was 9 when we first saw him, and not till 2 that afternoon did we get close enough for the *coup de grace*. Meanwhile he had adopted every tactic known to his tribe to throw us off his trail, passing through bands of other deer, and walking over every piece of bare ground he could find. Once he had succeeded in getting eight or ten caribou to walk all over his trail, so that in places it was completely obliterated, but it was easy work to follow it here compared to times when it passed over bare places where the ground was hard frozen and rocky.

Successful tracking is largely a matter of elimination, and at times the only way a trail can be followed is by considering all possible courses and striking out the less likely ones.

On our way to camp after sunset that night we jumped a moose on the edge of some green timber. Below us on the hillside we heard a thump, thump, that sounded like someone chopping, as he went off on a sharp trot. A moment later we came across the track, which proved that he was a big one.

It was three hours after dark when we reached camp, and we had gone through some vile holes to get there, but all was forgotten in the pleasure of the reunion with the other members of the party, and the big fire and generous supper.

Dec. 5 was our last day in camp. We got an early start and went up the brook four miles to the spot where the buck killed near the upper dam (which was the fourth on the brook) was cached. Hoisington and Du Bois took the job of dragging him to camp on the ice, and Dr. Wright and I set out across country for our buck.

The night before we had come out on the brook two miles below this point, but snow had fallen since then and made it impossible to retrace our trail. It seemed like a hopeless task to try to find the deer miles back in a country full of hummocks--meaningless ridges--and absolutely devoid of any striking natural features to serve as landmarks, but neither of us would give up while there was a ghost of a chance of success.

Laying our course by instinct, we struck off in a northeasterly direction through a part of the burnt lands of which neither of us had any previous knowledge.

The general character of the burnt land was the same here as elsewhere. The ground was broken into low, parallel ridges running for the most part northeast and southwest. These ridges are almost devoid of soil, and the salty under stratum is frequently exposed, its coverings having been consumed by fire. Narrow strips of lowland between the broader ridges are frequently swampy and wet, and here the forest has escaped the fate that was its lot elsewhere. These belts of green timber furnish a retreat for scattering deer and moose during the day, though probably the larger portion of game at this time was in the main body of forest surrounding the burnt area.

Game trails invariably run along the ridges in the prevailing northeast and southwest directions, and the walking is, of course, easiest on these trails. Everywhere are fallen trees, but these are mostly branchless stubs and lie flat on the ground, making the traveling easier that it would otherwise be. As a general thing these trees have fallen parallel with the course of the ridges, which no doubt accounts for the uniform direction of the game trails.

A three-mile tramp brought us about noon to a spot that seemed familiar. The country had assumed a rougher and more irregular character, and the ridges had lost their uniformity and were disjointed and peaky. We stopped for a moment in a little hollow where the snow was deeper than was the rule on the open ridges, and a depression that the recent storm had failed to quite obliterate attracted our attention. Dr. Wright kicked the snow with his foot, and there under its white covering we saw a few crimson spots of blood, proving that the deer had passed that way.

A short distance beyond we crossed a little ridge, and there sure enough was the buck hanging up against a birch tree just as we had left him. It was like finding a needle in a hay stack to go to that deer, and we felt rather proud of our achievement.

The buck measured 8ft. 4in. as he hung, and he was very fat. We estimated that he would dress 220lbs., and probably we were well within the limit. He had a very pretty set of antlers with a spread of 18in.

It was dinner time when we reached the buck and we were hungry. Accordingly, Dr. Wright broiled sections of the buck's liver, while I skinned out the head and forequarters.

Afterward I shouldered the hams, which, together with the skin, weighed 67lbs., and the doctor took the head, axe and my rifle, which was the only one we had along, and we set out for camp, six miles away by the shortest course we could take.

Two miles from the spot where we killed the buck we came out on the isolated bog which lies northwest of the burnt mountain. We walked through this in a southwesterly direction to take advantage of the smoother traveling afforded, and when near the end of the bog spied two caribou forty or fifty rods away.

In a jiffy we had dropped our loads, and just about then the caribou sighted us and ran up a little nearer to investigate. We had their wind, and feeling confident that they would give us a better chance for a shot, waited, crouching down behind some low bushes, the only cover that offered.

The doctor wore a read toboggan cap, which seemed to interest the caribou immensely. They trotted first to one side and then to the other to try and get a good view of this. Red caps evidently were a novelty in the burnt lands. The cap had not been intended to decoy caribou, but had rather been taken to neutralize the effect of a leather hunting coat which was a good deal the color of a deer. Hunters are sometimes mistaken for game by their companions, with distressing results, so the doctor adopted the precaution of wearing the cap as a distinguishing feature, warning us not to shoot at "red-headed deer."

The caribou ran up within easy shooting distance, and at 80yds. I let drive at the biggest one, who immediately wheeled and ran. I rose to my feet and fired twice more, and at the last shot the caribou went down in a heap. All three shots had taken effect, but all had gone low, and when we examined the animal we found the only way I had gotten him was by actually shooting his legs off.

The caribou which I had killed was a large bull, but unfortunately his antlers had already been dropped.

Apparently he had but just lost them, as the scars on this head were fresh. The second caribou remained near the first after he had fallen, and at one time I was within 30yds. of it and could easily have killed it. By the time Dr. Wright reached the spot, however, he had gone.

On our way back to camp we ran across a number of fresh moose tracks, including some very large ones. This was the third occasion that day when we had seen fresh moose tracks, and all were in or on the edge of green timber. One large track had passed near the spot where the first buck was cached.

Soon after striking the trail left by Du Bois and Hoisington when dragging their game down Wadleigh Brook on the snow-covered ice, we noted the tracks of two caribou which had come along more recently. These caribou had sniffed the depression left by the body of the deer, and with a singular hardihood followed the trail down the brook. For a mile or more as we followed we saw they had treaded its every turning, influenced no doubt by a morbid curiosity, but just before camp was reached they had turned aside and gone into the woods.

Later we learned that another band of caribou, numbering three or four, had crossed the road earlier in the day a hundred yards below the camp. There was no question then that caribou were present in numbers.

We left Trout Brook Farm for the outer world the following day, slipping along at a rapid pace over the 6in. of new-fallen snow. Though late in the season and time for them to be going into winter quarters, the deer were still moving about a great deal, and we were never long out of sight of fresh tracks.

Once while going down a hill with the horses trotting for all they were worth to keep ahead of the coasting sled, we ran right into a herd of deer, which scattered in all directions. A large doe stood within a few rods of the road in plain sight as we passed, and she waited until Brown had pulled up the horses and some of the party drawn out their rifles and loaded. Then she wisely concluded she had seen enough, and made tracks after the others.

At Trout Brook Farm we said good-by to Jock and Natey, and also to Du Bois, who stayed behind a few days longer in hopes of getting a moose. In company with Natey he went over to Sebois Grand Lake, but the lumbering operations in that neighborhood had temporarily driven out all the moose and he came home without accomplishing his object.

– J. B. BURNHAM

LUGGING BOAT ON SOWADNEHUNK

By Fanny Hardy Eckstrom, from *Atlantic Monthly*, April 1904

Fanny Pearson Hardy Eckstrom (1865-1946) was born in Brewer, daughter of Manley Hardy, a well-known Maine fur-trader and Maine Woods authority. She attended Abbott Academy in Andover, Mass. and graduated from Smith College in 1888, where she founded the college Audubon Society. From 1889 to 1891 she served as superintendent of the Brewer School Department, the first woman in Maine to hold that position. She then worked as a reader for the Boston DC Health Publishing Company. In 1893 she married Rev. Jacob Eckstrom of Chicago and they lived at Eastport, Maine then Rhode Island, where he died. After his death Fanny and her two children moved back to Brewer.

Back in Brewer, she began a life-long career of collecting and writing about her beloved Maine. In 1901 she published her first two books, The Bird Book and The Woodpeckers. A few years later she published "Lugging Boat on Sowadnehunk" in the April 1904 issue of Atlantic Monthly. The editors of that magazine contacted her and suggested she put together a series of stories that would chronicle the West Branch and later that same year, Houghton Mifflin published The Penobscot Man. It soon went out of print, was reprinted in 1924 and several times after, remaining a wonderful account of the men who drove logs annually on the West Branch of the Penobscot in the nineteenth century. "Lugging Boat on Sowadnehunk" became the first story in her new book.

This is a Penobscot Story.

When the camp-fire is lighted, and the smoke draws straight up without baffling, and the branches overhead move only as the rising current of heat fans them, then if the talk veers round to stories of crack watermen, and the guides, speaking more to each other than to you, decide that it was Big Sebattis Mitchell who first ran the falls at Sowadnehunk,---though full twenty years before John Ross had put a boat over and come out right side up,---do not, while they are debating whose is the credit of being first, let slip your chance to hear a better tale; bid them go on and tell you how Joe Attien, who was Thoreau's guide, and him who followed after and who failed, were the ones made that day memorable.

And if our guides are Penobscot men, they will tell it as Penobscot men should, as if there were no merit in the deed beyond what any man should do as to throw away his life on a reckless dare, and count it well spent when so lavished. For so are these men made, as it was in those days of the beginning, so is it yet even to the present among us.

You will have heard, no doubt, of Sebattis, he who from his bulk was called by the whites Big Sebat, and from his lazy shrewdness was nicknamed by his tribesmen Ahwassus, the Bear. Huge and round he was, like the beast he was named for, but strong and wise, and in his dark flat face and small, twinkling eyes there were resources, ambitions, schemes.

Scores of you who read this will recollect the place. In memory you will again pass down the West Branch in your canoe, past Ripogenus, past Ambajemckomas, past the Horse Race, into the welcome deadwater above Nesowadnehunk. There, waiting in expectancy for that glorious revelation of Katahdin which bursts upon you above Abol, that marvelous picture of the giant towering in majestic isolation, with its white "slide" ascending like a ladder to the heavens, you forget yourself, did not hear the tumult of falling waters, did not see the smooth lip of the fall sucking down, were unconscious that just before you were the falls of Sowadnehunk. Then, where the river veers sharply to the right, you felt the guide spring on his paddle as he made the carry by a margin, and you realized what it would have been to drift unguided over those falls.

So it has always been,---the sharp bend of the river to the right, blue, smooth, dazzling; the carry at the left, bare, broad, yellow-earthed. Crossing it forty rods, you cut off the river again, and see above you to the right the straight fall, both upper and lower pitches almost as sheer as mill-dams, and in front the angry boil of a swift current among great and thickset rocks. So it always stays in memory,---at one end the blue river, smooth, and placid, and the yellow carry; at the other, the white hubbub of tossing rapids below perpendicular falls.

One May day long ago, two boats' crews came down to the carry and lugged across. They had lugged three miles on Ripogenus, and half mile on Ambajemackomus, besides the shorter carry past Chesuncook Dam; they had begun to know what lugging a boat meant. The day was hot,---no breeze, no shade; it was getting along toward noon, and they had turned out, as usual, at three in the morning. They were tired,---faint; hot; weary with the fatigue that stiffens the back and makes the feet hang heavy; weary, too, with the monotony of weeks of dangerous toil without a single day of rest, the weariness that gets upon the brain and makes the eyes go blurry; weary because they were just where they were, and that old river would keep flowing on the Doomsday, always drowning men and making them chafe their shoulders lugging heavy boats. There was not a man of them who could not show upon his shoulder a great red spot where the pole used in lugging boat, or the end of an oar on which barrels of pork or flour had been slung in carrying wangan, had bruised and abraded it. And now it was more lugging, and ahead were Abol and Pockwockamus and Debsconeag and Passagamet and Ambejejis and Fowler's and---there are, indeed, how many of them! The over-weary always add to the present burdens the mountain of future toil.

So it was in silence that they took out the oars and seats, the paddles and peavies and pickaroons, drew the boats up and drained them of all water, then, resting a moment, straightening their backs, rubbed the sore shoulders that so soon must take up the burden again, and ran their fingers through their damp hair. One or two swore a little as relieving their minds, and when they bent to lift a boat, one spoke for all the others.

"By Jinkey-boy!" said he, creating a new and fantastic oath, "but I do believe I'd rather be in hell to-day with ninety devils around me, than sole-carting on this carry."

That was the way they all felt. It is mighty weary business to lug on carries. For a driving-boat is a heavy lady to carry. The great Maynards, weight eight to nine hundred pounds, and they put on twelve men, a double crew, to carry one. The old two-streakers (that is, boats with two boards to a side where the big Maynards had three) were not nearly so heavy, and on short carries like Sowadnehunk were lugged by their own crews, whether of four men or six; but diminishing the crew left each man with as a great a burden. A short man at the bow, another at the stern, with the taller ones amidships under the curve of the gunwale if they were lugging without poles, or by twos fore, aft, and amidships for six men lugging with poles, was the usual way they carried their boats; and it was "Steady, boys, steady; now hoist her!"---"Easy, now, easy, hold hard!" for going downhill she overrode John and Jim at the bow, and going up a rise Jack and Joe at the stern felt her crushing their shoulders, and when the ground was uneven with rocks and cradle-knolls, and she reeled and sagged, then the men at the sides caught the whole weight on one or the other of them. Nothing on the drive speaks so eloquently of hard work as the purple, sweat-stained cross on the backs of the men's red shirts, where the suspenders have made their mark; they got this lugging boats on carries.

But they bent their backs to it, wiggled the boat up and forward to her place, each crew its own boat, and staggered on, feet bracing out, and spike-soled shoes ploughing the dirt and scratching on the rocks. They looked like huge hundred-leggers, Brodingnagian insects that were crawling over that yellow carry with all their legs clawing uncertainly and bracing for a foothold. The head boat crowded Bill Halpin upon a rock so hard that he fell and barked his shins on the granite; that dropped the weight suddenly upon Jerry Durgan's shoulder, so that a good two inches of skin was rasped clean off where it had been blistered before; little Tomah Soc stumbled in a hole, and not letting go his grip, threw up the other gunwale so that it half broke his partner's jaw. Those boats took all the mean revenges wherewith a driving-boat on land settles scores for the rough treatment it receives in the water.

They were lugging that May morning only because no boat could run those falls with any reasonable expectation of coming out right side up. For up to that time they had chiefly used the Wallace boat, built low and straight in the gunwale, raking only moderately at the bow and low in the side. It is related that when the great high-bowed Maynard batteaus were first put on the river, short old Jack Mann, who was pensioned in his latter days by P.L.D.,[1] looked with high disfavor on the big, handsome craft, and then, rushing into his boat-shop, demanded an axe, and auger, and a handsaw.

"What' that for?" asked the foreman, suspecting that it was but one of Jack's devices for unburdening his mind in some memorable saying.

"Want 'em to cut armholes in that blasted boat," growled Jack, insinuating that the bows were above the head of a short man like himself.

But the old boat,---you may yet sometimes see the bones of one of them bleaching about the shores of inland ponds, or lying sunbaked in the back yards of country farms,---stable and serviceable as she was, was no match for this handsome lady of to-day. They run the Arches of Ripogenus now with all their boats, and have done it for years; but at the time when Sebattis came down to Sowadnehunk, such water no man ever dreamed of running. It is likely enough that Sebattis, just back from a sixteen year' at Quoddy, did not know that it had ever been run successfully.

Be that as it may, when Sebattis and his bowman came down, the last of three boats, and held their batteau at the taking-out place a moment before they dragged her out and stripped her ready to lug, what Sebattis, as he sat in the stern with his paddle across his knees, said in Indian to his bowman was simply revolutionary.

"Huh?" grunted his dark-faced partner, turning in great surprise; "you t'ought you wanted to run it dose e'er falls? Blenty rabbige water dose e'er falls!"

1 The Penobscot Log-Driving Association, known as P.L.D. to distinguish it from P.L.A., the Penobscot Lumbering Association. It is always called either "P.L.D." " or "The Company." It owns all dams, booms, etc., and annually sells the drive at auction to the bidder contracting to take the logs down at the lowest rate per thousand.

The bowman had stated the case conservatively. That carry was there merely because men were not expected to run those falls and come out alive.

But the bowman's objection was not meant as a refusal; he knew Sebattis, that he was a good waterman, few better. A big, slow man, of tremendous momentum when once in motion, it was likely enough that all the years of his exile at Quoddy he had been planning just how he could run those falls, and if he spoke now, it was because this was the hour striking. In his own mind he had already performed the feat, and was receiving the congratulations of the crowd. It was no small advantage that he knew an audience of two boats' crews waiting at the lower carry-end to testify, however grudgingly, to the authenticity of what he claimed to have done.

The bowman had faith in Sebattis; as he listened to the smooth stream of soft-cadenced Indian that cast silvery bonds about his reluctance and left him helpless to refuse (Sebattis being both an orator in a public and a powerful pleader in a private cause), the bowman caught the rhythm of the deed. It was all so easy to take their boat out into midstream, where the current favored them a little, to shoot her bow far out over the fall, and as the crews ashore gaped in horrified amazement, to make her leap clear, as a horse leaps a hurdle. And then to fight their way through the smother of the whirlpool below, man against water, but such men as not every boat can put in bow and stern, such strong arms as do not hold every paddle, such great heads for management, and skill in watercraft as few attain.

This was the oration, with its Indian appeal to personal glory. It was, as Sebattis said, "Beeg t'ing," and he fired his bowman with the desire for glory. The Penobscot man, white man or Indian, dies with astonishing alacrity when he sees anything worth dying for. And the name of "crack waterman" is a shining mark to strive for.

Thus at the upper end of the carry Sebattis and his bowman talked over at their leisure the chances of dying within five minutes. At the other end the two boats' crews lay among the blueberry bushes in the shade of shivering birch saplings and waited for

Sebattis. It did not worry them that he was long in coming; they knew the leisurely Indian ways, and how unwilling, though he weighed hard upon two hundred and sixty, and had strength to correspond, was Big Sebattis to lug an extra pound. They pictured him draining his boat and sopping out with swab of bracken the last dispensable ounce of water, then tilting her to the sun for a few minutes to stream out a trifle more before he whooped to them to come across and help him. I did not worry them to wait,---it was all one in the end: there would be carries to lug on long after they were dead and gone.

So, looking at the logs ricked up along the shores and cross-piled on the ledges, looking at the others drifting past, wallowing and thrashing in the wicked boil below the falls, they lounged and chaffed one another. Jerry Durgan was surreptitiously laying cool birch leaves on his abraded shoulder, and Bill Halpin was attentively, though silently, regarding his shins; there had not been too much stocking between him and the "big gray." The Indians, stretched out on their backs, gazed at the sky; nothing fretted them much. On one side, an Indian and an Irishman were having a passage at wit; on the other, two or three were arguing the ins and outs of a big fight up at 'Suncook the winter before, and Province man was colloguing with a Yankee on points of scriptural interpretation. It was such talk as might be overheard almost any time on the drive when men are resting at their ease.

"It was French Joe that nailed Billy; Billy he told me so," came from the group under the birches.

From among the Indians out in the sunlight arose a persuasive Irish voice.

"Why is it, Tomah, that when your folks are good Catholics, and our folks are good Catholics, you don't ever name your children Patrick and Bridget?"

And the reply came quick: "'Cause we hate it Irish so bad, you know?"

Off at the right they were wrangling about the construction of the Ark.

"And I'd just like to have seen that bo't when they got her home," said the Yankee; "just one door an' one winder, an' vent'lated like Harvey Doane's scho'l'ouse. They caught him nailin' of the winders down. 'How be ye goin' to vent'late?' says they. 'Oh, 'says he, 'fresh air's powerful circulation stuff; I callate they'll carry the old air out in their pockets, an' bring in enough fresh air in their caps to keep 'em goin'; an' that was all they ever did get's long's he was school agent. My scissors! Three stories an' all full of live-stock, an' only one winder, an' that all battened down! Tell you what! I'd 'a' hated to be Mr. Noah's family an' had to stay in that ole Ark ten months an' a half before they took the cover off! Fact! I read it all up once!"

Said another: "I don't seem to' member how she was built, 'ceptin' the way they run her seams. She must have ben a jim-dicky house with the pitch all on the inside's well as on the outside o' her. Seems to me a bo't ain't bettered none by a daub of pitch where the' ain't none needed."

"'T ain't the Ark as bothers me some," put in the Province man; "I reckon that flood business is pretty nigh straight, but I couldn't never cipher out about that Tower of Babel thing. Man ask for a hod o' mortar, an' like enough they'd send him up a barrel of gaspereau; that's"---

The religious discussion broke off abruptly.

"Holy Hell!---Look acomin'!" gasped the Yankee.

Man! but that was a sight to see! They got up and devoured it with their eyes.

On the verge of the fall hovered the batteau about to leap. Big Sebat and his bowman crouched to help her, like a rider lifting his horse to a leap. And their eyes were set with fierce excitement, their hands cleaved to their paddle handles, they felt the thrill that ran through the boat as they shot her clear, and, flying out beyond the curtain of the fall, they landed her in the rapids below.

Both on their feet then! And how they bent their paddles and whipped them from side to side, as it was "In!"---"Out!"---"Right!"---"Left!" to avoid the logs caught on the ledges and the great rocks that lay beneath the boils and snapped at them with their ugly fangs as they went flying past. The spray was on them; the surges crested over their gunwales; they sheered from the rock, but cut the wave that covered it and carried it inboard. And always it was "Right!"---"Left!"---"In!"---"Out!" as the greater danger drove them to seek the less.

But finally they ran her out through the tail of the boil, and fetched her ashore in a cove below the carry-end, out of sight of the men. She was full of water, barely afloat.

Would Sebattis own to the boys who were hurrying down through the bushes that he had escaped with his life only by the greatest luck? Not Sebattis!

"Now you bale her out paddles," said he to his bowman, and they swept her with their paddles as one might with a broom.

"Now you drain her out," commanded Sebattis, when they could lift the remaining weight, and they raised the bow and let the water run out over the slanting stern, all but a few pailfuls. "Better you let dat stay," said the shrewd Sebattis.

It was quick work, but when the crew broke through the bushes, there stood Sebattis and his bowman leaning on their paddles like bronze caryatids, one on either side of the boat. They might have been standing thus since the days of the Pharaohs, they were so at ease.

"Well boys, how did you make it?" queried the first to arrive on the spot.

Sebattis smiled his simple, vacuous smile. "Oh, ver' good; she took in lill' water mebbe."

"By gee, that aint much water! Did she strike anything?"

Sebattis helped turn her over. She had not a scratch upon her.

Then the men all looked again at the boat that had been over Sowadnehunk and they all trooped back to the carry-end without saying much, two full batteau crews and Sebattis and his bowman. They did not talk. No man would have gained anything new by exchanging thoughts with his neighbor.

And when they came to the two boats drying in the sun, they looked one another in the eyes again. It was a foregone conclusion. Without a word they put their galled shoulders under the gunwales, lifted the heavy batteau to their places, and started back across that carry forty rods to the end they had just come from.

What for? It was that in his own esteem a Penobscot man will not stand second to any other man. They would not have it said that Sebattis Mitchell was the only man of them who had tried to run Sowadnehunk Falls.

So they put in again, six men to a boat, full crews, and in the stern of one stood Joe Attien, who was Thoreau's guide, and in the bow Steve Stanislaus, his cousin. That sets the date,---that it was back in 1870,---for it became the occasion for another and a sadder tale. If only Steve Stanislaus had held that place for the rest of the drive, it is little likely that we should have to tell the story of the death of Thoreau's guide.

And they pushed out with their two boats and ran the falls.

But the luck that bore Sebattis safely through was not theirs. Both boats were swamped, battered on the rocks into kindling wood. Twelve men were thrown into the water, and pounded and swashed about among the logs and rocks. Some by swimming, some by the aid of Sebattis and his boat, eleven of them got ashore, "a little damp," as no doubt the least exaggerative of them were willing to admit. The unlucky twelfth man they picked up later, quite undeniably drowned. And the boats were undeniably smashed. Indeed, that was the part of the tale that rankled with Sebattis when he used to tell it.

"Berry much she blame it us" (that is, himself) "that time John Loss." (Always to the Indian mind John Ross, the head contractor of the drive, was the power that commanded wind, logs, and weather.) "She don' care so much 'cause drowned it man, 'cause she can get plenty of it men; but dose e'er boats she talk 'bout berry hard,"

That is how they look at such little deeds themselves. The man who led off gets the credit and the blame; he is the only one remembered. But to an outsider, what wins more than passing admiration is not the one man who succeeded, but the many who followed after and failed, who could not let well enough alone when there was a possible better to be achieved, but, on the welcome end of the carry, the end where all their troubles of galls and bruises and heavy burdens in the heat are over, not one man of them falling out, and lug them back a weary forty rods to fight another round with Death sooner than own themselves outdone.

Chapter 6

THE NORTH MAINE WOODS

The northern Maine Woods includes all the vast territory north of the West Branch of the Penobscot and everything north of Washington County. The western part of this region is a virtual wilderness of trees, lakes, ponds and rivers, while the eastern segment was opened up into vast fields, becoming one of the major potato growing markets in the country.

Few adventurers travelled to this northern region in the early 19th century as it was very inaccessible, and most sporting in Northern Maine was limited to the Allagash River. Access was made by going from Moosehead Lake down the West Branch to Chesuncook, then over the Mud Pond Carry into Chamberlain Lake, where an early depot farm was built. In 1831 Deane and Cavanaugh traveled down the Allagash to record the settlers on the St. John River for the State of Maine and this is the oldest known account of a trip on that river. In 1838 James Hodge also made a trip down the river on a geological survey of northern Maine, in 1844 William P. Parrot made a plan of the Allagash and in 1847 Noah Barker lotted out fifteen townships along the northern part of that river. Later accounts were written about trips down the St. John River and the Aroostook River.

The first adventurers into this vast forest were the lumbermen, who cut the many pumpkin pine and lumber camps were erected annually all through the woods to cut the lumber in the winter. These log camps were quickly abandoned when the snow left, waiting for the river drivers to float the logs down the rivers to the numerous saw mills at Old Town when the freshet began in March and April. These empty log camps were available havens for any passing sportsmen or paddler.

Travel to Aroostook County was generally made by the Houlton Road until the Bangor and Aroostook Railroad Company was formed in 1891. Three years later it reached Houlton and was extended to Van Buren by 1899. An alternate branch was completed in 1896, extending to Ashland and as soon as it was done, sporting camps began cropping up almost overnight, as now sportsmen in New York and Boston could take a train into the northern woods, getting off at Oxbow, Masardis and Ashland. It was later continued and stops could be made at Portage, Winterville and Eagle Lake, opening up the most northern part of Maine. From these stations buckboards and sometimes boats would take them to the lakes and rivers where they would "rough it," and later to sporting camps that were built on the myriad lakes and ponds for wonderful fishing in the spring and moose hunting in the winter.

After the pines were depleted railroads were completed right into the woods and would bring eager sportsmen into the woods and spruce pulp, game hides and returning sportsmen on the way out. Of the hundreds of sporting camps that were erected, many were closed before the 1930s, but a dozen of the original camps still offer hospitality to sportsmen and families. Some of these old quaint camps that are still open are Bradford's Camps, Chandler Lake Camps, Eagle Lake Camps, Libbey Camps, Munsungan Hunting and Fishing Club, Red River Camps, Umcolcus Sporting Camps and Willard Jalbert Camps. Today many tourists and sportsmen fly into the more remote camps or arrive after many hours and miles of travel on the lumber roads.

A BEAR STORY

By John Springer, from *Forest Life and Forest Trees*, 1851

Black Bear (From Springer's Forest Life and Forest Trees, p. 33)

After preaching for seven years, John S. Springer (1811-1883) settled in Boston where he ran a dry goods shop in 1851, the same year he published his well-known book Forest Life and Forest Trees. The book was so well received that a second edition was printed in 1856.

Springer's book, the definitive work on early eighteenth century lumbering in Maine, is divided into three parts. The first part, called The Pine Tree, or Forest Life, tells the history and value of the pine tree market, general life in the lumber camps, logging in the winter, the trials of getting logs out of the woods to the river and teamster driving. In this section Springer also included several stories of logger's encounters with bears.

This story takes place on the Madawaska River, which begins in Quebec and flows south to join the St. John River in northeastern Maine.

More sanguinary was the following encounter, which took place in the vicinity of Tara-height, on the Madawaska River. A trap had been set by one of the men, named Jacob Harrison, who being out in search of a yoke of oxen on the evening in question, saw a young bear fast in the trap, and three others close at hand in a very angry mood, a fact which rendered it necessary for him to make track immediately. On arriving at the farm, he gave the alarm, and, seizing an old dragoon saber, he was followed to the scene of action by Mr. James Burke, armed with a gun, and the other man with an ax.

They proceeded direct to the trap, supplied with a rope, intending to take the young bear alive. It being a short time after dark, objects could not be distinctly seen; but, on approaching close to the scene of action, a crashing among the leaves and dry branches, with sundry other indications, warned them of the proximity of the old animals. Within a few steps of the spot, a dark mass was seen on the ground--a growl was heard--and the confined beast made a furious leap on Jacob, who was in advance, catching him by the legs. The infuriated animal inflicted a severe wound on his knee, upon which he drew his sword, and defended himself with great coolness.

Upon receiving several wounds from the saber the cub commenced to growl and cry in a frightful and peculiar manner, when the old she-bear, attracted to the spot, rushed on the adventurous Harrison, and attacked him from behind with great ferocity. Jacob turned upon the new foe, and wielded his trusty weapon with such energy and success that in a short time he deprived her of one of her fore paws by a lucky stroke, and completely disabled her. Eventually she had a desperate cut across the neck, which divided the tendons and severed the spinal vertebrae. Having completed his conquest (in achieving which he found the sword a better weapon than the ax), the animal being unable to knock it from his hand, every attempt to do so being followed by a wound), he had ample time to dispatch the imprisoned cub at leisure.

During the time this stirring and dangerous scene we have related was enacting, war was going on in equally bloody and vigorous style at a short distance. Mr. Burke, having discharged his gun at the other old bear, only slightly wounded him; the enraged Bruin sprang at him with a furious howl. He was met with a blow from the butt-end of the fowling-piece. At the first stroke the stock flew in pieces, and the next the heavy barrel was hurled a distance of twenty feet among the underwood by a side blow from the dexterous paw of the bear. Mr. Burke then retreated a few feet and placed his back against a large Hemlock, followed the while closely by the bear but, being acquainted with the nature of the animal and his mode of attack, he drew a large hunting knife from his belt, and, placing his arms by his side, coolly awaited the onset.

The maddened brute approached, growling and gnashing his teeth, and with a savage spring encircled the body of the hunter and the tree in his iron gripe. The next moment the flashing blade of the *couteau chasse* tore his abdomen, and his smoking entrails rolled upon the ground. At this exciting crisis of the struggle, the other man, accompanied by the dog, came up in time to witness the triumphal close of the conflict.

Two old bears and a cub were the fruits of this dangerous adventure--all extremely fat--the largest of which, it is computed, would weigh upward of two hundred and fifty pounds. We have seldom heard of a more dangerous encounter with bears, and we are happy to say that Mr. Burke received no injury; and Mr. Jacob Harrison, although torn severely, and having three ribs broken, recovered under the care of an Indian doctor of the Algonquin Tribe.

A STORY OF THE MAINE WOODS

Anonymous, from the *Piscataquis Observer*, April 6, 1865

One of the oldest inhabitants of Northern Maine thus relates a race he once had with a catamount.

"Young man," said he, "when I first entered this town there were only three families living in it. You who now live here can never know the hardships and arduous scenes through which the early settlers lived. Come with me," he continued, "And I will show you the spot on which the first hut ever erected in this town was situated.

I followed silently, until this old man came to the bottom of the west side of a hill.

"There," said he, "on this spot was situated the hut. I shall never forget the first time I visited it and the story I was told."

"What is it?" I asked.

"I will tell you. When the first settler moved here, his nearest neighbor lived twenty miles distant, and the only road between the neighbors was a path that he cut through the woods, himself, so that in case of want or sickness, he might get assistance. One morning, I think it was the third season he had settled here, he was obliged to go for provisions. He arose early that morning and started for his nearest neighbor. People of the present day would not think it hard to make a journey of twenty miles for a bag of potatoes, and on foot too, such was the errand of the first settler. He arrived before noon and was successful getting his potatoes, got some refreshment, and started for home. But it was not easy to travel with a load of potatoes; and finally at sundown, he threw off his load and resolved to make a shelter and spend the night. I have been taken by him to the exact locality of it; it was situated on the other side of the stream.

"He built a shelter, struck a fire, and took out of his sack a piece of meat to roast. Ah! Young man," continued the narrator, "you little know with what relish a man ---tents his food in the woods; but as I was saying, he commenced roasting his meat, when he was startled by a cry so shrill that he knew at once that it came from nothing else but a catamount. I will now relate as nearly as I can in the language of the old settler himself.

"I heard every shriek," said he, "and it was repeated even louder, and it seemed nearer than before. My first thought was for my own safety. But what was I to do? I was at least ten miles from home, and there was not a single human being nearer than that to me. I next thought of self-defense, but I had nothing to defend myself with. In a moment I concluded to start for home, for I knew the nature of the catamount too well to think I should stand the least chance of escape if I remained in the camp. I knew too, that he would ransack my camp, and I hoped the meat which I had left behind might satisfy his appetite, so that he might not follow me after eating it.

"I had not proceeded more than half a mile, before I knew by the shrieks of the animal, that he was within sight of the camp. I doubled my speed, content that the beast should have my supper; although I declared I would not run if I had my trusty rifle with me. But there could be no cowardice in my running from an infuriated catamount, doubly furious, probably, by being hungry, and with nothing that could be called a weapon save a pocket knife.

"I had proceeded probably about two thirds of my way home, and hearing nothing more of the fearful enemy, began to slacken my pace, and that I had nothing to fear. I had left behind me about two pounds of meat, beef and pork, which I hope had satisfied the monster. Just as I had come to the conclusion that I would run no more, and was looking back, astonished almost at the distance I had traveled in so short a space of time, I was electrified with horror to hear the animal shriek.

"I knew then that my fears were realized. The beast had undoubtedly entered the camp, ate, and followed after me. It was about three miles to my log cabin and it had already become dark. I redoubled my speed, but I thought I must die. And such a death!

The recollection of that feeling comes to my mind as vividly as though I knew the animal was pursuing me. But I am no coward, though to be torn to pieces and almost eaten alive by a wild beast, was horrible.

"I calmly unbuttoned my frock with the determination to throw it off before the beast should approach me, hoping thereby to gain advantage of him by the time he would lose in tearing it to pieces.

"Another shriek and I tossed the garment behind me in the path. Not more than five minutes had elapsed before I heard a shrill cry as if he came to it. How that shriek electrified me! I bounded like a deer. But in a moment the animal made another cry, which told me plainly that my garment had only exasperated him to a fiercer chase.

"O, God," I said, "and must I die? I cannot, I must live for my wife and children;" and I ran even faster than I had done before, and unbuttoning my waistcoat, I dropped it in the path as I proceeded. The thought of my wife and children urged me to the most desperate speed, for I thought more of their unprotected state than the death I was threatened with—for should I die what would become of them?

"In a moment all the events of my life crowded through my brain. The catamount shrieked louder, and as fast as I was running, he rapidly approached me. Nearer and nearer he came, until I fancied I could hear his bounds. At last I came to the brook which you see yonder, which was double its present size, being swollen be recent freshets, and I longed to cool my fevered brain in it; but I knew that would be as certain death as to die by the claws of the beast. With three bounds I gained the opposite bank, and then I could see the light in my log cabin, which was not more than a hundred yards distant.

"I had not proceeded but a short distance when I heard the plunge of the catamount behind me. I leaped with more than human energy, for it was life or death. In a moment the catamount gave another wild shriek, as though he was afraid he should lose his prey. At that moment I yelled at the top of my voice to my wife, and in a moment I saw her approach the door with a light.

"With what vividness that moment come to my mind! The catamount was not so far from me as I was from the house. I dropped my hat, the only thing I could leave to stay the progress of the beast. The next moment I fell prostrate in my own cabin."

Here the old settler paused and wiped the big drops from his brow ere he continued.

"How long I laid after I fell, I know not; but when I was roused to consciousness I was lying on my rude couch, and my wife was bathing my head with cold water, and my children were gazing anxiously at me. My wife told me that when I was in, she had immediately shut the door and barred it, for she knew I was pursued, but by whom or what she knew not; and that as soon as I had fallen, and the door closed, a fearful spring was made upon it, but the door was strong and well barred, and withstood the spring of the beast.

"As soon as I recovered, I knelt down and offered the most fervent prayer to the Almighty that ever crossed my lips or ever will again. My family and myself shortly after retired, but no sleep visited me that night. In the morning when my little son, six years old, told me that he saw the eyes of the cat in the window that night, I knew the catamount had been watching to gain admittance; but our windows, you will perceive, are not large enough to permit a catamount to enter.

"When I looked in the glass the next morning, I was horror-struck at my altered appearance. My hair, which was the day before dark as midnight, was changed to the snowy whiteness you now see; and although I have enjoyed very good health since, I shall never recover from the effects of the fright I experienced on being chased by a catamount."

A MOOSE HUNT IN MAINE

By Senarius, from *American Sportsman*, January 31, 1874

The Mud Pond Carry (From Woods and Lakes of Maine, by Lucius Hubbard, p. 71)

In this short story the anonymous author gives us one of the earliest accounts of a fishing and hunting trip made to the wilderness north of Moosehead. The writer, remembering back twenty years to the mid 1850's, was apparently a little confused as he reiterated his account; from Moosehead Lake a traveler crosses into the West Branch, not the East Branch as he mistakenly called it. Also, to "pole up the river" would have taken them in the direction of Seboomook, not east and north to the infamous "Mud Lake Carry," the early entrance to the Allagash region. In spite of his geographical errors, he does give us a wonderful account of fishing and capturing a moose in the water.

Some twenty years ago, while visiting my native town, in one of the New England states, I received an invitation from two of my old schoolmates, who had never left the shade of their paternal tree, to join them in an expedition to the wilds of Maine. Glad enough was I to become one of the party, as after the excitement of meeting old friends, had passed my time hung heavily on my hands.

We left for Bangor by rail, thence by stage to Moosehead Lake, where our guides joined us with the boat and camping utensils. I well remember the excitement of our first camp on the east branch of the Penobscot. The efforts of the guides to make my two companions comfortable for the night, as it was their first experience in camp life; the novelty, together with the imaginary fear of some nocturnal visitor, keeping them awake, far into the night. The next morning we started in our batteaux, pushing up the river. When nearing a carry, so called, where we were to leave the river and strike the shores of Mud Lake, we came upon a party of twelve lumbermen, stopping for dinner near the mouth of the brook. After dinner, one of them told us that he had discovered a hole in the brook, full of trout, and we had better stop long enough to capture enough for supper. I looked round for their fishing rods to gain some insight into the way they took these highly esteemed fish. What was my astonishment, when I saw them jump into the water making as much noise and splashing as possible. Presently the trout by dozens, threw themselves upon the stones in the shallow water where they were gathered up by one of the men stationed there. Then the others by feeling among the rocks at the bottom, seized those that had taken refuge, and threw them on the bank. I must confess, unsportsmanlike as it was, my companions and myself, joined in the melee, and that night we supped upon delicious trout, some of them over two pounds of weight.

We accomplished the carry, and presently noticed one the guides coming toward us in the canoe, seemingly in great excitement. When within hail, he cried out "There's a moose in the lake." I caught up Boston's rifle, R. his double gun loaded with No. 4 shot and we, with the other guide, jumped into the canoe. What was my chagrin to find, upon examination, the rifle empty and the bullets ashore in Boston's pocket, there was no time to return for them, as the moose was making tall traveling for the shore, and it would be only by great exertion, that we could get near enough for a shot before he landed, fortunately as I then thought, I found a lead sinker in my pocket, large enough for a slug, and soon had the rifle loaded, and here we were, four men in a birch canoe bearing down to attack a bull moose, not exactly upon his native heath, but in one of his familiar lakes.

By hard paddling we succeeded in turning him from the shore, and when near enough, the guides said fire. After a quick aim, I saw my slug strike the water a foot over the moose's neck, while R.'s charges of No. 4, only made him more determined to land in spite of us. What were we to do? A noble moose within shot, a chance coming to one probably but once in a life time, and we with empty guns, R. however, soon found some buck shot cartridges in his pocket, and nervously succeeded in leading both barrels, then handing the gun to me, he said the game is too large, I feel that I shall miss, and he will escape. The moose was not perfectly enraged, and forced us to make way for him to the shore, I waited till his side appeared above the water, when the cartridge bursting only as it reached him, let out his life blood, coloring the water for yards around. The second barrel, fired in mercy, extinguished his life, and we soon drew his eight hundred-pound carcass ashore.

A DAY'S MOOSE HUNTING IN 1860

By Libbey, from *Forest and Stream*, February 17, 1876

Calling the Moose (From Paddle & Portage, by Thomas S. Steele, p. 93)

We had lain in camp ten days--three of us, with as many dogs; two noble moose dogs, having to judge from their looks, the blood of the bull-dog, mastiff, beagle, and stag-hound, and a brindled bull terrier, possessed of all the pluck and endurance of his race, but with no more knowledge of hunting than a sheep, having been brought from Rhode Island, where he had never seen anything in the shape of game larger than a woodchuck. We were buried in the heart of the great forest of Northern Maine, fifty miles northwest of Patten, in the vicinity of Telos Lake, and had waited for a "crust," through days of rain, thaw, and fog till we were perfectly desperate. At length it all cleared up, and on that eventful night we sat up till eleven o'clock, running out of camp every half hour to plunge our forefingers into the fast freezing snow to test the strength of the crust. When it became too hard for our fingers to penetrate, we retired satisfied to our berth to dream of moose.

At the first glimmering of daylight the next morning we were on the moose; but as the shadows of night retreated, and the pale sun illuminated the wintry sky, it became rapidly overcast, and we saw that a snowstorm before nightfall was inevitable; and a snowstorm in the neighborhood of Katahdin has to be seen to he appreciated. However, we pushed on, and as the snow-shoeing was all that could be desired, we soon placed six miles between ourselves and camp without striking the first signs of moose; but when, as we were striking the base of one of the numerous "spruce mountains" which are found in this forest, we suddenly missed our dogs. We had depended on them more than on ourselves to find a moose "yard," as instances have been known where a trained moose dog has scented the game nearly, or quite, two miles, and for the first three or four miles we had watched with eager eyes, but had latterly grown more careless, and their sudden disappearance somewhat disconcerted us, as their feet hardly made a mark upon the hard surface of the snow. To add to our perplexity the snow began to fall, rustling fine and dry through the boughs and withered leaves. We slowly retraced our steps forty or fifty rods, and stood undecided which way to steer, when all at once the voice of old Major fell on our glad ears, so faint as to be scarcely perceptible, and apparently miles away. It was impossible to distinguish the direction, and equally impossible that the dog could get the apparent distance in the time he had been gone. Then voices of the other two chimed in, seeming to float in the air overhead, and as we danced in circles over the snow, too excited to stand still, and too undecided to take any direct course, the noise grew suddenly louder, and at once burst on our astonished ears, filling the air with music, being not over one hundred yards away, and almost directly overhead. The mystery was solved. The dogs had run round the end of the mountain, (we being near its eastern extremity) and had started their game on the back side, which had bounded up its steep and almost inaccessible side directly toward its summit. Of course the intervening ridge had all but cut off the sound, but when the animal and its pursuers reached the top the sound poured down on us in a flood.

To climb the mountain at the point where we were was simply impossible, and we tore around its eastern end, while the deep and measured baying of the big dogs and in incessant barking of the terrier aforesaid, told us the game was at bay. We quickly divested ourselves of our snow-shoes, and commenced to clamber up the steep ascent. Being encumbered with a heavy rifle---the only one we had taken from camp--I fell behind my comrades, and their shouts, as they reached the top, instead of hastening my ascent, as was intended, very nearly caused me to tumble back to the place from which I had climbed with so much labor. Bathed in perspiration, and panting for breath, I at length gained the summit, flung myself on to my snow-shoes, and bounded forward, hearing, as I ran, the voice of Bill (the Rhode Islander) frantically endeavoring to call off his dog, which mingled with the barking, snarling and yelling of the dogs, made a din more easily imagined than described. I soon reached the scene of action, and the sight which presented itself to my view still has the power to provoke a smile, although a gap of fifteen years stretches between. The dogs had roused up a yearling moose, which, making up in agility what it lacked in weight, was fighting as only a moose can fight. The old dogs, Major and Rolls, war both from instinct and experience, had escaped almost scatheless; not so with the unfortunate bull-terrier, Jim sharp. He had rushed in on that moose as he would a pig or a sheep, and the consequence was *frightfully* apparent---cut through the muscles into the cavity of the abdomen with dividing the tough skin and the entire intestines apparently protruded against the loose exterior integument. How he preserved his equilibrium was a wonder, and still more wonderful was his indifference, or rather utter unconsciousness that anything was wrong. He rushed around and barked and bit as though his internal arrangements were in their normal condition, and appeared, in fact, delighted. My first care, after taking in the situation, was to endeavor to shoot the moose without sacrificing the dog. No such opportunity presenting itself, the animal gradually worked its way to the western extremity of the mountain, and maddened by fear and pain, jumped from the summit upon a ledge about four feet below, which was perhaps six feet wide, and stood with his head looking over an abyss of three hundred feet in depth, the mountain projecting over its base at this point thirty or forty feet. On finding itself in this frightening position, the animal planted all its feet firmly and stood as if carved in stone, with its back just above the level of the summit. Old Major calmly walked up behind the beleaguered and helpless animal, and fastened to him. By dint of command and hard words the other dogs were kept off, but Major proved utterly refractory. We dared not advance for fear the moose would leap into the air, taking the dog with him, and the same consideration restrained me from firing. At length I lost patience, and with a peremptory command from Joe to "risk it," I brought the rifle quickly to my shoulder. A glance through the double sight, a report like the crack of a whip, with no echoes on that height to return the sound, and the animal dropped lifeless in its tracks, with its head hanging over the cliff, pierced through the neck. We removed the skin and disemboweled it where it lay. Then, in view of the difficulty of getting it upon the summit and down the steep sides of the mountain, we determined to throw it over the cliff, which we did, hearing a dull thud far below as the mass of flesh which so lately was a moose descended to the earth. We retraced our steps to where we ascended, and on getting round to our venison found it in a badly battered condition; but we hastily quartered and buried it. The snow by this time had fallen to a depth of three or four inches, and we struck out for camp taking a more southerly course than the one we had passed in the morning. I had forgot to state that, after shooting the moose, we held a "medical consultation" over the case of the unfortunate dog, Jim Sharp. His owner advised shooting him on the spot, but we outvoted him two to one. Poor Jim was stretched out on the snow, and at the end of half an hour we had the pleasure of seeing him restored to his natural shape. A handkerchief---which two weeks before was white---was tied around his body, an old mitten furnishing a pad, and with a rope attached to his collar, he trailed along behind his master's snow-shoes, his looks expressing sheepishness and disgust. We had accomplished nearly half our return to camp, and were crossing an outlying spur, which rose gradually to the south into the Wassataquoik Mountains, and had just reached its crest, when we came suddenly on the tracks of a large moose. It was evident that the only snow in them was that which had just fallen; but as that was the first which had fallen in a fortnight, it was of course, not easy to tell whether the tracks were ten hours or as many days old.

We were discussing in eager, but suppressed voices, whether it was best to hunt them out, or keep on our course and return on the morrow, when the two dogs, which had been lazily pushing their noses into the old "dents," suddenly faced to the south, raised their noses high in the air, and with tails extended straight behind, walked a few steps, swinging their heads from side to side, quickening into a trot, and then bounding forward with almost audible whine. Major lost the scent within a few rods of his starting-point, and ran a circle to recover it; but Roll kept straight on towards a knoll, which I observed at that moment, about a hundred yards distant. When within three yards of it, it rose as if blown into the air with gunpowder; the snow fell off, revealing a magnificent bull moose, blacker than any I ever saw. A wild yell from the astonished dog brought Major round like a flash, while the excited terrier spun round like a top, tugging and biting at his rope like a dog possessed. I started at once in advance, Joe being encumbered with the hide of the moose we had killed, and Bill with his dog. The noble game started directly along the ridge, which rose but very little for the first half mile. The snow had blown and melted nearly all off it, the old snow or crust not coming above his fetlocks---just enough in fact, to steady his feet. But with all this advantage he could not gain on the dogs one inch. So close was old Roll to his haunches when he bounded to his feet that he could not even settle into that long, ungainly lope or trot, which carries him over all ordinary obstructions, and which the animal will keep up hour after hour in a depth of snow that those to whom the wonderful powers and endurance of this "king of the forest" are unknown, would deem impossible. The first leap from his bed would measure fully eighteen feet, and this style of running he kept up greatly to my surprise, for the old hunters had informed me that moose never galloped when pursued, but always trotted, and in my subsequent experience I have never seen the thing repeated. How long this could have been kept up will never be known, for a circumstance occurred which brought the race to an abrupt termination. Like all the broken and mountainous countries, these wilds are subject to tremendous gales, which leave their traces in windrows of giant trees, upturned or broken by their force. Two of these tornadoes blowing from different quarters, had turned up two rows of trees in the form of a V. Into the apex of this trap the animal had rushed in his blind haste. As it was nearly twenty feet high at this point, to leap over it was impossible, and before he could retrace his steps the dogs were upon him. He had run perhaps one hundred rods; I had made half that distance, so he was hardly out of my sight. There was no baying this time. The first intimation I received that the game was brought to, was the peculiar savage snarl a dog gives when he seizes it. At the same instant my ears were saluted by the heavy roars or "grunts," as hunters call it, of the enraged bull. The sound cannot be conveyed on paper; but the dull, heavy thuds produced by a sledge-hammer on the end of a post, when driving it into the ground, comes nearer to it than anything else I can think of. This is the animal's call as is made in the pairing season, and I have never heard it uttered at any other time, before or since; but this fellow seemed an exception to his race in color, form, and actions. Upon reaching the spot where the fight was raging, all the stories I had ever heard of the activity, fury, and power of this noble animal were more than verified. Perfectly fresh, his short run not having blown him in the least, with no snow to impede his movements, roaring with rage first at one dog, and then the other, he appeared the very incarnation of fury, and I looked upon him with a sort of fascination. Not less wonderful was the conduct of the dogs. The first charge made as I came in sight happened to be at my dog, and I involuntarily held my breath, for the windfall was directly behind him, and his destruction seemed inevitable; but the instinct of the dog was superior to my reason. He stood perfectly still, facing the moose, and as he rushed upon him, sprang between his fore legs, then out at one side, and fastened to his back before I had time to realize that he was not brushed out of all shape. This, which seemed to me a mere chance escape, I afterwards came to know a good moose dog will do every time. The moose, in charging on the dog, invariably strikes directly downwards with each fore foot. This of course leaves the width of his breast between his feet and through this space the dog darts, and usually contrives to fasten to him before the bewildered animal is aware that he has not trampled him under foot. Just as my companions reached the spot, old Major gave a tremendous upwards spring, and fastened to the animal's hinder parts; but his hold gave way and he fell back. The moose, as he felt him strike his haunches, delivered a tremendous kick, which, had the dog been at any distance from him, would have brained him on the spot; but edging, as he did, upon his leg, the effect was to launch him into the air as if propelled from a mortar. Had he struck a tree in his course, his fate would have been sealed. Luckily the coast was clear, and he flew over and over like an acrobat, clearing the windfall in his course and alighted with a force that completely bewildered him for some moments. His absence produced a momentary cessation of hostilities, which gave me the wished for opportunity of delivering the fatal shot. The bullet struck him behind the fore leg, and going slightly "quartering," broke the opposite shoulder as it came out. He pitched forward on to his nose, came up again instantly, endeavoring to stand on the broken shoulder, failed again, then reared upon his hind legs, and fell over backwards to rise no more, still uttering his "grunts," which only ceased with his breath. We quickly dressed and buried him, and taking his nose, as a bonne bouche, started once more for camp, where we arrived long after dark, tired and hungry, but well pleased with our day's moose hunting in the wild of Northern Maine.

– LIBBEY

HIRAM TELLS A STORY

By Thomas Sedgewick Steele, from *Paddle and Portage, from Moosehead Lake to the Aroostook River*, 1882

At Night By the Camp-Fire (From Paddle and Portage, by Thomas S. Steele, p. 66)

In the fall of 1870, when Thomas Sedgwick Steele (1845-1903) took a long canoe trip through the northern Maine woods, he hired three guides, Thomas Nichols, an Indian from Old Town and two brothers, Hiram and John Mansell from Greenville, "the former officiating as cook and the latter as man of all work." Steele went on to describe Hiram as "clad in a pair of blue pants with red stripes at the sides, a souvenir of military life, and looked like a relic of Bull Run. He wore a jacket of brown duck with a leather strap about his waist, to which was slung a long bowie-knife, whose sheath was a deer's leg with a hoof attached. He stood five feet five inches in his stockings--how high with his shoes we are not prepared to say - was thirty-one years of age, and weighed just one hundred and forty-eight pounds, before dinner."

Having finished lugging their gear and canoes over the Osgood Carry, which took them from the head-waters of the St. John to those of the Aroostook River, they crossed Echo Lake and made camp. After dinner Hiram, who was one of the earliest guides at Moosehead Lake, recited the following account of his early days. Johnny, the unfortunate chap, was John M. Way, who later created and published the first Guide and Map to Moosehead Lake in 1874.

"Ye never heerd me tell about the man who fust tried to make maps o' these 'ere woods, did ye?" said Hiram, as he tossed an extra log upon the fire. "Wall, it's a long story; but I'll try and load the car'idge so the bullet won't go far, as I see Nicholas a-blinkin' over there like an owl at high meridian. It was 'long about the autumn of 1870, if I remember right, that a feller by the name o' Way cum up from down below an' took board at Greenville, foot o' Moosehead Lake. He was quite a spruce lookin' chap for these 'ere regions, an' though still under twenty-one years of age, had seen a deal o' the world in his little day. Wall, Johnny (that was his name,) had come to rough it, an' take his chances for life with the rest of us, though it was said he'd heaps o' money, an mighty fine fixins' at home; but he was one of them advent'rous splinters as are allers flyin round a-wantin' to see more an' more, an' git into wuss an' wuss every step they go. Us boys was mighty busy that year a-loggin', and he enj'yed the fust winter so rattlin' well that among us that he cum back the next season. When the snow got good an' deep in Jan'wary, an' snow-shoein' was just fine, we two arranged a huntin' trip an' started out with our rifles an' all the provishuns we could truss on our way backs toward Chamberlain Lake. We hunted about there some days, but finally made a hand-sled, strapped our kit on to it, and by dint o' pushin' and haulin' made our way over the fruz surface o' Chamberlain and Eagle Lakes to Smith Brook. Next day we pushed on to Haymoak Brook an' as it cum on to rain we built a hut of bark and camped.

"Johnny was a restless feeler, an' fur all tired out with the pull through to camp, thought if we were goin' to stay long and hunt we'd better lay in more provishuns. He was a plucky little feller, too, an' 'though not much used to the woods, could foller a 'spotted line' with the best o' ye. So he made up his mind to switch back to Chamberlain Farm an' git enough provishuns to last out the trip. I thought this a rather crazy freak, for I felt pretty sartin we could manage to pan out with what we had. But Johnny wanted to be sure. Like all city fillers he had a peevish bread-basket, an' spirit enough to rough it in other ways, he couldn't weather the trial of goin' without his straight meal no-how. I did all I could do to hold him back, but it was no use; then I offered to go back with him, but he was bent on don' the trip alone, and' leavin' me to rest in camp. So, after buryin' his part o' the kit in the snow, he stood ready to start.

"He didn' want to go back the same way we had come, but had planned to skirt round back o' the lakes, you know--a mighty uncertain kind of bizness, boys, for a feller raised in a hot-house.

"But he plead so hard I finally give in to him, an with the point o' my ramrod I marked out his course in the wet snow. Says I,

'You see here, Johnny, that mark I jist made goes across Haymoak Lake to Stink Pond. Now don't you forget it,' says I, 'to keep right on your course to Fourth Lake, for that there line leads into Little Leadbetter Pond, an' by a foot-track, will take ye to Chamberlain Lake, an' then yer all hunk. There's an old log camp on the Leadbetter, right there,' says I, diggin' the rod into the snow. 'Don't go further than that to-night. Camp there, no matter how early ye reach it; lie over till mornin' and then push on."

"It was the wuss snow shoein' I ever did see, and I ought not to've let the boy go, but I'd said yes, an' I'm not one of them fellers who goes back on his word.

"I buckled on Way's haversack, filled it with graham bread, stuck his hatchet in his belt, slung his rifle over his shoulder, and with many misgivin's saw him disappear in the woods. After he'd left I commenced to get kind o' nervus like, an' wish I hadn't let him go. Afore night I begun to feel terrible skittish about him. I lit my pipe, cleaned my gun, cut boughs and bark from the trees to make our camp more snug, an' tried by fussin' round to git the lad out o' my mind; but 'twnat no use--it didn't work wuth a cent. So buryin' the balance of our kit in the snow I started back to Chamberlain Farm by the old path and camped that night on Haymoak Lake, reaching the farm the next night.

"You will bet boys I was scared to find that Way had not got in, but I thought 'p'raps he was restin' at the old log camp--don't you think, he hadn't seen a hair of him either. Wall, the way I got into them snow-shoes was a caution--the deer's hide has gathered over my toes and heels quicker that a trout takes a fly, and I was a-slidin' off into the woods like mad. I kept goin' and goin' hour arter hour, as if the devil hisself as arter me; it was the best time I ever made on snow-shoes, even on a moose track.

At 2 o'clock I reached Way's camp of the night before, and follerin' his sloat' (track) I kept on arter him and in two hours saw him stumblin' along through the snow in front o' me like a lost sheep. I give a shout of joy, and then a wild haloo, as I dashed on arter him. But he plunged on without turnin' a head--he didn't seem to hear me. I hailed him again with no better effect, 'Somethin's up. He's not hisself by a long sight,' I said to myself; an' the way I put forrard through that snow would have done honor to a pair of the seven leagued boots. Just as I come up with him, an' was about plankin' my paw on his shoulder, I heerd him give a gasp, an' stumbled an' fell in a parfect heap at my feet.

"Johnny! Johnny!' says I, 'Brace up, Hiram's here and yer all safe.' But he was so far gone, he skarce knew me. To his belt was tied a partridge; but this was all the provishuns he had left, an' with his half froze hands he could but jist hang on to his rifle. I took his gun an' haversack, an' goin' before broke down the big drifts with my snow-shoes, an' cleared a track for him to foller. But he was so weak an' benumbed with cold, that every little while he dropped in the snow like a wounded animile, an' begged me to let him alone.

"Hiram,' he moaned, 'I can go no further. I am so tired. I feel so sleepy. Go on yourself an' leave me here.' But I warn't a lad o' that kind, I knew pesky well what that there sleepiness meant; it meant nothin' less than a closin' of eyes once an' forever; he would have been cold, stiff, stone dead in half an hour. It didn't take me more'n a brace o' minutes to find a remedy for this. Whippin' out my old knife I cut down a stick from one o' the young trees on the road, an' the way I laid it round that poor feller's body would have been a sight for the chicken-hearted, I tell ye. I beat him like an old carpet until his bones were sore. I fairly warmed him, which was jist what was wanted; an' what with whippin', kickin' him, an' at times cartin' him along on my back, we soon made mile after mile on our way.

"Those were long hours flounderin' on through the snow; but at last we reached Chamberlain Farm, though to tell a gospel truth I felt we never would git in.

As luck would have it there was a doctor there from East Corinth, an' with his help we were soon at work with snow gittin' the frost out of Johnny's hands an' feet, an' pumpin' life into him. In a week he was up and about, good as new, an' hunted with us till the followin' April afore goin' out of woods.

"As I learned from him afterwards, Johnny had lost his way between Fourth Lake and Leadbetter Pond. The snow was over three feet deep, an' as the rain had clogged his snow-shoes he turned into an old loggin'-road that he diskivered an' this took the poor feller right smack off his course. He follered the old road till dark, an' not comin' across the old log cabin I told him about, made for the base of a decayed tree, which he reckoned was fifty foot high at the least. This he set fire to, an' sat all night watchin' it burn down. Fallin' asleep towards mornin', when he woke up he found the merk'ry had gone a long way below zero, an that is feet, though wrapped in four pair o socks had both frozen. What the poor man suffered till I found him must have been terrible. Afore leavin' Greenville that Spring, John Way made the fust of a lot o' maps o' Moosehead Lake an' all its surroundin's. Aterwards he jined these all into one, which I used to sell on the boats, and this is the orthority for nearly all the late maps of these 'ere regions."

MOOSE HUNTING IN AROOSTOOK

By Arthur James Selfridge, from *Outing Magazine*, Aug 1889

Arthur James Selfridge

Arthur James Selfridge (1859-1934) was a well-respected Boston attorney. Born in California, he attended Philips Academy and then three years at Hamilton College in Clinton, New York, but was forced to leave due to illness. He later studied at the Boston University Law School and graduated in 1884, specialized in mining law, but also handling criminal cases. In 1924 he was appointed as Licensing Commissioner for the city of Boston, a position he held for ten years.

An active athlete, Selfridge belonged to the University Club of Boston, the Braeburn Country Club, Crown Point Golf Club and Boston Art Club. An avid fisherman and hunter, he was an active member of the Stadacona Fish and Game Club in Quebec and upon his return to Boston from moose hunting in the northern part of Maine, he submitted the following account of his trip.

On the 10th of September, 1887, we left Presque Isle, the terminus of the New Brunswick Railroad, for Junkins' Farm, the last settlement on the Aroostook River, forty-five miles distant. At this season of the year the Maine rivers are very low and shallow. Oftentimes one of the party will have to wade and pull the canoe, while the others go through the woods. It is a disagreeable and unpleasant way to navigate.

Our guide, an old Frenchman who could speak little or no English, "socked" the canoe up the river, while we tramped fourteen miles through the woods to a point on the river nearest Chandler Brook Lake, our destination, where we made our home camp. We rested here for a day and 'cached" our valuables, consisting mostly of canned vegetables and onions. Next morning each of us rolled up a pack which contained all the paraphernalia for a week's tramp--blankets, frypan, coffee pot, pork, flour, bread, baking powder, coffee, sugar and a can or two of condensed milk.

Our path to the lake lay over an abominable old "tote" road mostly corduroy, which was slippery, rotten, and treacherous. At one time we would be wading in mud to our knees, at another balancing on a slippery log, trying to avoid some dangerous honey hole. After five-hours' walk we reached an old lumber camp, five miles from the river, which we selected as our abode. Nearly a day was consumed in trying to find the lake. Road after road was followed up, invariably leading to some log yard. It was evident that some of us must climb. Selecting the tallest spruce on the highest hill, the guide began to climb. For forty feet there was not a branch or a twig.

After a struggle of ten minutes, he reached the top. "Me see de gross mont. Look lake, for sure; dis way," pointing north. He meant "I see a large mountain at the foot of which appears to be a lake, the direction from here is north."

The following morning the guides and I started through the woods over hill and through swamp, due north, blazing our trail which led us to the lake, a sheet of water containing about four square miles of surface. The point at which we struck it was "no good for de bull moose, he like de lilly," the guide's expression for "it is an unsuitable place for calling." We followed the shore of the lake, seeking a shallow spot filled with later lilies or "cow lily pads," surrounded by a swamp that gradually rose to a high hill. Our path led us through moss-covered ledges, stunted trees, and over trails that had actually been worn by moose, deer and caribou; traveling up and down the lake. It excites wonder and admiration for these wary denizens of the forest to see the place they have selected for their lairs and beats. At one time you are walking lightly over a soft bed of moss; without any warning you slump through between two great rough boulders that scrape your legs the whole length. Slowly you extricate yourself and select a log to be sure of your footing, when all of a sudden both feet head for the starry sky. Oh, how your head aches! Our pack, which we took turns in carrying consisted of one "lit-ly hach" (a belt axe), one rubber blanket, one thin, moth-eaten army blanket, two pounds of salt pork, plenty of hard bread, and a few biscuits. It weighed about ten pounds, and seemed to weigh a hundred. After the first ten minutes of this wretched tramp drew the cartridge from my rifle to prevent any accident, so frequent were my falls. You may judge of the pleasant paths we trod when I tell you that it took us nearly six hour to do two miles.

We were rewarded, however, by finding an ideal place for calling. An arm of the lake made in between two hills that sloped gradually to a cedar swamp that was, perhaps, a mile across. We chose for our location a little bare spot under the branches of a great leaning cedar, just behind of tuft of alder bushes. Marking the place by a tall pine that stood near we retreated a quarter of a mile to select a camp. We found a level spot underneath two great spruce tops (trees felled the previous winter, from which logs had been cut), which had fallen across each other. With the aid of the belt axe we cut the small limbs that grew downward and soon had a cosey little nest, with at least a foot of soft, fragrant fir spread for a bed. We threw our rubber blanket over the logs and fastened it securely, as we thought, and swung around the hill to be a mile from the calling spot, for a quiet smoke.

We lit our pipes and were dozing off, picturing ourselves the moose we were going to have. We could almost smell the delicious odor of a broiling steak, when we were brought to our feet by a terrible crash and a terrific peal of thunder, followed immediately by the most vivid lightning I ever witnessed. Quickly I selected a leaning tree, placed my rifle, axe and compass there, so that they would not attract the lightning to me, and rushed for some fallen logs to avoid the pelting rain. For twenty minutes a most frightening thunderstorm, with a terrific rain and wind accompaniment, was passing. Trees were blown down, limbs were falling, and here and there great trees were splintered by the lightning. We were soaked by the torrents of rain. As soon as it cleared off we went out into the bright sun and back to our camp, where we found that the rain had driven underneath our rude tent and drenched our bed.

All the old hunters tell me that if moose smell smoke they will leave its locality. Whether this be true or not I am not sure. They have been known to yard for the winter within three miles of a lumber camp, where they must have smelt smoke. Once two deliberately walked into my camp when the fire was burning merrily. I have never tried building a fire within three miles of a place selected to call. For this reason we did not dry our bed nor cook our supper. Do not be disgusted---it consisted of raw pork, hard bread and "Old Medford." It was not bad, because every sign indicated a dead moose before morning.

It was growing dusk. We went to our stand, carefully marking our path by bits of birch bark curled about the bushes. Reaching our ground we waited in silence for dark. When it came, my guide wet the horn, which he had carefully made in the afternoon by rolling a piece of birch bark into the shape of a funnel. Fitting the horn to his mouth and holding it to the earth he gently and softly uttered the plaintive, amorous call of the cow moose, given only at this season of the year. Raising his head, so that the end of the horn described the curves of the letter S (beginning at the bottom of it), he gradually increased the volume of sound; then lowering the horn to its original position, the end have traced a gigantic figure 8, he gradually decreased the volume until near the end of the call, when he suddenly burst out with a plaintive, seductive grunt that went rolling over the swamp and up the hill, bidding any bull moose to come. After a wait of perhaps ten seconds he gave a second of the three parts of the call. This began with an impatient expression of intense eagerness, quickly changing into one long note, which combined quavering complaint, pathetic longing and unrequited affection, and sunk into a confiding appeal. The third followed the second at a shorter interval and commenced with a tone of scolding impatience, which gradually swelled in intensity, approaching fierceness. It closed with an upward toss of the head and a shriek, terminating in a rising inflection, almost a roar that seemed to say decidedly: "Come, now or never!"

The note is peculiar to the moose and can be compared with nothing in nature. It is made by shaping the mouth as if to pronounce the French u, then forcing the syllable "her" through the vocal organs by the use of the abdominal muscles, giving it a decidedly nasal twang. The idea of beginning with the horn held toward the earth is taken from the habit of the cow moose, as is the number of parts of the call.

After waiting until every echo had died away and the oppressive silence had again filled the woods, perhaps half of three-quarters of an hour, a second call was given. It seemed to roll over the hill and valley and come echoing back for an interminable length of time. Patiently we waited for an answer, but nothing save the drip, drip, drip, from the wet leaves, the occasional splash of a musk rat, or the lonesome hoot of an owl was heard. Again and again the call was given. The response was the same. For two hours this monotony continued. After a call louder, longer and more intense than the rest, an answer came in the form of a flash of lightning that illuminated the entire landscape. We could distinguish a flock of ducks on the water within one hundred feet of us. Then followed a peal of thunder and again the rain fell in torrents. We huddled together under the great leaning cedar and held a consultation in whispers.

"Tunner bon for the bull moose. No 'fraid. Come lymly. You try call. No come for me."

We shivered for half an hour before it stopped raining. When it did I began. The guides voice was a heavy bass, mine a baritone. Putting the horn to my lips I gave the call. Scarcely had the sound died away when the answer came rolling down the opposite mountain to us---clearly and distinctly. A heavy silence of ten minutes followed. Just as I was putting the horn to my mouth for a second call, the answer was repeated, this time nearer and more distinct. I replied to it with a plaintive grunt full of satisfactory longing. The response was shorter and quicker. For the next fifteen minutes there was not a sound except the dripping of the leaves and the croaking of the frogs. Raising the horn I gave an inquiring grunt. The answer came so clear that we judged the moose was within a quarter of a mile. Taking a dipper I dribbled some water in the edge of the lake. The old bull fairly roared in his eagerness, the brush began to crack and we could hear this majestic creature walk back and forth. Again I poured the water; an eager answer was the result.

The guide then took my horn and with the power of a ventriloquist gave a furious challenge that sounded as if it came from another bull far in the opposite direction. Almost before it was finished an angry, smothered roar broke from the now infuriated bull, which dashed into the water. Our flock of ducks took flight and scattered with discordant quacking. "Be ready for shoot. No shake. I trust you," whispered my guide.

Carefully cocking my rifle I stepped out from under the dense shade to be sure of a good light. I thought I could distinguish the moose crossing the space between us and the other shore. For a better light I took another step, and down into a honey hole I went above my knees. I pulled one foot out with a pop. The other was deeper in the mire than ever. I had sunk below the alders and could see nothing. I made another frantic effort. The moose was coming. Alas! I was slowly sinking in the filthy, black mud, utterly unable to extricate myself. "Why no shoot?" I tried to make him understand, offering my gun. I had settled to my waist. "Moose there---shoot!"

I spoke loud enough to make him realize my predicament. The faithful fellow, disregarding the coming moose, pulled me out by main strength. The noise we made was frightful. No wonder the moose stopped coming. When I stood on terra firma everything was silent. We resorted to pouring water again. We could hear his retreating steps. We applied the horn, giving every conceivable variation from an angry challenge to a gentle, plaintive moan expressing abject misery. It was useless; he had departed. After another hour of patient waiting we gave it up. Oh, how bitter cold it was! It seemed as if I should freeze. There were no spreading horns to carry home in triumph. It was a wet, gloomy, nasty night. I hated myself for my careless stupidity. The old man tried to comfort and encourage me: "Come next day; no scard I bet ten dollar."

THE WILD MAN OF LUCKY BROOK

By C. C. Munn, from *Maine Sportsman*, April, 1898

From "Pocket Island, A Story of Country Life in New England" by Charles Clark Munn, 1901 (Courtesy of Boston Public Library)

Charles Clark Munn (1848-1917) was born and raised on a farm in Springfield, Massachusetts, where he received a country school education. Leaving home at the age of seventeen, he worked for over thirty years as a commercial traveler, having married and settled in Springfield. About 1900 he began writing novels and after having spent several vacations in Maine, he set some of his novels on the Maine coast and in 1903 published "The Hermit, a Story of the Maine Woods."

There were two of us--an old fishing chum and myself--and with good guides, canoes and all the necessary outfit for a month of camp life, we had journeyed fifty miles from civilization into the very heart of the Maine wilderness,--pitched our tents beside a pretty lake known as Lucky Pond and settled down for a month's rest and wildwood life.

The lake was a gem in its way: of clear, cold water, about four miles long, sandy and pebbly shores completely surrounded by low mountains. The primeval forest had never been marred by the hand of man and naught but the occasional cry of a loon on the lake or the chatter of a squirrel disturbed its silence. It is amid such surroundings that the true peace and poetry of camp life are felt. The ruthless lumberman's tracks and any sight or sound of humanity always mar the picture.

I had heard of this lake on previous trips into the woods, but as it was almost inaccessible except by a long and hard up-stream canoe journey, had never before visited it. We were more than charmed by the situation and lost no time in getting ready to take comfort in true backwoods style and stock a larder. A deer and a nice string of birds were soon in store and then we proceeded to enjoy life.

Comfortably settled by the camp fire, one of our guides that evening told us a queer story of how he had once come upon a strange creature: half man, half bear, with a hideous ape-like face; how it had uttered a strange mournful cry as it stood upright in the shadow of the thicket and glared at him a moment, and then with a blood-curdling scream plunged into the forest and disappeared. It was a well told tale and while it might have made the low, quavering cry of a wild cat, in a distant swamp, sound a little more uncanny, it did not disturb our rest, for such stories float around among the backwoods guides and are told and retold to all who visit the woods, a part of the stock in trade of all good guides. We thought little of it, in fact had almost forgotten it, until one day, a week after, we were startled by some very unusual and mysterious discoveries. The first was the finding, among a tangle of driftwood at the mouth of a stream, just across the lake from our camp, and called Lucky brook, the handle of a broken paddle with the end cut, carved and stained into a most hideous semblance of a human skull. The top was formed of the round end of a bone set into the wood; the teeth were the real teeth of a wild-cat, inserted into a grinning mouth, and to make it more hideous, between them the wood was stained a deep red. The eyes were formed of bits of round bone, with little circles of black about them.

It was an uncanny bit of handiwork and much we marveled at it. This stream, at the mouth of which we found this odd bit of driftwood, we had never explored; partly because we had not gotten around to it and partly because it was of a forbidding look. The water was black and looked treacherous, and why it had been named "Lucky" brook was a query. It looked unlucky. It entered the lake between two rocky banks, one of which had a sloping face of rock, perhaps twenty feet, and back of these a flat swamp.

We were still discussing the queer bit of drift when one of the guides, who had been crawling around the face of the boldest of the cliffs, called to us. We hastened to him and found he was examining a peculiar, faint outline drawing on the face of this rock. It had apparently been intended to represent a skeleton. The skull was merely a ring with holes for teeth and eye sockets, the ribs and bones of arms and legs rudely cut in the rock and yet rough and rude as it was, it had an ominous look.

We studied it long and carefully and marveled much. Had this pretty lake once been the hiding place of some pirate in years gone by, or what? We looked and talked and looked again at the queer figure on the rock until the sun had crept down in the west, and it was time to start for camp.

That night I noticed the guides were unusually silent and my chum had less to say than usual. Somehow the story of the queer creature our guide had claimed to see, forced itself into our thoughts.

But when the first smile of sunlight peeped down upon us through the treetops next morning, and wakened the birds as well as us, all uncanny fears of hidden pirates or skull and crossbones fled away. There is nothing like bright sunshine to chase away any and all hobgoblins in the woods. Our supplies were running low and we resolved to hunt for more.

My chum started for the foot of the lake for birds and my guide and I headed the other way. There was a stream entering the lake about a mile above Lucky brook, along the banks of which was a favorite feeding spot for deer. Toward this we paddled and entering it I laid my paddle aside and, with rifle in hand, sat and watched the opening vista of forest, swamp and thicket through which the stream wound its way. It is a most charming pastime, this sitting on an air cushion in a canoe with one's back resting against a thick blanket folded across a thwart, a trusty rifle in your lap, the prospect of a deer ahead, and naught to do but feel yourself floating on air, as it were, while you watch for him and all the varying landscape views at the same time. Now it is a stretch of swamp alder where bunches of blue heather color the brown bush background, and dead trees at intervals stand like whitened sentinels to watch your progress. Now it is a dark and shadowy passage beneath the bending tops of stately fir trees; again it is a broad opening, where the stream forms a tiny lake a dozen rods across, bordered by a luxurious growth of rushes bending in billows beneath a breeze;

a flock of ducks disturbed here, rise with sudden splashing, and circling around head away to some other lakelet they know well where to find; a muskrat, scared from its house building, plunges in from a bank and swims across in front of you; and still again you enter the shadows and the deep, silent mystery of the dense woods is all about you; the chattering of a red squirrel fifty rods away almost startles you with its loud distinctness; you can hear your own heart beat, the silence is so absolute. The guide makes no sound with his paddle, he simply twists and turns it and almost without a tremor the canoe moves on and on up the stream with the thick shadows of the wilderness beside you on either hand. It is like a dream, a continuous succession of surprises, a voyage into fairy land.

A mile of this and we come to a sloping hillside where once a mountain tornado had swept down the forest like reeds; a hunter's fire had later on burned the dead and dry tangle and a fresh growth of young scrub mixed with patches of grass, had take its place. And while we slowly passed beside this low opening, suddenly I spied a young buck nipping the still green leaves, from a low cluster of maples. The guide sees him as soon as I, the canoe is halted by a firm back stroke, I raise the rifle; a sharp crack follows; the deer leaps in the air and with two loud bleats makes two bounds and plunges into a hollow.

Our hunt is ended, but even at this supreme moment and just as the guide has forced the canoe up into the tangled brush bank and I rise to step out--suddenly from the edge of the forest growth and not twenty rods away, there breaks upon the stillness an unearthly scream, so strange, so frightful in its suddenness, that I forget in an instant the deer I have shot, and look at my guide in silence. I have had many strange experiences in the woods; I have learned many sounds of wild animals, wildcats, panthers, and such gentry, screaming at night in some swamp, but in all my experiences I have never heard such a cry as that! With a sudden sense of fear I sprang out, pushed the canoe back clear of the brush, leaped in, seized a paddle, and shoved out into the open stream. I looked at my guide, he looked at me. "Great Scott! Levi," said I, "what was it?"

There was not a sight or sound of the forest that Levi was not familiar with. He could tell them all by day or by night, be it bobcat, panther, wolf, bear or deer. He could paddle a canoe so still the breaking of a twig rods far away could be heard. He could tell the points of compass the darkest night that ever blew, but for the first time he was plainly beaten.

"I give it up," he replied, as he shook his head. For ten minutes we waited and listened in breathless silence for the cry to come again. Not a sound broke the stillness.

"Shall we go?" he said, finally.

"And leave the deer?" said I.

His face was a study as he still watched the shadowy forest. The hunter's instinct finally won and he pushed back into the bushes and stepped ashore. It was needless to say we crept cautiously through the undergrowth. We found the deer and quickly slitting its tendons, trussed it on a pole, regained the canoe and started back. But hardly had we passed the open stretch, ere there came to us from far away in the forest that same unearthly scream, loud and clear, but repeated again and again. We paused not, but putting ever ounce of strength into each stroke, we sped on and on until the open lake was reached and a good mile of clear water separated us from the shore. Then we paused to take breath.

I am not superstitious. I do not believe in ghosts, or hobgoblins of any sort. I am familiar with the peculiar cries of any and all "varmints" that roam in the Maine woods and yet as I sat in the canoe that day and wiped the perspiration off my face, in spite of all sense and reason I felt peculiar. I noticed also, as Levi was filling his pipe for a smoke that his hand shook. Mine did, also, and as I scanned the shadowy ravines that opened between the low mountains all about, I confess they looked sinister. But a mile of open water is a great tonic after a fright of that sort and I finally breathed easier.

"Hang it all, Levi," said I, as we resumed our paddles. "It was most likely a panther that was after that deer, the same as we were." He shook his head. "It wasn't a panther," he replied.

But we got a worse scare later on. Our course to camp, toward which we now headed, brought us close to a point on one side of which was a bit of sandy shore and just inside it a tiny brook entered the lake. We had shipped some water in getting the deer in, or else in our hasty rush down the stream had knocked a hole in the canoe and as there was two miles of lake to cross I thought it best to go ashore and examine our craft. We found a tiny leak and while the guide caulked it I took a look about and a peep at the little brook. The lake was low and out on the edge where the brook and lake joined was a bit of sandy shore the size of a table. I came suddenly upon it and then more suddenly two immense tracks recently made there, fully fifteen inches long and spreading at the toes at least six.

They looked like those made by a barefooted giant, but the toe marks showed claws like a bear, only longer. I called to Levi. He came, and without a word went down on his knees, out with his knife and began picking out the sand to see how deep the claw marks were. He then went back to the canoe and returned with both rifles and silently handed one to me. Then he looked intently across the brook to the swamp, back on the other side full twenty feet over; turned up the brook, crossed, came back opposite to me, looked carefully into the long tangled grass and beckoned me. I followed.

There I saw the same footprints where the creature had evidently leaped across the brook and struck into the soft bog bottom. The tracks were deep and the mud had been splashed over the tall grass. It was a terrible bound the animal had made from one set of tracks to the other, full twenty feet!

Then we looked further up the stream and found the same tracks on harder bottom, where only the faint heel mark and sharp, distinct toe mark were visible. We looked and listened and looked again.

"What is it?" I finally whispered. Levi's face was drawn and pinched. He slowly shook his head. "Let's get out of this," he said finally. We lost no time, but loaded and launched our canoe and headed for camp.

Now a piratical carved paddle might be a freak of some idle trapper, and a skeleton picked out with a knife on the side of a rock, the pastime of a lazy hunter, but those blood-curdling screams uttered by some creature unknown to an old woodsman like Levi, and freshly made tracks of a size and ferocity that made a bear's or panther's track seem like a rabbit's in comparison, were stern and startling facts that would not be downed. That night as I sat by our campfire and told my day's adventure, I noticed my chum also watched the dark shadows of the forest all about, and long after we had turned in I heard the guides still talking in low tones, still keeping the fire burning brightly, and when the gray light of early morn crept into the tent and I crawled out, I found them both fast asleep on the ground close beside the still smoldering fire.

After breakfast we held a council. All the circumstances that had disturbed us were discussed in length. It seemed probable that we had some sort of strange neighbor that haunted the woods and streams of Lucky Pond and the more we discussed him the less attractive the creature proved. The guides were for packing up and quitting the lake at once. My chum and I were undecided. We finally settled it by the toss of a coin.

To hunt for the "bogie" won the toss. To hunt, I say, and yet where? The signs we had for a clue were miles apart and on the three sides of the lake. The one and only tangible evidence was the fresh tracks. But they led into an impassable swamp. We resolved to explore Lucky brook. We started light, carrying only our rifles, and crossed the lake. At the mouth of the brook we paused, to examine once more the rudely carved skeleton cut on the cliff at the entrance. For the first time we noticed that one bony arm was evidently cut to point up the stream. It was not an encouraging signpost, by any means, but four men and four Winchesters are quite a battery and we kept on. For a mile the stream wound in tortuous curves through a swamp, with here and there dead trees standing like ghostly sentinels, whose branches had for years been beaten by storm and sun until they looked like bleached skeletons on guard. A crow on top of one cawed dismally.

Beyond the forest shut in and the dark waters of the stream took on a blacker hue. Half a mile more and the stream narrowed into a brook that gave us the first music of running water and the banks began to shut in high and rocky beneath the tangle of fir and spruce. Soon we came to a foam-flecked pool, into which the brook tumbled in a way, which at any other time and place would have sounded cheerful. Here it seemed to utter defiance. We drew our canoes out on a mossy rock and with rifles in hand paused to consider.

It was a weird spot; gray and green moss-covered rocks about our heads on either side; gnarled and twisted cedars forming a thick tangle crowning them; long tufts of grey moss hanging from their branches and twisted trunks like beard on the faces of some gnome, and over all the shadowy silence and deep, dark, mystery of the wilderness. Beyond and above us the brook opened a narrow passage.

Cautiously we crept up the bed of the stream over the wet rocks slippery with the perpetual dampness of the forest, twisting and turning for a few hundred rods while the rocky banks grew more shadowy. And then an opening showed ahead and soon we entered a circular, crater-like space, perhaps ten rods in diameter, walled in on all sides by sheer, rocky banks. In the center, the brook formed a pool deep and dark; and floating across it from the tiny cascade at the farther side, patches of white foam kept a slow-moving procession. It was a spot fit for the bath of a Diana and her goddesses, but the shadowy solitude and the mystery of our quest left no space for poetic contemplation.

We paused, and huddled together like scared children gazing wonderingly about at the grandeur of the spot. The black, twisted roots of cedars like the arms of a devilfish crawled over the rocky banks; the long tufts of mossy beard hung from their branches; the white patches of foam circled slowly around the dark pool; the music of the brook as it entered was the only sound that broke the silence and even that had an unnatural sound.

We listened and looked, and listened again and then suddenly I felt Levi grasp my arm and point to a white object that was perched high on the top of a rock away up on one side of the tall bank that walled us in. It was the skull of a moose, with the spreading antlers bleached almost white, and beyond it laid two more of the same ghostly objects, and back of them what seemed like the dark entrance of a cave. And then as we held our breath, suddenly from out the opening in the rock, there rose a hideous, gray, shaggy haired and bearded head and face! An ape-like face, in the grinning mouth of which the white teeth showed clear and distinct, and then slowly a massive, hairy body followed. We held our breath, our eyes riveted to the horrible sight.

One instant and then the creature slowly turned its face and seemed to look down at us and then suddenly it uttered a scream, the fierce rage and intensity of which I have never heard before and never want to again.

What I felt or thought, I can never tell. I only know that the next instant we were in a mad scramble back over the slippery way up which we had come, and at every bound that wild screech repeated in rapid succession only hastened our flight.

How we ever got back to the canoes without broken bones, I never knew, but we got there, wet, bruised and sore from many falls; and tumbling into them never ceased paddling till the open lake was reached and we breathed once more.

We broke camp that day and I never visited that lake again. I spent many nights in camp by forest lakes and streams since then--for all this happened years ago--and many a time have I sat by the campfire and heard the night cries of some prowler in the forest, and hearing them always brings to mind that mad rush and the vivid memories of the Wild Man of Lucky brook.

– C. C MUNN, Springfield, Mass.

Chapter Seven

DOWN EAST REGION

The Down East region of Maine basically encompasses the northeast part of Hancock County and all of Washington County. Known as the Sunrise County, due its being the most eastern most piece of land in the United States, it is the only region of the Maine Woods that reaches from the ocean to great forests filled with lakes, rivers and mountains, and with only a few inland towns on Route 9, better known as the Airline, and Route 6 in the northern part of the county.

The Grand Lake chain was the first focus of fishing in this region, especially known for its salmon. Unfortunately in the mid-eighteenth century, due to the vast amount of hemlock trees, a tannery operated at Grand Lake Village and made fishing very poor due the increase of tannic acid in Grand Lake Stream. Once the tanning business closed, the river regained its health and it then became a center for fishing, with several sporting hotels and camps operating within the village at the head of Grand Lake Stream.

The problem for sportsmen was getting to Grand Lake, but a stage coach business began operating from the railroad at Bangor, which went across the Airline, bringing more and more sportsmen. Later camps were built at Great Pond, Alligator Lake, Mopang Lake, Nicatous Lake, Duck Lake Sysladobsis Lake and Pleasant Lakes. As the railroads got built it opened up sportsmen to the region around Princeton and the Chipputnecook Lake Chain on the Canadian border.

Today some of the sporting camps that are still operating are Great Pond Wilderness Lodge, Nicatous Lodge, The Pines on Sysladobsis, and Wheaton's and Rideout's Camps in the Vanceboro region. There are a cluster of camps offering hospitality at Grand Lake – Grand Lake Lodge, Leen's Lodge, Indian Rock Camps and Weatherby's, with Chet's Camps nearby on Big Lake.

A BEAR STORY

Anonymous, from the *Piscataquis Observer,* April 16, 1862; originally published in the *Calais Advertiser*

From In the Maine Woods, 1906, p. 25 (Courtesy of Boston Public Library)

As Mr. Nickerson Peters of Baileyville, was returning home from the woods with his axe on his shoulder, he espied an animal near the foot of an old tree, a little way off, and on going to the spot discovered it to be a large bear which had taken refuge under the roots of the tree. He furthermore found two or three of the varmints under the tree and that they had two or three of egress and ingress to the den.

His dog commenced the attack by stationing himself at one of the holes and barking furiously. Mr. Peters stationed himself at another and with the axe in hand, should any of them attempt to leave the den to give battle. Soon the oldest and largest essayed to run the blockade, when Mr. Peters struck her a blow between the snout and the eyes, which cut through the lower jaw, and drove her back to her den with a growl, where she remained some time. She then attempted to escape by one of the other holes, but Mr. Peters was too quick for her, and dealt her a blow on the small of her back, which laid her out, dead.

In the meantime, one of the other bears got out and Mr. Peters immediately gave it his attention, dispatching it with a blow of the axe just back of the fore shoulder, the axe penetrating to the heart, and producing instant death. By this time it had gotten quite dark, and the other one showing no disposition to leave his den, he concluded to suspend operations for the night. So shouldering the smallest one, he started for home.

Next morning he returned with three of his neighbors to the scene of his previous night's exploits. They found the old one where he had left her, dead. On looking round, they soon found the other one up in a tree. The party had two guns with them, but neither of them would go off. Presently Bruin began to descend the tree, and as soon as he struck the ground, Mr. Peters again raised the fatal axe and dealt him a blow which killed him. Thus Mr. Peters killed all three of the varmints with his own right arm. The largest would weigh 300 pounds, and each of the other two were as big as a large sheep.

LAND-LOCKED SALMON AT GRAND LAKE STREAM

By R. R., from *Forest and Stream*, July 2, 1874

In the Maine Woods, Boston and Aroostook Railroad, 1908, p. 7 (Courtesy of Boston Public Library)

By your request I will give you the result of our trip to Grand Lake Stream. My intention was to extend the trip to the Provinces, but finding fishing so entirely satisfactory at Grand Lake Stream, I did not hanker for any better sport. We left Boston May 25th, going by rail to Calais, Maine. There learning that Mr. W. W. Sawyer, Superintendent of the St. Croix Railroad from Calais to Princeton, had this season placed a small steamer on Big and Long Lakes, to run in connection with the P. M. train to Gould's Landing, where Grand Lake Stream empties into Big Lake, I called on him and he at once made arrangements to make a special trip the next morning. We took an early start by the first train to Princeton, reaching there a little past eight o'clock, and the landing about half past one, P.M., having had a splendid run up the lakes, favored not only by the beautiful weather, but by the company of Mr. Sawyer himself, together with two ladies of his family. We found Mr. S. obliging and courteous, and to say that the ladies were not agreeable and entertaining, would be both ungallant and untrue, and we acknowledge our obligation.

The usual preparation and delay in pitching tent left only a short time for fishing that afternoon, May 27th, but enough, however, to kill a dozen or more salmon before sundown. Our party, by the way, was made up of Mr. Alfred Rowe, Springfield, Massachusetts; Mr. Walter S. Barnes, Somerville, Massachusetts, and myself. The first two named never before trailed a fly over the Schoodic waters, and were highly delighted at the good opening of their first campaign at Grand Lake. I have little doubt that they were playing salmon (in dreams) all night, judging by the broad grin on the countenance of one of them, and the almost boisterous laughter with which he was convulsed while handling and witnessing the "leaps" of his first salmon. Fishing improved and our scores increased every day.

One morning, on learning that the gates were not to be hoisted that day, I said to Joe, my guide:--

"Joe, do you think that there will be any one fishing down to the little falls today?"

"No," said Joe; "don't think anybody will be there today."

"Why, said I; can it be possible that among so many anglers as there are here, there will not be some one or more who knows there will be good sport at the little falls to-day, with the gates closed and no logs running?"

"Well I guess nobody down there." said Joe.

"Why not?" said I.

"Nobody here, (meaning among the Indian guides,) like lug canoe," replied Joe.

"Oh, I see," said I; "you mean all the other guides here are too lazy to carry their canoe down there."

"Yeas," replied Joe, laughingly.

"I think I can do some execution there without a canoe," I said.

"Can't do much without a canoe," said Joe.

"Well said; and do you want to carry yours down?"

"Yeas," says Joe pleasantly.

"We can have good sport there with canoe."

I felt as confident of that as he did, but wanted not only to have him confirm my belief but to see how he felt about carrying down his canoe, a distance to carry of over a mile. I knew from the way he spoke he was glad to take his canoe down if he could by so doing, give me a good day's sport. Now I did not think it worth while to lug a canoe so far if the chances were more than ever that there would be others there, but I knew I could place great reliance on what Joe said. Joe can speak volumes in one word. If he mars the English language he never wastes it. I think I have seen a more demonstrative display of affection between Romeo and Juliet that I should imagine could possibly take place between Joe and his, "or any other fellah's squaw. He will never be brought into tribulation by his gossiping. He goes straight at the point in speaking. I shall never forget when once we were together I asked him to paddle me into a little deeper and more rapid water, and when there I insisted on sitting up on the cross bar of the canoe. Joe looked me calmly in the face, and with a gravity and waggishness, for which he is noted, asked: "Can you swim?" I never comprehended three words quicker and better than I did those three. Accordingly I lost no time in replying that swimming was part of my early education, and immediately dropped into the bottom of the canoe. I had learned that 'twas useless to argue with him.

As I was saying, I can rely on him. I have tried him well. We have tented together five seasons. We have been in the middle of Grand Lake in a heavy north-easter, with a full sail up in the canoe, when it looked scarey, and when one of the guides himself looked ominous, and when our canoes shipped many a heavy roller, drenching some of the party (ask Prouty.) We have camped on an island for the night, to find, on awaking, our only paddle gone, and "nary" a board with which to make another, anywhere to be found. Another guide, by mistake, had taken it with him on his departure the evening before. This was no joke, judging by the strange mixture of languages and worse grammar Joe used on that solemn occasion, in which it is more than probable I joined. We were in a hurry to proceed on our journey. We were entirely surrounded, not so much by pleasing incidents and circumstances of travel, as by water. We could both swim some, but that wouldn't do.

One may be mad clear through, and get resigned in a measure, because he can't help it. Such, I think, was Joe's condition, and I felt like a politician when he says "he is in the hands of his constituents;" I was entirely at Joe's service. But he proved equal to the emergency again, hewed out a cedar paddle and we were soon on our journey again. But I see I am drifting away from Little Falls. After breakfast I said to Joseph, and if we have good sport, "you shall be a Bishop Joseph." Our canoe was lightly set upon the pool just above the falls at 8 ¼ o'clock. Sure enough, as Joe predicted, no one was there. What a privilege! To be alone on such a splendid pool, with none to foul you in casting, and no pork-slingers slashing round--enough to frighten the spots out of the fish. We had scarcely got pushed out into the current, my leader had not measured its length on the water, before a salmon took my leading fly. He fought well and was landed, when a third or fourth cast took another, and he made my reel sing lively, doing some smart jumping before surrendering, when he proved to be like the other, a male fish. I saw at once there was game as well as music in that pool. We would scarcely get out into the current before Joe had to paddle slowly ashore out of the current to land my fish, and in this way I took nine males in succession, all about the same weight and of a dark, greenish color, all of which were the gamiest fish I ever handled on the Schoodic waters. Then came along, now and then, a female fish much fatter and brighter color than the others. I am certain that the fish in that pool were the smartest I have ever seen. Why, I cannot say. They seemed to vie with each other in seeing which could leap the highest. One among them deserves not only freedom, which he got, but special mention here. After hooking him he made two such brilliant dashes and leaps, running full sixty feet, that he thrilled my very nerves, and convinced me that he "meant business," and to become master of the situation if possible. He made one more run, ending in a leap, which almost startled me and brought forth from the stoic Joe an expression of wonder and satisfaction. It was a different leap from any I had ever seen before. Now, in telling this, I don't forget that more than half of the fish stories are not credited, except with being inflated. I don't forget that the "noble man." Joe, was witness to the contest and can be interviewed relating thereto any time; neither was I excited. He came out to the water much as a frightened duck does when rising to fly, making very much the same splash or sound, only instead of being head first he appeared to me to go sidelong and at an angle, which left him at the terminus of his leap at least five feet high in mid air, making a jump after coming to the surface of fifteen feet sure, nearly going over the falls, and freeing himself. That fish was a success, either a jumpist or as a lively and accomplished performer on "leaders" and fly tackle. I should say that an honest pair of scales would accord him three and a half pounds. I played and landed several more, all of which gave lively satisfaction; and when a quarter to one o'clock we heard the whistle, (desiring to ride home on the express,) I ceased fishing and counted up and found the score to be thirty-nine, and no small ones among them. That part of the day not employed here I fished around the dam and took sixteen, making my whole catch for the day fifty-five salmon. From that day I lost interest, not fishing with the zest and keen relish I had done before, it being almost a matter of indifference to me sometimes whether I landed a fish I hooked or lost him off in playing, believing half the sport be in the rise.

The day before leaving I fished below the tannery, telling Joe I should not keep over one dozen or one and a half dozen, and when I had reached that number and began to put back all I got after, Joe scowled (I had returned many before) and twisted uneasily, but being "boss of that job" I continued until I had taken in all twenty-three, returning seven to the water to live and be happy, or make some other sportsman happy.

"It was here," says Joe, "where you took eight pair one day two years ago;" and Joe knows.

The following day, June 5th, I broke camp and started homeward, my companions have preceeded me a few days; therefore, I cannot give their full numbers, both having had, like myself, excellent sport and good success. Mr. Barnes having killed, the day before he left us, sixty salmon, the largest number taken by any one in our party. My record was for the eight days, two hundred and three, not counting the little yearlings of course. Of my two hundred and three, fifty were returned to their native element. I will say here that I took all but one of my fish with a fly, nearly or quite all around me using bait for the first two or three days. Of the one hundred and fifty-three I killed, and many more Mr. B. and Mr. R. took, we did not consume at our camp more than two dozen, the rest, after Mr.

B. taking home with him to our Boston friends about seventy five, we gave to neighbors, from whom we had received favors, and to our guides, not permitting a single fish to be wasted. I mention this because I am often asked what I do with so many fish, besides, many hearing of so large a number being taken, might suppose our object was slaughter. Such is not the fact, our whole party being unanimous against such wickedness. I left Grand Lake two days earlier than I should have done, more by reason of entertaining some compunction of conscience against what seemed to be almost slaughter, than because of becoming satiated with that kind of sport, although I must say that since that day I bent my first pin hook into shape, attached a piece of twine, bare-footed and bare-headed, I crept cautiously on to the old rickety, decayed log-bridge spanning the little brook near the old homestead, and fiddled my line down between the stick and experienced my first "tug" at the line, landing my first trout, (I didn't think to use a pin hook after that,) and probably marched home with my happy trophy so near being satiated with fishing as now.

I never expect to enjoy such fishing again at Grand Lake. It seems to me only a question of time when these beautiful fish will become scarce, unless some further protection is given them. Would it not be a good way to have enacted a law limiting the catch per day per anyone person, say not exceeding two dozen, and to fly and bait fishing? Indeed it would not lacerate my feelings to see such measures taken as to insure good fishing there for all time. It can easily be done. It is my honest conviction that all persons who are actively engaged in the propagation of food and game fish, and the procuring of enactments for their protection, are public benefactors.

In closing I my say that on my way home by the short route up Grand Lake, Junior Lake and Stream, Duck Lake and Stream to Carroll, thence by stage to Lincoln Station on E. & N. A. Railroad, I stopped over one day at Springfield, and by driving ten miles to where I struck the Baskahegan Stream near the dam, I took over twenty pounds of spotted trout, averaging over a half pound each. Thus ends a most enjoyable trip.

– R. R., Boston, June 22, 1874

A FEW DAYS FISHING ON THE SCHOODIC LAKES

By Thomas E. Lambert, from *Forest and Stream*, December 3, 1874

Maine Sportsman, July 1900 (Courtesy of Ernst Mayr Library, Harvard)

The accounts this year from the Schoodic Lakes, in the Northeastern part of Maine, were so grand that the writer and two Boston friends, old associates in angling excursions, determined to give this rather unfrequented locality a trial themselves.

The requisites for a few days' camping out were despatched before hand, and by communicating with a farmer residing close by Grand Lake, two experienced guides were engaged. The weather promised well, being during that delightful spell we had in the latter portion of the last month, and our journey was very enjoyable with the prominent exception of the last six or several miles, performed in a wagon innocent of springs over an awful road of the corduroyest pattern. It was my worst experience of this species of travel, and has fully impressed on my mind the capacity of the human frame to resist the force of shocks. Were the journey over this wretched apology for a road to continue much longer, as at the acme of the ordeal we went, plump, crash, jolt, over a dreadful piece of corduroy, I felt body and soul could not be kept together, when the joyful cry, "There they are!" reached my ear. The lovely scene there presented to our view--the calm beauty of the Schoodic Lakes, bathed in Autumnal haze--soon dispelled all thought of our late torture. In every ripple of the glistening lake fancy pictured the silvery splash of a landlocked salmon.

It was nearly 5 P.M. when we arrived at Lakeville Plantation. There something to eat was got ready for us, but our desire to do some fishing that evening was paramount to all considerations of appetite or rest, and after a hurried snatch at the viands, we were soon busily engaged in getting out rods and tackle, when a decided wet blanket was thrown upon our movements by our host, who, with sententious unconcern, coolly informed us that fishing on Grand Lake "wasn't worth a cent." With blank disappointment we looked on one another, mutely questioning. "Can this thing be?" Did this tally with Fred C.'s glowing account of his exploits on the Schoodics? Were we but the victims of a fiendish self? With tacit consent we deemed it inexpedient just then to press further enquiry on our terrible informant, beyond asking where we could find the guides. We rose full of bitterness and gall, Ned silent, but Charlie's mutterings betokened intention of going for some one's "skulp" when we got back to Boston.

Gathered together on an indicated point of the shore whence the guides could be hailed, we gave vent to our oppressive feelings in a rousing halloo, which soon met the desired answer. From behind a headland, a hundred yards or so distant, a canoe with two stalworth Indians on board shot forth and quickly reached where we were standing. One of them, Peter, was of the Mohawk tribe; the other, a white man, who had taken to his bosom a dusky squaw, and lived wholly in Indian fashion. Both, we afterwards discovered, were fully up to this business, skillful hunters, first-rate cooks, too, and withal very agreeable attendants especially Nicholas, who was brimful of humor and sporting anecdotes.

The farmer's statement, that Grand Lake did not amount to much, was fully corroborated by them, but Duck and Pleasant Lakes, they confidently assured us, would afford plenty of sport. Nothing further could be attempted that evening, and so, with somewhat restored good spirits, we retired to our night's quarters at the farm house.

By six o'clock next morning everything was snug on board the two canoes. Ned being the heavy weight of the party was left in undivided possession of one, with Peter at the paddle, while Charlie and I placed ourselves under the guidance of Nicholas in the other. We were lucky in our captain, whose amusing proclivities kept us well entertained the whole way up. Not much conversation took place, apparently, in the eternal fitness of things, he took untiring care to inform the woods and waves must occur before he would "ever cease to love."

The breeze was well in our favor and we skimmed along the waters at a rattling pace. Grand Lake has no particular pretensions to the picturesque, being an open, undiversified sheet of water, about five miles long by three in width, the shores on either side low-lying and densely wooded with pines. The monotonous said through it left us quite in mood to enjoy a change of scene, and this was well gratified by the sight of Duck Lake. It is not more than half the size of Grand, but is infinitely more beautiful. Just at the entrance, on the right hand side, in marked contrast to the continued evenness of the lower lake, and bold wood-crowned headlands jut out in all directions, forming in the numerous indents of the shore the most inviting nooks and quiet sheltered coves.

Here at the lake's outlet a short halt was called for lunch, it being our intention to proceed with the least possible delay to Upper or Pleasant Lake, as it is called. There our man said was the real good fishing of the places to be found. But the time here devoted to the meal was of the shortest duration. The splash of a salmon a little distance out made us all jump to our feet. Previous intentions were knocked on the head. We could stand suspense no longer, and in a jiffy, three sets of flies were doing their prettiest to tempt that fellow to show himself again.

For ten minutes at least we plied in vain. The speckled beauties of Duck Lake seemed to utterly disregard the city dainties we so assiduously offered. At length a decided splash was heard. An appalling stillness followed. No time for questions now. "Ha! I've got him," broke from Charlie, and so he had, and a good one, too. Out went his line with a whiz, and the quivering bend of his rod showed that the customer he had to deal with would require every care to bring him to terms. C.'s appeal to take in my line, for fear of a possible foul, was not be resisted. I was winding up in a very miserable frame of mind at the prospect of delay until I could again commence operations, when, splash, tug, I was no longer a spectator, but in active business on my own hook. We both soon had our fish well at play, and were offering occasional consolation to Ned for the loss of the pool for first lake, when "good, sir!" ejaculated the taciturn Peter, and Ned was also in the race.

Then began in earnest the struggle for the grand prize which by the way, consisted of a purse of one hundred and fifty cents. Every move of our game was watched with an intensity that made the nerves feel as if rod and line were conductors to a first class electric battery. Charlie's enquiries for the landing net were becoming frequent; he was evidently on the home stretch. I had fair hopes of making a good second, or possibly by a sport, a rush in for first. My fish was already yielding to a slight pressure, as I commenced playing with a shortened line, when on a sudden he made for the surface and sprang clear out of the water. This well directed move to get free did not meet with success, though it was uncomfortably near it, and causing, by the sudden energy of the effort, the top of my rod to give way, left my chance of first place rather precarious indeed. The contest now lay between Charlie and Ned. But as the latter's was much the lighter fish, it was not long before the words, "Consolation boys." "Better luck next time," etc., were heard, mingled with abominable guffaws, from his direction. We suggested that a head and tail ought not count against five and six pounders, as our prizes turned out to be, but this point was not pressed, as later examination showed that between the head and the tail of Ned's fish lay three and half pounds of good salmon. That victorious gentleman was also kind enough to commiserate me on my damaged rod, which was in fact of more show than good, and had been won at some fair or other. Eyeing it, he observed it was worth about as much as it cost me, namely--the dollar for the chance--nor was he wrong.

The sport continued good and we remained here nearly two hours, hard at work, each rod in that time averaging the respective amount of about a dozen, all strong and full of play. We then resumed our journey towards Pleasant Lake. Crossing over we reached the mouth of the stream that unites both waters. There parting from the guides, who were to carry up the canoes and fire camp. We started, under full directions how to proceed, to walk the intervening distance, something close on three miles. On arriving at the shores of Pleasant, the wind was just the right thing, allowing us to fish from land. A short time at work here, and proof was abundant that the high character of it given by the Indians was every whit deserved. We met with first-rate success, as good a day as ever it was my luck to cast a line, and when the approach of evening compelled a cessation, and a return march for camp, we were laden with spoils, and in the highest possible spirits at the excellent prospects for the next day's regular set-to.

Following down the rugged course of the stream for a considerable distance we were glad enough at length to descry the camping ground, and the welcome form of Peter, crouched before the fire, preparing the dinner. No prettier site could have been selected, and pledging Peter's health in full pumpers of Gibson's good old Monagram, we testified our approval of his judgment. The test was pitched in a small clearing by the stream side, the dark woods behind, and right in front a cascade, down which dashed the waters that came struggling through the boulders from the upper portion of the stream, visible some distance, till lost in among the overhanging trees; further down, below the little waterfall, was a placid pool, its sombre fringes flecked here and there with the bright red of the maple's fall foliage, and over it leaned an immense old vine-tangled pine tree, as if in his quiet nook seeking rest from long continued battle against time and tempest.

We were all as hungry as hawks, and made a right royal feast. The fish was cooked in real woodcraft fashion, and were we an exhibition jury on that occasion land-locked salmon would stand a capital chance of honorable mention for "delicious flavor." A "little game" in which all took a hand, followed in due course, and of said little game, I must say, our noble red men showed a knowledge, which, I have no doubt, if occasion required, could be displayed even to an oriental extent. With song and story we kept it up until the "wellness" of Nicholas, as manifested in the increasing tallness of his narratives, and the miscellaneously loose manner in which another person's little dogs wagged their tails in front, gave the signal for hammock.

Among friend Ned's many little peculiarities was an alarming predisposition to cramps, which could only be subdued by a certain remedy. A violent attack came on at an admirably early hour next morning, just about daybreak. The fuss he made looking for his particular medicine soon drove sleep from the camp. He would have us also use it as a preventive. Growls and abjurations to signify he did not then, at least, require the treatment, his tender solicitude for our welfare would not let him understand. His henchman, Peter, too, by this time fortified against all danger from "cramps," so joined in the shout of "tickets" that even "Old Nick" had to turn out from his birchen bark couch, though he remarked he was "a powerful sound sleeper." With a shake and a stretch, toilets were complete, and all were ready for breakfast. The amount of provisions demolished at that meal rendered it absolutely necessary to put in force the adage, "After breakfast rest a while." It was not safe to venture immediately where there was a possibility of slipping. So placing a bottle as a mark some twenty yards off and lighting our pipes, we went in for a little pistol practice. After a half an hour's shooting the target remained in tact, though the trees for a circuit of fifteen feet showed evidence of our work, and we came to the conclusion that it was a pity to injure such a bottle after the noble defence it had made, and letting it remain in its glory, the subject of pistol sharpshooting was by mutual consent allowed to drop.

Now we started for the lake, but on arrival there found it as smooth as a mirror; not a ripple ruffled its glassy surface. In the still air above here and there soared a fishhawk, and now and then one came down with whirring, like arrow like dash on its prey beneath, and floated of with it to the shore. These, and an occasional loon, were the only objects to break the morning quiet of the scene. Fishing for the present looked of little use. However, rather than be idle, Ned and I determined to make a circuit of the lake, and try what trolling would do. Charlie selected a spit of rock a little out from the shore to fish from, and having left him perched there, we went on our way. Our success at trolling was very poor. An occasional shot at a loon did not help in the slightest to increase the amount of our game, though unexpectedly the last shot we devoted to the black-headed diving fowl, afforded us a bit of amusement that well repaid for all the powder and shot we had wasted on them. Not far from the promontory that separated us from the spot where we left Charlie, we espied a solitary loon, banged at him, and down of course he went, but not on the 'never to rise any more" plan, for just as we were rounding the point, we heard his infernal screech as he again came to the surface, and at the same moment, to our utter astonishment, up went Charlie's arms in the air, and flop went he into the lake. We immediately pulled to his assistance, helped him ashore, and endeavored to get an explanation of the mishap. He shook himself repeatedly, but appeared totally regardless of our questions, and for some moments looked with a steadfast gaze on the water. "Well, I thought it was the devil," at last escaped his lips. The mystery was solved. The roars of laughter that followed this short speech were enough to exorcise all the evil spirits, if any there were, in that neighborhood. It was our "devil" of a loon that had done the trick. Master Charlie, finding fishing no go, had allowed himself to drift into a delicious little reverie, half in thought, half in easy enjoyment of the scene around, when his pensive lucubrations were so unceremoniously disturbed by the unexpected popping up, just under him, of the diver's ugly head, accompanied by that terrible scream.

No breeze yet springing up, we employed our enforced idleness in going about the lake. It is much of the same character of Duck, but of great extent, and a bolder class of scenery, to which is the picturesque addition of high wooded hills rolling far away in the distant background.

By the afternoon things got more lively, and soon we had our hands full of exciting business. We were into it up to the handle--chock full of occupation until almost dusk. The fish took lively, and most of them were game to the back bone, especially one splendid fellow that after a magnificent fight, that lasted, I am sure, quite twenty minutes, finally yielded himself captive to the noble Ned.

Our third day was good from beginning to end, and when next morning we had to pack up our traps for home, it was no small regret we felt that imperious business would not permit a longer stay.

– THOMAS E. LAMBERT

SYSELEDOBSIS AND PASSADUMKEAG

By F. C. P., from *Forest and Stream*, May 13, 1880

"Camping in Washington County" From American Scenic Magazine, 1901

Through the genial landlord of the Lincoln House, Mr. David Stockbridge, familiarly known as "David," we secured canoes and a man to do general work, who proved efficient in the canoe and an excellent cook. Under David's good management we had the canoes and supplies properly loaded and sent on ahead, and on the arrival of the train, Tuesday, Sept. 9th, he was in readiness with a first-class team to convey us to Gowell's. It had rained during the previous night sufficient to lay the dust, and we had a most agreeable ride through the green wilderness, over a good road, reaching Duck Lake about 3 P.M. On the shore of the lake is a club house, owned by Boston parties, under the care of Mr. Gowell and twice a year they visit here, having fine success and exhilarating sport hunting and fishing. We shortly had the canoes afloat, loaded and under way. Our man Henry was in charge of one canoe, and "Brick Top," having been over the route before, was appointed guide of the squadron, and took the lead in the other canoe. Besides the two mentioned, our party consisted of Mr. E. V. Cross, of Lawrence, Mass., an expert disciple of "Izaak," and a thorough sportsman, and Prof. Mills, well known in Eastern Maine as a "dead shot," and taxidermist, and for his agreeable loquacity on hunting subjects, which afforded us much enjoyment and instruction. We paddled leisurely across the lake and entered its stream, nearly hidden by dense alders, and being exceedingly narrow and rapid we soon reached the beautiful, clear water of Junior, as the sun, sinking behind the high ridge on our right, was illuminating the entire surface in gorgeous colors, which we accepted as a welcome and good omen for our success. About a mile below the mouth of the stream we found on our left an excellent camping spot and while some were engaged in gathering boughs and making camp, the rest were busily employed in getting supper. David had accompanied us thus far for the purpose of being with us one night in the camp, and he proved a pioneer in the work.

Camp and supper were soon in readiness, and under the combined inspiring effects of juniper tea, camp fire and a feeling of freedom from all care, the Professor began a relation of some of his wonderful experiences by land and water. He had the field entirely to himself, and we listened long in admiration until he began a thrilling narration of his experiences at Bar Harbor during a gale of wind, when we quietly dropped out one by one, and left him talking to the stars. We had an excellent bed, and slept tranquilly until the rays of the rising sun, shining in our faces, awakened us to a day of sport. While we were seated about the breakfast table an exclamation from the Professor turned our attention to the lake. His experienced eye had discerned in the distance a flock of ducks approaching us. We all made preparations for their reception, and began the day with seven black ducks, handsomely stopped by the Professor and "Brick Top." While Henry was gone to Gowell's, with David, we broke camp and were ready to start on his return. The day was warm and clear, and the six mile stretch of water before us was calm and transparent as glass. The numberous islands at the head of this lake, closely crowded together, somewhat interfere with its outline, but after passing them it expands into a beautiful shape nearly two miles in width and the shores handsomely wooded. Near the islands, land-locked salmon are found in plenty, of good weight and game. Vose tried them with good success, while the Professor and the rest of us gave exhibition of skill in shooting kingfishers on the wing.

The high ridge on our right, about a mile in width, is all that separates us from the Syseledobsis lakes, and is the home of the deer in great numbers, many of them being taken every season. We paddled lazily along, reaching Junior Stream at noon, and proceeded down its placid length, not a sound disturbing the solemn quiet about us - conducive to reflection and study. Near its mouth, the stream widens considerably, its shores becoming meadow and marsh. This place seemed a perfect rendezvous for wood, black duck, and blue-winged teal. The Professor shot very handsome specimens of wood drake and blue-winged teal, while our success was excellent in shooting snipe and sheldrake. A tongue of land about twenty feet wide on our left extends up the stream nearly a mile, and we heard the waves of Grand Lake beating on its shore long before we entered it. Passing through just a narrow break in this narrow strip of land, we entered at once on the lake, most appropriately named Grand. Looking by the point of Big Island, the expanse of water seems almost limitless until we notice the high hills about the stream at the foot of the lake, blue in the distance. The shores of the lake seem almost straight, looking like a huge canal, but there are deep coves, in crossing, which a person with a canoe will have to exercise due caution when there is any wind. We took dinner on the beach, with this handsome view before us, and Vose, noticing the peculiar formation of the point of land opposite us, drew from the Professor this story, which he told with thrilling effect: --

"Several years ago the enterprising lumbermen of Calais sent men into this region to secure the pine. During the season of rafting, men were employed in squads of three or four to pick up the scattered logs. One of these squads, while so engaged went ashore on this point to prepare their breakfast. Just as they got it in readiness they discovered their batteau adrift, and one of them started to recover it, saying in reply to one of his mates, who urged him to eat his breakfast first, that he 'would get that batteau or eat his breakfast in h---.' He swam out to the boat, and put his hands on it to get in, when he gave one despairing yell and went down. After several hours' search his mates recovered his body, and took it back to the point, and tied it to a tree with a two-inch hawser, and then started to the settlement to procure a coffin. They returned the next day, bearing the coffin, but found their mate gone and the hawser broken in two. They left the coffin and retraced their steps to the settlement, saying their mate had been dragged into the lake by a large serpent, whose track they plainly saw."

From that day the point has been known as "Coffin Point," and the story of the man's disappearance is firmly believed by the Professor and every one about the mills below. The Professor confirms this story by finding the bottom of the coffin five years afterward, while there winter fishing, and using it to make a pair of snow shoes.

We passed into the lovely Pocompas Lake, apparently as primitive and wild as when the Indian alone canoed its waters and hunted its majestic shores. Entering the stream, we passed up two miles and camped for the night. While supper was in progress, "Brick Top" started on an exploring expedition on his own account, and shortly returned with the intelligence that we were on the right stream, but a few rods below Syseledobsis dam. This so relieved the anxiety of Vose and the Professor that they became at once animated and happy, particularly the Professor, who felt somewhat limited in time, having an engagement to deliver a lecture on natural history toward the close of the month.

Thursday morning was bright and warm. Soon after breaking camp we reached the dam. We found Mr. Ball here, one of the assistant fish commissioners, who has admirably arranged breeding houses, and being an enthusiast in his work, is very successful. He also has care of the house owned by the "Dobsis Club," which club is composed of several prominent gentlemen of Massachusetts, who visit here regularly. Their catch of land-locked salmon in May was fully up to the average for several years, which is large. We passed the morning here, visiting the hatching works, and getting much useful information from Mr. Ball. He and his wife remain here the year round, twenty miles from any settlement, their mode of locomotion being canoes in summer and snowshoes in winter. We left the dam, accompanied by them, about 3 o'clock, and started around Big Island and up the lake to our camping spot, selected for us while at the dam. We met here two gentlemen from Boston, returning from a cruise in Chain lakes, reporting excellent success. Reaching the head of Big Island, we bade adieu to Mr. Ball and wife. Following their instructions, we trolled for salmon in both canoes, and caught several beauties, some weighing five pounds.

We reached our camping spot about dark, and found it a dry, sandy beach. After supper we prepared birch bark torches, and lashing the canoes together started around the shore of the lake to spear any luckless fish we should see. Vose made a striking tableau as he stood motionless in the bow with the spear poised aloft, the lurid light of the torches casting a brilliant halo about him, showing him in bold, relief against the surrounding darkness. Suddenly he made a vigorous thrust, and in a second speared a huge sucker. So we fished for an hour, catching nothing but those listless fellows who gave up the ghost with a squeak like a guinea pig.

Friday morning was rare and beautiful, even in this, our best season of the year in Maine, and the glorious prospect before us of water and wilderness was sufficient to repay us for our journey thither. After an early breakfast, Vose and Henry went up the lake to try the salmon, while the Professor and "Brick Top" took the high ridge behind us. In two hours we were assembled about the camp fire comparing notes, with the following results: Five landlocked salmon, averaging three pounds; two salmon trout, weighing respectively one pound and one pound and a half (these last named are the handsomest fish that swims); seven partridges, one white-headed eagle, shot by the Professor on the wing, and one red-headed woodpecker. While the Professor was busily employed with knife and scissors preserving the eagle and woodpecker, we had camp broken and were in readiness to start.

Pushing out into the lake, we had a beautiful scene presented to us--six miles of perfectly calm water stretching away to the blue hills in the north, with a width of two miles or more, its shore accurately portrayed in its blue depths. We had no hesitancy in declaring this the lake of lakes in Maine. Its Indian title, Syseledobsis, is most significant, meaning "a lake with big rocks in it." The water is clear as crystal, and to a depth of forty feet we clearly discern great shelving rocks; in many places they would seem to rise abruptly before us, with little or no water over them, when in truth they were many feet below us. The lake was unusually high, and our catch of fish limited in consequence.

We reached the head of the lake and our first carry after a delightful sail and getting canoes and luggage out, started over a good road to the dam, about a mile distant. We had everything over in three hours, and finding sufficient water at the dam to float our canoe into the lake above, we settled on camping there for the night and fishing the stream. While supper was in progress, Vose caught trout enough to last us several days, some of two pounds.

Saturday morning found us abroad early, and in readiness for the Passadumkeag range of hills before us. The maps erroneously give Syseledobsis as one lake, about twenty miles long, while in fact it is separated by a stream narrow and rocky, and navigable only from the dam to the lake above, called Crooked on the maps, which is about as large as Syseledobsis. We pushed across this lake to Porter's Landing, and made preparations to pass the day and night. Vose and "Brick Top" climbed the high ridge above us, the watershed between St. Croix and Penobscot waters, and proceeded to Mr. Porter's camp, receiving a hearty welcome from this gentleman, who, reared in luxury, prefers the solitude of the woods. Securing his hound, they went out on the ridge, running parallel with the lake for two miles, and letting the dog loose, returned to our camp by the shore. The Professor readily left his specimens and arsenic, and accompanied "Brick Top" in his canoe to a station down the lake favorable for the entrance of the deer, while the other canoe was placed at an equally favorable point above. We had been in waiting scarcely half an hour, when we heard the baying of the hound, gradually becoming more distinct, and apparently in a direct line with the point covered by the Professor and "Brick Top." Before we got our guns in readiness a noble buck was in full sight of us. Pausing only a second to sniff the air about him, he plunged into the lake. We waited patiently for him to swim by the point, but he must have discovered our camp fire, for he turned suddenly about and swam toward the shore he had left. The canoe containing the Professor shot by the point like a flash, and while it was in rapid motion he took quick aim and fired, killing the buck in his tracks just as another spring would have taken him into the woods again. The hound appeared at this instant, and received our praises in dignity and silence. Reserving only such portions of the buck as we could use in a short time, we gave the rest of the noble animal to Mr. Porter, and retired to our bed of boughs to enact the chase in dreams.

We were awakened Sunday morning by the rain beating upon our canvas roof. Getting breakfast with the rain dripping down our necks and off the end of our noses into the frying pan was one of the slight discomforts of our trip. But as we were all volunteers, we made the best of it with good grace. Mr. Porter soon appeared with his team to convey our canoes and belongings across the three miles between the Passadumkeag River and us. After many break-downs and several trips, we got everything in sight of the river about 4 o'clock, and were all tired and wet after our hard work. The rain ceased shortly after we got our traps into the woods, and we quickly had a rousing spruce log fire, and dried boughs enough to give us a comfortable bed for the night, which was duly appreciated by us all.

We decided to remain at this point for a day or two, and as the river was unusually high we argued that the trout pools below would be flowed out, and our best fishing would be above us. The result proved our wisdom, as we caught during Monday nearly two hundred handsome fellows, some of three pounds. During Tuesday we remained about the camp, fishing a little, sleeping a good deal, and at work loading shells for duck shooting below. The numerous creeks and streams along the stream are an excellent feeding ground for ducks, large numbers and several varieties frequenting these places during the season. It rained heavily again during the night, but Vose's waterproof tent sustained the reputation of the maker, and we passed the night as dry and comfortable as if we had been at home. During the evening the Professor was engaged in packing the specimens preserved by him during the trip. They contained arsenic enough to poison the entire population of the township which we were in.

Wednesday was cloudy and cold, with strong indications of more rain. We broke up our comfortable home in the woods and commenced our descent of the river, whose Indian name, Passadumkeag, meaning "Meadow River," is most appropriate, and if they could have extended its title to include "very narrow and extremely crooked," it would have been described completely. There is quite a current for its entire length, and its deep, dark water is full of excellent breeding and feeding ground for the trout. We reached the Taylor Brooks about noon, and caught a few nice trout, while the rain fell on us in torrents. The mouths of these brooks are reputed places among a few anglers earlier in the season, and were fished by distinguished parties, containing Judge Clifford of the Supreme Court, and Senator Hamlin, of Maine, during May and June, with splendid success. We passed several parties gathering cranberries, which grow on the meadows in vast quantities. The river in many places is very picturesque, and for a time we follow its crooked course far into the open meadow, turn suddenly about and enter the woods to continue for two or three miles, its width in no place exceeding one hundred feet. These changes from meadow to forest are most agreeable, and break the monotony of the trip. The flora of this region, although somewhat meager, was learnedly analyzed by the Professor as we glided quietly along. We made camp early, and after a royal supper of broiled duck, partridge and trout, our wet clothes were forgotten, and we contentedly sought the shelter of our canvas home.

Thursday morning was bright and beautiful, and, after the cold rain of the previous days, was thoroughly enjoyed by us all. We started early, having a day of hard work in prospect. We passed the mouth of Nicatous stream, which runs ten miles from the lake of the same name, and reached Grand Falls about noon. These falls pitch suddenly down the river to the lowland below, nearly three hundred feet. The water was high enough to enable us, with care, to drop down to the dam, but it proved a rough place for canoes. The Professor and "Brick Top" were obliged to get out after a few rods and wade their canoe through the boisterous current. There is a good carry road on both sides of the falls, and we should have got by more comfortably had we carried the whole distance, about a mile. Taking out the canoes at the dam, a short carry took us to the calm water below, and getting a hasty dinner, we were in readiness to leave for our intended camp on the shore of Saponic Lake, eight miles away. We had seen but few ducks above the falls, but made preparations to encounter them on our way down, as we heard a party who left a few moments ahead of us firing repeatedly. Judging from their excessive shooting, we concluded we should get nothing but cripples. We had gone but a few rods, when a handsome wood drake flew up from the grass ahead of us, which the Professor tumbled into the stream with a well-directed shot. In about five miles of our journey from the falls we shot five wood drakes, four black ducks and two blue-winged teal.

To any one in a hurry a trip down this river would prove most exasperating, as its torturous course continues for its entire length, while the distance must have been computed in air line, as in traversing the eight miles to Saponic we were unanimous in the opinion that we had traveled twelve. The river makes one more abrupt turn to the right, and opens immediately into a lake of which we had no previous warning. It is nearly circular in shape, and about a mile in diameter, abounding in pickerel and white perch, the trout being exclusively confined to the water above the falls. The settlement of Burlington, on its north shore, gives us our first intimation of returning to civilization. We found the party encamped near the spot we intended to occupy, and while we were getting camp in readiness the Professor was interviewed by them, and his conscious smile of superiority must have been blighting when, in comparing notes of the shooting, they brought forth two black ducks, having expended powder enough, as they admitted, to supply a company of infantry, while he silently pointed to our eleven with an air of pride he could not conceal.

After the excellent supper prepared for us had been full discussed, the Professor was soon learnedly discoursing upon the different methods of taking fish, deer and other game, with our united parties as auditors. We listened with admiration to his excellent ideas, clothed in graceful language, until, his entire absorption in relating his experiences, he got into repetition, and as he commenced to relate, for the fortieth time, his experience at Bar

Harbor during a gale of wind "most terrible, gentlemen, yes, sir," we of our party quietly withdrew to our bed, leaving the other party spellbound at his thrilling narrative of events that only occurred in his imagination.

Friday morning found us early astir, as this was to be our last day out, and, although we were but fifteen miles from the town of Passadumkeag, where we were to take the cars to our several homes, we had before us several rapids and one or two carries, for which we must make due allowance of time. We were across the lake at an early hour, and encountered at the outlet the first of the several rapids in our path. This rapid was short, like them all, but very rocky, and it required considerable skill to keep our frail craft clear of the white-crested rocks that stood up all around us, by which we rushed with railroad speed; passing one other safely we reached the town of Lowell. Carrying over the dam, a few rods below, we had canoes afloat again and in readiness to start about noon. Before leaving we called on Mr. J. Darling, whose home is here. We found him busily engaged in building a canvas canoe, several of which he had in his workshop completed. He has acquired a reputation as a builder of canvas and birch canoes only equalled by his reputation as a successful hunter and guide. No better man could be engaged for a hunting or fishing trip anywhere in Maine, as he is familiar with all the lakes and rivers.

Taking our places in the canoes for the last time, we reluctantly started for our destination, ten miles below. Passing in safety many rapids in quick succession, we arrived at Passadumkeag, at the junction of the river with the Penobscot, in good season for the train which was to break up our party.

We had enjoyed the best of health for the entire trip, and felt our bodies and minds renewed by our rough experience, storing up the pleasantest of reminiscences, to be recalled during the long winter night before us.

– Lincoln, Me., Oct. 1st, 1879., F. C. P.

MY FIRST DEER

By J. B., from *Forest and Stream,* March 16, 1882

A Scene in Washington County (From American Scenic Magazine, 1901)

In 1840, for Tippecanoe and Tyler too, I cast my first Presidential vote, and shot my first deer. I was residing at the time in the pleasant seaport town of Machias, then and now the shire of Washington County, Maine. One of the peculiarities of its denizens was that what you had not done you could not do, particularly if you were young folks; this, with my love for a "still-hunt" and "we'll give you fellows fifty cents a pound for all the deer meat you'll kill," were strong inducements to try what could be done.

Early morn, July 10, found my companion "Bob Foster," and the writer, with the necessary accompanying documents footing it up to Whitneyville, four miles. Placing our birch canoe in the water we began to load and get ready for a start. As the upper deck of a "birch" consists entirely of air, it is important that the cargo should be packed in the hold, and just as near the bottom as possible. Everything in place, we took positions as follows: F. in the stern, myself in the bow, wedged in between the ribs just as far as my own ribs would admit—sitting on my heels with knees and toes on the bottom—midships occupied by camping and cooking utensils, rations and "Jack," a little wiry Scotch terrier kindly loaned by Mr. W., the postmaster, who was also Jack's master and one the syndicate making the above liberal offer of 50 cents per pound. Jack was of the kind a great deal of dog done up in a very little skin, and next to being assistant postmaster, deer hunting was his forte.

Constant paddling, a few carries, a sharp lookout on the banks of the river for game, and in it for rocks and logs, made our arrival at the mouth of a spring brook quite satisfactory. Here we caught, cooked and ate a good trout dinner, and decided our manual of action in case the object of pursuit was found. Before sundown we reached an elevated point on the west side of the river a little below "Great Falls," nearly forty miles from home, where we were to camp first night.

After an examination, unpacking supper, fixing the cedar boughs and making a big smudge for the use if not benefit of the pre-occupants, we took a look at the "big carry," which would be in order early in the morning, and a stroll by the river side to see if anything was lying around loose, then returned to quarters feeling satisfied with the day's work. Listening to the mosquitoes never was my best prescription for sleep. Jack stood watch the best of any of us being more experienced and at home, and keeping off the amazons fell principally on humanity.

Toward daylight we heard a noise—pat, pat, great big drops—soon it became wet rain, very wet, and we found our camp well adapted to letting in the rain as well as letting out the dark; there being no "deacon's seat, we hitched up back, but all to no purpose.

Having been up the river the previous autumn, I knew there was a good camp a few miles above and we decided to go for it. Taking a hasty bite and tying up the gunlocks with our pocket handkerchiefs, the birch was reloaded and soon we were at the foot of the carry on the opposite side of the river. The narrow path and high bushes wet the last dry thread we had on. After tipping the water out of the birch no time was lost in relaunching. Soon after, as we turned a bend in the river and looked up to an island perhaps 600 yards distant, there in the tall grass, broadside too, stood a big buck in his bright, well-fitting summer coat, the handsomest animal yet seen in my life, alternately feeding and raising his head, looking several times, as we thought, down upon us, when not a motion was made or hardly a breath was drawn, and no sharper or more anxious eyes looked that look than Jack's, apparently boss over all. When feeding, we put in the double quick and worked for deer life; we were obliged to, not that we were out of meat, but the current was strong against us.

Thinking we were within 200 yards, I removed the handkerchief, laid the muzzle over the bow, and took "any position." Soon went the crack of the rifle, out of it went two patched conical bullets, "60 to the pound," one entering just back of the fore shoulder, the other passing through the top of the neck. At the same instant out jumps Jack, taking in "right smart" water, and within two of getting all of us into the river. The deer jumped sideways and fell flat out of sight. "You've fixed him," said Foster. Hardly had he spoken before the deer was up, looking directly at us. He got off the island, swam the river, and in climbing up the bank, fell over backward twice. Being successful in reaching the top, I took Foster's smoothbore loaded with buckshot, had him set me on the shore, and soon reached his beat, where the blood spurtings were plainly visible from every leap he made. In the meantime Foster goes out into the river again to pick up the dog, who was hardly able to hold his own, but soon called me back as the buck had returned to the water. I stepped down and into the birch, we were soon near our game, he having laid himself panting and kicking on a little tuft or hassock part way across the river.

As we approached he partially raised his head. The look that came from those eyes is not forgotten, and with feelings of regret I pulled the trigger and ended his sufferings. Jack jumped on to the body, holding a sort of post mortem. We put a cord around his neck, took him in tow, and paddled for the shore, were we met the most numerous reception in all my life. Black flies! Oh, the black flies! Both air and woods were full of 'em. We lost no time in letting them have other blood besides our own; and, while removing the entrails, taking off the head, the horns, being in their soft and velvet state, "no good," decided our trophy should be got home that same day before dark, the obstacles to which were rain still pouring, two journeys at each carry, forty-two miles' travel, more cargo and a head wind; in our favor was the current, not yet seven o'clock, and at least one "extra pluck."

Placing the deer's head on top of a big stump, tying his legs so to admit of a "shoulder pole," never having tied Crockett's method (on the bottom of the river), we made no attempt to reload anything but the canoe; that accomplished we started without a single good-bye to the flies, mosquitoes, etc. What would that have been among so many? After a few hours work, an internal feeling reminded us we had little or no breakfast. The rain ceased, we made a landing, then a big fire, and intended fried deer's heart to be part of the menu; but Jack, having been very busily engaged guarding the birch, had appropriated that part to himself, so salt pork was in order. No time was to be lost. With a square meal, we were soon on the way, and plied the paddles with a will that meant and was business. About two P. M. the sun came out; this increased our zeal and gave another steady boost. Before sundown we reached Whitneyville, hired a team to take us home, "before dark" being part of the bargain, which was faithfully performed, and arrived at eight P. M.

Our return "with the largest deer ever brought into this town" was soon noised about. Hundreds came to see it. It was nicely dressed, and weighed a little under 200 lbs. Jack returned to his post-office and we to our homes. The next morning distributions were made. Some parts of the meat (which in color much resembled veal, having been killed in fine condition and without running) were slightly salted, making the best corned meat I ever tasted, and finally the skin made into soft, serviceable leather, well adapted to slippers and dry weather.

– J. B.

GRANDFATHER'S STORIES, FOURTH EVENING: A REMARKABLE ESCAPE

By Charles A. Stephens, from *Youth's Companion*, 1885

Charles A. Stephens

A prolific writer of children's tales, Charles Asbury Stephens, began writing under a number of pen names including Stinson Javis, Marcus Vanderpool, Charles Adams, Henrietta Crosby and Charlotte H. Smith. Many of his tales were written as series, such as his outdoor tales in the Camping Out series, The Knockabout Club and The Moose-Hunters.

Borrowing from his childhood farming experiences, Stephens produced several other series set in a more rural atmosphere. The Old Squire series and the Grandfather's Tales series were very popular children's books for many years. While staying on Grandfather's farm, each evening the children would gather around Grandfather and request a tale. Stephens, who wrote many odd tales, used this forum to introduce a number of unconnected stories.

"Fifty years ago said the old Squire, "when the Maine forests were the theatre and emporium of the Eastern lumber business, it was customary every fall for little parties of three or four to go off 'prospecting' in the wilderness, for the purpose of looking for favorable places to conduct logging operations during the following winter. I went on several of such 'timber cruises,' and it was during one of these that the dangerous and extraordinary adventure that I am about to relate befell our party.

"There were with me that time two young men of not far from my own age, whose names were Caleb Bearse and Eben Winslow. Our party that year was confined to the region about the Pocumpus Lake, one of the western Schoodic Lakes, which form the head waters of the St. Croix River. The country about the Pocumpus was very wild, and covered for the most part with dense growth of mixed woods. We were obliged to camp out for nearly three weeks.

"On referring to an old diary, I see that on the morning of the 27th of September, as we were taking breakfast at our camp on the lake shore, Bearse espied two bears on the opposite side among the dead trees on a flowed tract, caused by the dam at the foot of the lakes. They were both on the trunk of a very tall sugar-maple, climbing it; and I recollect that as we looked, one of them lost his hold and slid back into the water with a splash.

"There's game for us!" Bearse exclaimed, hastily swallowing the coffee in his dipper, then jumping up, he loaded his old musket. Winslow and I charged our shot-guns. Bearse had a young dog with him, which he whistled for. We got into our bateau and pulled out onto the lake, making our way with as little noise as possible, for we hoped to get a shot. Meantime, the bear in the water had again regained the tree, and was clambering clumsily up after the other. We could see the first bear near the top of the maple.

"We were not many minutes crossing. The maple stood among other trees. The dog espied the bears before we were half over, but so intent were they on whatever was inside the tree, that they did not see nor hear us till we were within about two hundred yards of them. Then the topmost one faced about, growled and turned to get down. But the lower one had not yet seen us, and was trying equally hard to get up, whimpering to his eagerness.

"Shoot!" exclaimed Bearse.

"All three of us fired, and both bears either jumped or tumbled off the tree into the water.

"Pull in!" shouted Winslow.

"The dog had become so excited with the firing that he leaped out of the boat and swam for the game, though he could hardly keep up with us, for Winslow was doubling over his paddle, and shouting, 'Close in, fellows! Close in on 'em!'

"Bearse stood up, and reloading, fired a second shot, getting aim after a fashion. The bears were swimming for the shore. We had not seriously injured either of them. The boat could not readily be paddled among the dead trees and fallen brush. The scared animals got to the shore in advance of us. Bearse fired a last shot just as they were jumping out of the water. It hit the smaller one of the bear, apparently, for he turned with a snarl, and for a moment seemed disposed to fight; but before Bearse could reload, he ran off after the other. We heard them racing through the woods, smashing the twigs.

"It was next to useless to chase them now. The dog had climbed out on a stranded log, and stood quivering, with an occasional whine, as he looked off and heard the bears running away. Suddenly he gave a shrill yelp and jumped into the water, and just then I felt something strike my hat and heard and angry buzz. We looked up and saw bees darting about. The air was full of them, and a deep humming issued from the tree tops.

"Bee-tree,' said Bearse, making a leisurely observation. 'Fellows, that's what these bears were after—after the honey!"

"Honey!' cried Winslow, 'If there's any honey, we will be looking for it.'

"The dog came swimming to the bateau. Bearse pulled him in. Winslow had taken up his paddle and worked the boat up towards the foot of the maple, which stood four or five feet deep in the water.

"Hollow tree,' Winslow remarked.

"Bearse now struck it several times, making the whole shore resound. The jar aroused the bees again. A black stream of them issued from the hole and filled the whole leafless top of the maple with a threatening cloud, making a deep, solemn- sounding hum.

"A big swarm!' exclaimed Bearse.

"But the bees began to see us, Buzz-z-z came one and rapped on Bearse's glazed cap. Tiz-z-z came another and hit the dog. A yelp followed the sting. I caught up a paddle, when spat struck one on the back of my hand. Another hit my cap.

"Out if this!' shouted Bearse; but a bee hit him on the nose before he could make a stroke. At that we all three jumped up and fought them with both hands. The harder we fought, the faster they came. Everywhere they touched they stung, and they came so fast that we could not beat them off.

"Phew!' panted Winslow, with both hands flying like a windmill. 'I—can't—stand—this!' and over he went, at a jump, into the water. It was up to his waist. Bearse and I leaped after him. By dint of a heavy spattering of the water, we drove the little torments off; and after a time they went back into the tree. Thoroughly soaked, we waited awhile, then waded to the bateau and climbed into it. The dog was shining on a log, a long way off. We went to take him in.

"Well,' said Wnslow, 'let's have that honey, somehow!"

"We paddled ashore to consider the subject.

"Must screen ourselves in some way,' Winslow proposed, and to effect this, slim poles of alder were cut and bended over the bateau, forming a sort of frame. Bearse felled a fir, and with the long, fan-like boughs we thatched the bateau over completely—making a hut of boughs over it. Getting under this, we then worked the bateau beneath the maple, which we concluded to cut down if we could without getting stung.

"Winslow shoved the bateau alongside the trunk of the tree and thrust his paddle down into the mud, so as to hold the boat close against the tree. Bearse then pulled away the boughs a little, so as to expose the tree, and then taking up the axe, began to cut into it. The blows soon roused the bees again. We could hear a furious buzzing outside our bough-house with light pats into the thatch.

"After a good deal of hacking Bearse cut through the outer shell of the maple into the decayed hole inside. There was a dark cavity, with bright drops of honey on the black punk. It smelled both sweet and rotten. Occasionally a drop of honey dripped down from the mass of comb above; but there were no bees in the hole below the comb, which was evidently near the top of the tree.

"By peeping cautiously out through the boughs, we discovered that the tree stood nearly or quite perpendicular. Which way it would fall was uncertain. We wanted it to fall in towards the shore, instead of outward into the deep water, where it might sink down and submerge the honey. Fifty or sixty feet out, there stood a dead fir. A foot and a half, perhaps, in diameter, and a little beyond this, a very large black ash—one of the largest I ever saw, nearly or quite four feet through and very tall. It had been dead so long that the top had mostly fallen. The smaller and nearer fir seemed, we thought, to lean inward, towards the maple that the honey was in; and Bearse now suggested felling the fir against the maple, so as to help push it over shorewards.

"So, after cutting the maple partly off, on both sides, we pushed the bateau along to the butt of the fir; and then set to work, to cut that off, so that it might fall against the maple and force it over. There seemed no special danger; yet as the falling of trees, particularly dead trees standing in the water, is often attended with some little risk, it was agreed that I should get out of the bateau and stand, while cutting the fir, on an old fallen trunk which lay alongside it, and that my two companions should push off in the bateau a little distance for safety in case the fir should not fall as we expected. They did so, and went back, out past the great black ash, a distance of some fifty feet.

"Meanwhile, getting as good a footing as possible on the old log—which lay just above the surface of the water—I chopped away until the fir began to crack. Stepping hastily back on the log, I looked up, when to my surprise and alarm I saw that it was going to fall outward towards the great black ash, instead of inward against the maple; we had been deceived in the 'cant' of it.

"Look out! Look out, fellows!' I shouted. 'It's falling out towards you!"

"From where I stood, the bateau seemed to be just in line of the big black ash; both Bearse and Winslow were sitting on the thwarts, looking towards me. When they saw the fir coming over, they started partly up, as if to jump out. Bearse had an oar in his hand. The fir fell against the big ash and would have hung upon it, if that had held. But it was rotted away at the roots; and when the fir struck against it, I heard first a loud, dull crack, then over it canted-—towards the bateau!

"To this day I feel a shudder of horror when I recall the sight—that great pillar of lumber, certainly fifty feet high, sailing, rushing down, through the air onto the boat, with those two fellows looking helplessly up at it—as if petrified with fear!

"The great ash struck the water, just alongside the bateau, barely clearing it; and the force of the wave which it threw up, toppled the boat over, as lightly as if it had been a chip. I had a glimpse of the boys and of the dog as they went over with it. Then the fir-top and with it another smaller ash—which had been struck by it, and which delayed its final fall a second or two—came down, with a crash and a sullen souse, over the spot—and all was still!

"For an instant I stood speechless; then I ran hurriedly along on the fir; the trunk of which lay on the surface of the water, towards where I had seen the bateau disappear. The water was full of brush and floating bits of bark; and amidst the brush I saw something struggling up to the surface. It was the dog. He came up with a pitiful yelp, and I pulled him out upon the log.

"Poor thing!' I thought, 'you are the only one left alive, I'm afraid; and then I shouted, 'Cale! Eben! Are you both dead?

"In response there came the strangest sound which I ever heard—from down in the water. It did not sound like the human voice. It was a dull, dead sound—and yet it was divided off like words.

"*Are you alive*?' I shouted.

"Again those dull, strangely muffled noises came struggling up to the surface. There was also a great rise of bubbles.

"I ran back for the axe, and then fell to work chopping off the fir-top. I could see the bottom of the bateau, down three or four feet under the water; yet the water was so muddy that I could not tell exactly how the boat lay. With might and main I chopped and cleared out the stiff fir limbs, standing nearly up to my knees in water on the black ash trunk.

"Two or three times, as I cut and hacked, I heard those same strangely muffed noises. I cut off the fir in two places, both above and below the point where if held the bateau down, and then by a great effort hauled the log aside, also a large limb of the second ash-tree which had fallen under it; and no sooner had I started this latter stick, then up came the bateau bottom up to the surface of the water, and I saw a hand thrust out from under the gunwale!

"Seizing hold of the boat, I partly lifted it, when, to my inexpressible joy, I beheld both my companions struggling from beneath it, bruised a little, it is true, but not seriously hurt!

Yet it was very simple. The bateau had been turned over, and had not only taken them down beneath it, but had taken down sufficient air under it to keep them from suffocating, till I could cut away the brush and let it up.

"What with the violent exertions which I had made, and the great shock of joy of seeing them alive, I sat down with my legs in the water, and for some moments could not utter a word. Indeed, we scarcely spoke, any one of us, for some time. Then the first thing Bearse said was, 'Well, let's get the bateau up, and then go back to camp and let that bee's nest alone!'

"Yet I feel sure we all three felt most profoundly thankful for so manifest a preservation. Aside from a few scratches and bumps, neither of them was injured, nor was the bottom of the bateau broken so as to leak.

"In reply to my questions, they said that when they saw the great ash start to fall, their first impulse was to jump overboard; then they saw that it would just clear the bateau, and so stood still. The instant it struck the water, they found themselves underneath the bateau, and then felt the fir top strike on the bottom of it, over their heads! The gunwales of the boat rested partly on some sunken logs, but their heads were up, inside the boat, and they lay there half-stunned, till they heard me shouting, and then heard the strokes of the axe. Thinking that I would free the bateau, they wisely made no effort to crawl out from under it.

"We had no further desire to hunt bees that day, though we subsequently took up the nest and got over a bucketful of clear, white, well-filled comb from the hollow in the maple. It was probably a runaway swarm of bees from Mattawamkeag or Topsfield."

A BEAR HUNT IN THE MOPANG REGION

By H. F. W., from *Shooting and Fishing*, August 16, 1888

Maine Sportsman, Nov 1899. (Courtesy of Ernst Mayr Library, Harvard)

Cherryfield, Me., August 13.

Noticing a sketch in the columns of SHOOTING AND FISHING of a bear hunt in the White Mountains, it put me in mind of a like experience which two sportsmen and I had in the Mopang region last year, which, perhaps, would be of some interest to the readers of your paper. It was in the latter part of September, 1887, when I received word that two gentlemen, who had been fishing at Moosehead Lake, desired my services as guide, on a short trip to the Mopang region, and that they would meet me at North Beddington, a small settlement 20 miles away and about ten miles from the noted Lake Mopang.

So making a small pack of necessary articles needed on such a trip, I started, reaching North Beddington in time to have a few hours' rest before going into the woods. The gentlemen I met there proved to be Mr. B. F. Smith and his son Clifford, a Harvard student. After making known their plans we procured a team and made our way for about seven miles over a rough road, which terminated at the foot of what is called Second Lake, where I had a canoe in readiness for such occasions. After loading our baggage in the canoe and making arrangements with the teamster to meet us on the following afternoon, we paddled up the lake. In the meantime the wind commenced to blow from the northwest and by the time we reached the head of the lake, the wind was blowing very heavily. Here we paddled up a small stream and out upon the broad Mopang, where we found it difficult proceeding, on account of wind and waves. However, with our united efforts we reached the north arm of the lake without accident, but wet, tired, and hungry. Thence we proceeded up a small stream to a lumbering camp, reaching there about one o'clock in the afternoon.

After getting dinner and preparing for the night, Mr. Smith wished to try the lake for fish. Directing him to good fishing ground, young Smith proposed taking a trip in search of game, which abounds in this region. Taking my repeater and he a double-barrelled shot-gun, we took a trail leading north through the woods to a burnt country, where there were plenty of bear signs. We had traveled about a mile when we struck numerous fresh signs where bruin had been seemingly but a few hours previous. About a half a mile further on we climbed a little hill that overlooked quite an extensive country, and sat down to rest. We had scarcely seated ourselves on an old burnt log, when looking to my right I espied a large bear on a neighboring hillside, walking along and feeding on blueberries and pigeon plums, which cover this burnt country. As near as we could judge, bruin was about 400 yards away and I did not dare to try so long a shot, and as the bear was coming towards us we waited patiently for fully twenty minutes, till his bearship was within 200 yards of us, in plain sight. I was aching to try him at that distance, but Smith thought he would come nearer; instead, he just walked along behind some bushes and went into a little swamp and was out of sight. I waited as long as I thought prudent for him to come out, and as he did not make his appearance we started on a run for a high rocky bluff that ran parallel with the swamp, about 200 yards to our left, where we could have a better chance to shoot. We had scarcely reached the summit, when, within 60 yards to our left, another bear started from behind a large boulder upon the run for some hackmatack sprouts that were within 20 paces from where he started. In less time that it takes to tell it I brought my .38-Bullard to bear on him and, thanks to my Lyman sight, which showed off to such good advantage on his black carcass, I had two bullets through him before he was out of sight in the bushes and just as he disappeared. Smith, being some 15 paces behind me, let both barrels of buckshot at once after him, which mowed the bushes down at a great rate, having no effect on the bear but giving Smith a lame shoulder from the recoil. I started on the run and called to Smith to follow, which he did. We penetrated the thicket for about 20 yards where we found our game in the agonies of death, which was something terrific. As I neared him he raised himself on his fore legs and tried to get at me, but being disabled, could not; however, I stood ready with my trusty rifle to put a bullet through his brain if necessary. We watched him till he expired, and then proceeded to remove his skin, which was quite a task as he was a very large bear. On examination I found the bullets struck him about a foot back of the right shoulder and came out forward of the left, which I should thought would have caused instant death. After removing his skin we went in search of the first bear mentioned, but I suppose our shooting scared him away, for we did not succeed in finding him. As it was getting late we concluded to start towards camp. I let Smith take my rifle, I taking the barrels of the shop-gun to aid me about carrying the bear's skin. We made a circuit of about three miles and when the distance was about half traveled, Smith going in advance of me about 20 yards, had just gone down in a little ravine, which I had looked across over 40 years ago, and saw a bear rise up from behind an old log. I spoke to my companion telling him to shoot that bear, and as I spoke the bear raised on his haunches, looking Smith square in the face, as much as to say "are you looking for me, sir?" I don't know whether Smith was scared or excited, but it seemed he forgot he had a rifle, till the bear started to run, when he fired, but missed. The bear, with a few bounds, reached a swamp and was out of sight. We then proceeded on our journey, and as we neared camp I saw a large porcupine clambering a little hill about 60 yards distant; Smith, being somewhat provoked at his ill-luck, shooting at the bear last mentioned, turned his pent-up fury on that old porcupine and the way the quills flew, proved that he had not missed his mark this time. As it was now nearly dark we hurried on toward camp, where Smith senior, whom we left fishing, was anxiously waiting our return, he having a fine lot of fish as a proof of his efficiency with the rod. We soon had a roaring fire in front of the camp, and not a small quantity of the fish were soon sizzling in our long-handle frying pan. When cooked we proceeded to gratify our appetites, which had been sharpened by our tramp over the rugged country. After talking over the events of the day we retired to our "down couch" of spruce boughs. Rising early next morning we spent a few hours in fishing and target shooting, after which we packed up and started down the lake to meet the team which was to convey us back to the settlement, and thus ended our two days' cruise in the Mopang region.

– H. F. W.

CPSIA information can be obtained
at www.ICGtesting.com
Printed in the USA
BVHW09s1753150718
521677BV00007B/67/P

9 781939 166258

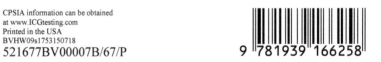